TRIUMPH

Other books by this author include:

ISBN 1 85960 850 7
£19.99

ISBN 1 85960 997 X
£19.99

HAYNES CLASSIC MAKES SERIES

TRIUMPH

SPORT AND ELEGANCE

BILL PIGGOTT

TH ₍cᶜ H5

First published in August 2006

A catalogue record for this book is available from the
British Library

ISBN 1 85960 969 4

Library of Congress control no: 2005926141

Published by Haynes Publishing, Sparkford, Yeovil,
Somerset BA22 7JJ, UK
Tel: 01963 442030 Fax: 01963 440001
Int. tel: +44 1963 442030 Int. fax: +44 1963 440001
E-mail: sales@haynes.co.uk
Website: www.haynes.co.uk

Haynes North America Inc., 861 Lawrence Drive,
Newbury Park, California 91320, USA

Edited by Jon Pressnell

Printed and bound in Britain by
J. H. Haynes & Co. Ltd, Sparkford

contents

The roots of the *Triumph company*

A sporting version of the very successful Triumph Super Seven model dating from 1929. Note the Triumph globe motif on the radiator, and the Calormeter thermometer and mascot.

As with so many of the older-established car companies, the Triumph company can be traced back to the 1880s, in Triumph's case via bicycle manufacture and the importation of sewing machines.

Triumph was founded by a German émigré living in London, Siegfried Bettmann. Multilingual Bettmann arrived in the UK in 1884, and as a budding entrepreneur it was not long before he was appointed the overseas representative for US-manufactured White sewing machines. He travelled widely within Europe and North Africa, making contacts which stood him in good stead when within a year or so he went into

business on his own account, taking on the UK agencies for several German manufacturers.

At this time the bicycle boom was reaching its zenith, and Bettmann was not slow to realise the potential of this revolutionary and relatively cheap form of transport. Accordingly he resolved to export cycles, having them specially manufactured in the Midlands. By 1887 he had taken on fellow German Mauritz Schulte as a business partner, Schulte being an engineer and thus offering a perfect complement to Bettmann's sales expertise. Schulte quickly convinced Bettmann that the real money lay in manufacturing cycles rather than just selling them – and where better to establish a works than in Coventry, already the centre of the bicycle industry?

The company needed a snappy name for its products, and Bettmann came up with 'Triumph', a name he claimed could be understood in all European languages. While this may have been stretching the truth, 'Triumph' certainly had positive and upbeat connotations and as a car marque name it was to last more than 60 years; indeed, it may yet be revived, if rumours are to be believed. The premises obtained by the partners in

Coventry belonged to Alderman AS Thompson, the then mayor; he later became a Triumph director while, in a strange twist of fate, Bettmann himself later became Coventry's mayor.

The invention of the pneumatic tyre by Dunlop gave a giant fillip to the cycle industry, and by 1895 Dunlop was putting money into the successful Triumph Cycle Company – something which both helped Triumph expand and provided more outlets for Dunlop's products. By the late 1890s Triumph had become one of Britain's largest bicycle manufacturers. But how to expand yet further?

In 1902 Schulte fitted an engine to a Triumph bicycle. He had previously investigated acquiring the manufacturing rights to an existing motorcycle, but these plans came to nothing, and so in the third year of the new century the first Triumph motorcycle took to the road, equipped with a Belgian-made 2¼hp Minerva engine.

Over the next few years several different proprietary engines were tried, but the directors concluded that their own design would prove superior as well as offering greater profit. By 1905 a 3hp Triumph motorcycle, wholly made in-house, was on the road, and by 1909 more than 3,000

Sporting pre-Gloria: a four-seater Southern Cross for the 1933 model year. Power comes from the Triumph-built Coventry Climax inlet-over-exhaust (IoE) engine, in 1122cc form – for 1934 it dropped to 1087cc in displacement.

Triumph motorcycles per year were being built at the Coventry factory, and manufacture was rapidly overtaking that of bicycles as the company's main business. By the end of the Edwardian era Triumph had become one of the leading names in the industry, and was well placed at the outbreak of the war in 1914, for the military had an insatiable demand for all types of motorised transport.

It was as a direct result of a war office contract that a man who became a seminal figure in the Triumph company first comes into the story. Claude Holbrook, at the time an army captain, met Bettmann on many occasions during this period, and Bettmann was so impressed with Holbrook's all-round talents that in 1919 he persuaded the Triumph directors to appoint him manager of the firm.

The military had purchased the amazing total of 30,000 of Triumph's 550cc motorcycles during the war, ensuring the company's secure post-war financial position and its place as

It just looks right, doesn't it? This 1935 Southern Cross has a 1232cc version of the IoE 'four', and is here in tuned Vitesse form – meaning 50bhp from the engine and a cockpit enhanced by big 5in main dials. Detailing is lovely, and includes paired 'Continental' rear numberplates and a dipped rear crossmember wrapping around the twin spares.

a leading and trusted motorcycle manufacturer in the eyes of the general public. Under Holbrook's managership, production continued to increase and by 1923 had reached 300 units per week, or 15,000 per annum. The time was right to branch out, and where better to go than into motor car manufacture?

Schulte was the more entrepreneurial of the partners and pushed for the

company to branch into four-wheelers as soon as possible. Holbrook was also in favour, but the conservative Bettmann took some persuading, being content to rely on the proven bicycle and motorcycle businesses. Eventually won over, in 1921 Bettmann acquired the premises of the defunct Dawson car company, in Clay Lane, Coventry. Incidentally, at about the same time, William Morris

had hit financial difficulties and it is said that Morris Motors Ltd was offered to Bettmann as a going concern. Had he not turned this down, how the face of British motoring would have changed!

The prototype of Triumph's first car, to be known as the 10/20, was running by 1922; it was a well-constructed but conventional vehicle of 1393cc, with its sidevalve engine designed by

This six-cylinder Gloria tourer also dates from 1935; thus it lacks the dipped front bumper and vertical radiator slats introduced for 1936. A clever feature of the body is a patented arrangement whereby the cutaway doors convert to a high-sided configuration when you pull up the hinged filler-panel nestling in the door-trim aperture.

respected engineer Harry Ricardo. Only rear-wheel brakes were fitted, but a four-speed gearbox with an easily-mastered change was an up-to-the-minute feature. Three body styles were offered at the car's launch in April 1923 – two-seater and four-seater tourers, plus a fabric-bodied saloon, all constructed by the Regent Carriage Company in London.

In relation to the Austin Seven and the Bullnose Morris, the Triumph was a relatively expensive car, costing between £430 and £460, but it was expected that the company's excellent reputation for quality products and good workmanship would attract the top end of the small-car market, and this indeed proved to be the case.

The 10/20 Triumph was not by any means a sporting car, but it could top 50mph, which was better than many light cars could manage at the time. Sales were steady rather than brisk, but were sufficiently encouraging to warrant development of further models, and in late 1924 a 13/30 model appeared, significant in that, along with the 1925 model-year Horstman, it was the first British car to be fitted with hydraulic brakes – and on all four wheels, too. The 10/20, the 13/30 and a bigger 2.2-litre Triumph

Donald Healey himself, by then in his late eighties, is reunited with one of the Dolomite straight-eights near the beach at his native Perranporth, Cornwall. Designed under his direction, this hugely expensive car did not reach production, only three prototypes being constructed. From the rear the car looks even more Alfa-ish – but the body was an in-house Triumph design.

Fifteen continued through to 1927 – finding particular favour in the colonies, where their ruggedness and quality engineering counted for a lot.

However, Bettmann and Holbrook wanted to produce a top-quality small car to sell at a price that would encourage mass sales. This they finally achieved for the 1928 season with the Triumph Super Seven. Selling for £150 as a complete well-equipped four-

seater tourer, and for as little as £113 as a running chassis, it was able to compete head-on with the more popular makes, especially as it offered superior Lockheed hydraulic braking and such niceties as electric windscreen wipers, pneumatic seat cushions, and dampers for all wheels, items frequently absent from cheap cars. The miniature sidevalve engine was of only 832cc but it sported a three-bearing crankshaft for smoothness and longevity and produced enough power to propel the car to nearly 50mph. It was a quality product at an affordable price and sales took off at once. The Super Seven was also the car that started Triumph's 50-year competition career.

In Australia and New Zealand the Super Seven established a number of endurance records, the most amazing being a 10,000-mile run in which a 250-mile trip across a mountain range was accomplished 40 times non-stop by a team of six drivers! In Britain, it was the later-to-be-famous Donald Healey who campaigned the little Triumphs with most success, winning more than one major rally outright with a supercharged version of the car. These victories led to Healey being appointed experimental and competition manager of Triumph at the end of 1933. Meanwhile, a Super Seven was driven more than 3,500 miles in eight and a half days from Vancouver to New York, covering an amazing 450 miles a day. The Super Seven was an excellent little car, and with over 18,000 sold it established Triumph as a manufacturer to be taken seriously.

In 1933, Bettmann was succeeded as managing director by Holbrook, and three years later Bill Sangster purchased the cycle and motorcycle business from what was by then the Triumph Motor Company Limited, with Bettmann becoming his new chairman. Thus in 1936 the Triumph motorbike and car companies became separate enterprises.

Holbrook's first venture as the man in charge had been the Triumph Scorpion, an unsuccessful small 'six', but it was with the 1932-on Super Nine range and subsequent Ten that Triumph finally found the way forward. Powered by a Triumph-built Coventry Climax inlet-over-exhaust engine of 1018cc or 1122cc, these were satisfactory enough small cars, and the Super Nine spawned a sports model known as the Southern Cross. Capable of cruising at 60mph, at £225 this model was good value although no MG rival.

Triumph's breakthrough came with the Gloria range introduced for 1934. Essentially a cocktail of bought-in proprietary parts, these mid-sized Climax-powered four-cylinder and six-cylinder models carried elegant Triumph-built coachwork and were a resounding success. Offered in a bewildering array of different versions, the Gloria was sold under the slogan 'The Smartest Cars in the Land' and the range included lower-slung and more powerful Vitesse models and a cobby little two-seat sports car perpetuating the Southern Cross name. For the 1934 Monte Carlo Rally Donald Healey created two hybrid Glorias based on the old pre-Gloria Southern Cross; in one of these he

The fabulous supercharged two-litre engine of the straight-eight Dolomite, a car which owes more than a little to the 8C-2300 Alfa Romeo.

Dating from November 1935, this shot depicts the 1936 Triumph Gloria 12hp saloon. Sporting pretensions are evidenced by the knock-off wire wheels. At this stage the engine was still the IoE 'four', but in 1937 the Gloria received a 1496cc version of the ohv engine, and was renamed the Gloria 1½-litre.

The Standard Motor Company

The Standard Motor Company was the product of one man's foresight, industry and engineering expertise. Reginald W Maudslay received a sound engineering training in London, and at the age of 31 came to Coventry in 1902 with the specific intention of manufacturing motor cars on his own account. Sensibly, he purchased examples of other people's vehicles, dismantled them, and set about improving on their design. By the following year he was in a position, both in terms of knowledge and finance, to take a small factory in Much Park Street, Coventry, where he put in new machinery and took on a small staff. The Standard Motor Company Limited was formally incorporated in March 1903.

From a simple single-cylinder 6hp prototype Maudslay rapidly progressed through twin-cylinder and four-cylinder vehicles, and by 1905 a 20hp six-cylinder car was also in production. Small numbers of these various models were sold, the Standard car gaining a deserved reputation for being soundly constructed, well engineered, and yet not in any way revolutionary or experimental – in fact just the sort of solid, middle-ground, middle-sized vehicle that would appeal to the moneyed classes who by the late Edwardian era were taking an interest in the motor car as a serious means of transport.

From somewhat shaky beginnings, finances improved, and by 1911 Standard had even received royal patronage, the new King George V using a 20hp model on his overseas coronation tour. By 1913 Standard had entered the new 'light car' market as well, and by the outbreak of the Great War production had reached 50 units per week. However, car production had to cease, the several Standard factories turning to aeroplane manufacture – including the new Canley plant, established in 1916, which was to become familiar to all Standard-Triumph enthusiasts. By 1921 the company employed over 2,500 workers, and Canley was being rapidly expanded to produce the vehicles demanded during the expansionist 1920s by a new generation of motorists.

In 1929 Maudslay took on as his right-hand man Captain John Black, the man who was to transform Standard from being a middle-ranking car-maker to one of the 'Big Six' UK car builders of the 1950s. Owing largely to Black's efforts and energy, Standard weathered the depression of the early 1930s, but Maudslay's health was declining. Black became managing director in 1933, and took full control after Maudslay's death the following year. Car production continued to increase, with manufacture now largely concentrated at the ever-expanding Canley plant, and 1934 was a record year for the company. Under Black's leadership, Standard had progressed by 1939 to being a company on a very sound financial footing, with modern manufacturing facilities, selling the sort of solid, dependable but uninspiring cars that the public wanted, at prices that they could afford. That was an enviable position to be in, compared with the state of Triumph at the time.

came home third overall, and first in class, an achievement that did much to raise Triumph's profile.

One spectacular model that must be mentioned is the straight-eight supercharged two-litre twin-cam Dolomite sports. Evolved by Healey, this fabulous 115mph two-seater was Britain's answer to the Italian Alfa 2300 models – indeed it owed many of its design features to the Alfa. The plan was to use this model to win major international events outright, with a limited production run to be available at the enormous price of £1,225. Healey drove the first car himself in the 1935 Monte Carlo Rally and would doubtless have done well but for hitting a train on a level crossing. In 1936 he tried again, finishing in eighth place, but by then it was all too late and no further development finance was available. Sadly, only three examples of this legendary beauty were ever built.

A more modern assembly plant known as the Gloria Works was bought on Holbrook Lane, Coventry, and an ever wider range of Triumph models was made, the Gloria and the Vitesse continuing in production after the 1936 introduction of the overhead-valve Dolomites, with their striking 'waterfall' grille. This glamorous model was designed by Walter Belgrove, the company's in-house stylist, a man whose name will be encountered on a number of future occasions.

Financial difficulties loomed, however. Colonel Holbrook was relieved of the managing directorship and made chairman, and the company's day-to-day affairs were taken over by London car dealer Maurice Newnham. He had taken on a sick company, and there was little that he could do to prevent fortunes further declining. In retrospect Triumph – in the same way as rival Riley – was simply making too few examples of too many models in the late '30s, and it was making money from virtually none of them. They were fundamentally good cars of sporting demeanour – well respected in enthusiast circles and well-liked by their owners. But with the money-making bicycle and motorcycle business gone by 1936, there was not the cash to keep Triumph afloat.

A last-gasp lower-priced model, the Triumph Twelve, was hastily cobbled up to try to regain middle-market sales, but it had little showroom

The sole surviving Flow-Free, of perhaps 22 such cars made for the 1935 model year. The body was originally fitted to a Bentley, after Triumph had hastily discontinued the poorly-received model and sold its stocks of bodies; today this ill-fated Triumph foray into 1930s aerodynamic faddism sits anachronistically – but to good effect – on a 1938 Gloria Vitesse six-cylinder chassis.

Below: The Dolomite saloon in 1991cc six-cylinder form. For 1939 the body was lightly revised and a luxury Royal model – with a wider body and a higher roof – joined the range.

Above: This 'waterfall grille' Dolomite Roadster Coupé is a four-cylinder car first registered in July 1940. The Hudson-style front created some controversy at the time.

Left: Cubbies either side of the characteristic dickey seat open out to allow golf bags to be stowed across the car; a fold-out step is on the other side, to aid access.

Sir John Black and Standard-Triumph

Sir John Black was the individual who had the greatest influence on the course taken by Triumph Cars in the post-war period.

Born in 1895 in Surrey, John Paul Black was initially destined for a legal career. However, the First World War got in the way, and he became a tank commander after fighting – and being gassed – in the trenches. By 1917, aged 22, he had achieved the rank of Captain, reputedly the youngest in the Army. He returned to the UK at the end of 1918 a war hero but a man whose personality had been irrevocably changed by his dreadful experiences.

He entered the motor industry in the mid-1920s, taking a management job with Hillman. His rise was rapid, and doubtless not hindered by his marrying one of William Hillman's

daughters. By 1928 he had become joint managing director of Hillman, but when at the end of that year Humber took the company over, Black departed to join Standard, where his boundless energy, hands-on management style and commercial acumen ensured the company's success.

His manner was autocratic and mercurial; he could be exceedingly difficult yet he was well respected and fair. As was once said, 'He could be the kindest or the cruellest of men,' and the word that perhaps best sums up his temperament is unpredictable. Whatever his personal traits, he was a superb industrialist, as was recognised in 1943 when he was knighted for his role in the war effort, Standard having played a huge part in wartime aircraft manufacture. Without

Black, there would have been no Standard-Triumph to make the vehicles that form the subject of this book.

One of Black's many master-strokes was to purchase from Ward's, in late 1944, the remaining assets of the old Triumph company. At the time many in the industry were sceptical of the value of such an acquisition, but it was principally the name that Black was after, and the Triumph Motor Company (1945) became a wholly-owned subsidiary of Standard, which henceforth became known colloquially as Standard-Triumph. Sir John announced that as soon as the war was over, a new range of Triumph cars would be revealed.

He had the foresight to realise that the way forward post-war for Standard was to adopt a one-model

The interior is beautifully crafted. Details include quick-action window winders and sprung-flap door pockets; it is thought that the dashboard should be leather-covered on a model of this period.

appeal and rapidly flopped, leading to the whole company being offered for sale in July 1939 as a bankrupt but (just about) going concern. The major asset was probably the services of Donald Healey, but even he could do nothing to save the situation. The great days of the pre-war Triumphs were the years 1934 to 1937: ultimately the company suffered from being neither small enough to contain costs and cater for a niche market nor large enough to gain the economies of scale of the Austins and Morrises of the world. With the right management, Triumph could have survived, as Jaguar did, but instead, as with Riley and so many others, it went to the wall.

The wreckage was purchased in August 1939 by a firm of engineers and steelmakers from Sheffield, Thomas W Ward and Company. A few dozen more Triumphs were put together largely from parts in stock, but by November 1939 all car production had ceased and the factory turned to war work. The first Golden Age of Triumph cars had ended – and had it not been for the war, that may well have been that. But the great bombing raids on Coventry during the war caused major damage to the Triumph factories, and by 1944 Ward's was ready to dispose of the remains: it had no particular interest in car production, having purchased Triumph merely as a long-term speculation. At that time, few in the motor industry would have put money on there ever being any new Triumph cars, but they reckoned without the intervention of a formidable character, Sir John Black . . .

policy, and accordingly he commissioned the revolutionary Vanguard, a rugged, do-anything car that could seat six, cruise at 70mph and give nearly 30mpg. Although for a couple of years the company had to produce revised pre-war cars, once Vanguard production started in 1948 the wisdom of Black's policy became apparent: the Vanguard was a huge hit and a great export success. This, coupled with his decision to team up with Harry Ferguson on tractor production (to utilise the 'shadow factory' at Banner Lane, Coventry where Standard had made aero-engine parts) laid the foundations of Standard-Triumph's post-war prosperity, and provided the background against which the new Triumph models could be produced. Triumph was to be the up-market end of the company's range, and to be the name gracing future sports models.

Sir John Black, although theoretically answerable to his board of directors and thence to the shareholders, tended to treat Standard-Triumph as his own personal fiefdom. He lived in a grand manner at the company's expense and entertained lavishly, and he was known and feared for his high-handed treatment of middle management. On the shop floor, however, where he was reputed to know many of his employees by name, he was held in some reverence, and many would not have a word said against him.

Above all, Black was a man who got things done and made things happen, and his nine years in charge of the regenerated Standard-Triumph company must be considered a major success. Sadly, he could sometimes treat his fellow directors with disdain, on occasions taking major decisions without their knowledge, and it was this that ultimately led to his downfall at the end of 1953.

Having suffered injury in November that year when a passenger in a Swallow Doretti sports car driven by Ken Richardson, his absence allowed his co-directors to hatch a scheme to oust him, and an enforced retirement ensued in early 1954. His place was taken by his right-hand man Alick Dick, long groomed as his successor. Sir John Black lived a further ten years, succumbing to a heart attack on Christmas Eve 1965 at the age of 70, one of the last of the old school of motor-industry autocrats.

The Razor-Edge era

A *pre-production Triumph 1800 Roadster from 1946 shows its stylish lines and pontoon shaped front wings. The additional windscreen for the dickey seat passengers is seen erected.*

The pre-war Triumph had always been a middle-market car, more so than the Standard, and whilst Black envisaged a one-model Standard policy with the new Vanguard announced in 1947, he also, correctly as it turned out, wanted a more up-market and exclusive sideline, and more particularly he wished – at least latterly – to produce a sports car to penetrate the lucrative US market. It must nevertheless never be forgotten that without the financial success of the Vanguard (and the Ferguson tractor) there would not have been any serious post-war Triumph production.

It was the new Triumphs that were to hit the showrooms first: the Vanguard involved much new and complex

1800 Saloon
1946–1949

ENGINE:
Four cylinders in line, cast-iron block/head

Capacity	1776cc
Bore x stroke	73mm x 106mm
Valve actuation	Pushrod
Compression ratio	6.7:1
Carburettor	Single Solex
Power	63bhp at 4500rpm
Maximum torque	92lb ft at 2000rpm

TRANSMISSION:
Rear-wheel drive; four-speed; column change

SUSPENSION:
Front: Independent by transverse leaf and wishbones; lever-arm dampers
Rear: Live axle and semi-elliptic springs with anti-roll bar; lever-arm dampers

STEERING:
Cam-and-peg

BRAKES:
Front/rear: Hydraulic drum

WHEELS/TYRES:
16in steel disc wheels
Tyres 5.75 x 16in

BODYWORK:
Coachbuilt over ash frame; aluminium panels
Tubular chassis

DIMENSIONS:

Length	14ft 7in
Wheelbase	9ft 0in
Track, front	4ft 2½in
Track, rear	4ft 6¾in
Width	5ft 3in
Height	5ft 3½in

KERB WEIGHT:

PERFORMANCE:
(Source: *The Autocar*)

Max speed	75mph
0–50mph	18.7sec
0–60mph	29.1sec
30–50mph in top	14.7sec

PRICE INCLUDING TAX WHEN NEW:
£927 (April 1947)

NUMBER BUILT: 4000

2000 Saloon
March–October 1949

As 1800 saloon except:

ENGINE:

Capacity	2088cc
Bore x stroke	85mm x 92mm
Power	68bhp at 4200rpm
Maximum torque	108lb ft at 2000rpm

TRANSMISSION:
Three-speed gearbox; column change

2000 Renown
1949–1951

As 2000 saloon except:

TRANSMISSION:
Overdrive optional from June 1950

SUSPENSION:
Front: Independent by coil and wishbone; anti-roll bar; lever-arm dampers
Rear: Unchanged

BRAKES:
Front/rear: Hydraulic drum

DIMENSIONS:
Track, rear: 4ft 6in
Wheelbase 9ft 3in from 1952

KERB WEIGHT:
26.6cwt

PERFORMANCE:
(Source: *The Autocar*)

Max speed	74mph
0–50mph	19.8sec
0–60mph	30.0sec
30–50mph in top	13.5sec

PRICE INCLUDING TAX WHEN NEW:
£991 (February 1950)

NUMBER BUILT: 6501

1800 Roadster
1946–1948

As 1800 saloon except:

DIMENSIONS:

Length	14ft ½in
Wheelbase	8ft 4in
Width	5ft 4in
Height	4ft 8in

NUMBER BUILT: 2501

2000 Roadster
1948–1949

As for 1800 Roadster but incorporating 2000 saloon engine/transmission

KERB WEIGHT:
21.96cwt

PERFORMANCE:
(Source: *The Autocar*)

Max speed	77mph
0–50mph	17.7sec
0–60mph	27.9sec
30–50mph in top	13.6sec

PRICE INCLUDING TAX WHEN NEW:
£991 (February 1949)

NUMBER BUILT: 2000

Triumph Mayflower
1950–1953

ENGINE:
Four cylinders in line, cast-iron block and alloy head

Capacity	1247cc
Bore x stroke	63mm x 100mm
Valve actuation	Sidevalve
Compression ratio	6.7 to 1
Carburettor	Single Solex
Power	38bhp at 4200rpm
Maximum torque	58lb ft at 2000rpm

TRANSMISSION:
Rear-wheel drive; three-speed all-synchromesh gearbox; column change

SUSPENSION:
Front: Independent by coil and wishbone; telescopic dampers
Rear: Live axle with semi-elliptic springs; telescopic dampers

STEERING:
Cam-and-lever

BRAKES:
Front/rear: Hydraulic drum

WHEELS/TYRES:
15in steel disc wheels
5 x 15in tyres (5.5 x 15in for export)

BODYWORK:
Two-door saloon
Steel monocoque

DIMENSIONS:

Length	12ft 10in
Wheelbase	7ft 0in
Track, front	3ft 9in
Track, rear	4ft 0in
Width	5ft 2in
Height	5ft 2in

KERB WEIGHT:
18.8cwt

PERFORMANCE:
(Source: *The Autocar*)

Max speed	65mph
0–50mph	23.9sec
0–60mph	42.6sec
30–50mph in top	16.3sec

PRICE INCLUDING TAX WHEN NEW:
£505 (April 1950)

NUMBER BUILT:
33,990 (additionally 10 dropheads)

technology and engineering, whereas the Triumph 1800 Saloon and Roadster were built in smaller numbers by much more traditional methods.

Work on the two new Triumphs commenced as early as the 1944/45 winter, at a time when war was still raging; indeed, a press release giving details (later modified) was issued as early as February 1945. Of necessity, the Triumphs were compelled to use as many existing Standard components as possible, and this included the 1776cc ohv engine that Standard had produced for Jaguar from the 1938 model year. Black had sold Jaguar the tooling for the 2½-litre and 3½-litre engines Standard also made for William Lyons's company, only capriciously (and fruitlessly) to change his mind a short time later; but fortunately he had retained the rights and tooling for the 1776cc unit. A well-proven engine, it was relatively modern and would suffice for the Triumphs pending supplies of the all-new Vanguard unit. Coupled to this was the four-speed gearbox found in the larger Standards, but adapted to give a right-hand column shift, much fashionable at the time as a way of allowing three-abreast seating. The transverse-leaf independent front suspension developed for the bigger

A photograph dated 1 March 1946 depicts the tubular chassis frame used on Triumph's first post-war models, the 1800 Roadster and saloon.

Standard saloons in the late 1930s was used, as was their leaf-sprung spiral-bevel rear axle, together with many other components from the company parts bin.

What was essential was a new chassis to tie all these well-tried components together. As sheet steel was in such short supply, the plot was to use more readily available steel tube, Standard having gained much experience in the art of fabrication from steel tubing during wartime aircraft production. Part of the brief was to produce a chassis easily adaptable to different wheelbases, for the proposed Roadster would be considerably shorter than the saloon. The new chassis was to be made in-house, no problem given the highly skilled men coming off military work who were available to undertake production. With its extensive use of existing components, the new chassis could be readied swiftly, but the bodies presented a greater problem.

In 1945 Walter Belgrove, the company's chief stylist and the man who had designed the 1937 Dolomites, was still having to undertake war work, and thus the task of drawing the Roadster was entrusted to Arthur Ballard and Frank Callaby, later to become the company's chief photographer. Callaby produced the overall sketches and dealt in detail with the front half of the car, including the unusual pontoon front wings, whereas Ballard designed the rear,

including the by-then archaic dickey-seat, incorporated specifically at Sir John Black's insistence. The set-back radiator grille, close-mounted headlights and twin chromed horns, coupled with the low build, the dickey seat and the rear-hinged doors, certainly gave the 1800 Roadster a different look, one that was either loved or hated.

However, in the shortage-of-everything world of 1946, the new car was bound to sell irrespective of what the public thought of it.

Launched in March 1946, the Roadster 1800, as it was called, was into production first simply because its body was produced in-house at Canley by traditional coachbuilding methods, in other words an ash frame clothed with aluminium panels, these being shaped on the rubber presses installed during the war for aircraft manufacture. It was labour-intensive, to be sure, but made sense given the good supply of skilled men and the fact that aluminium sheet was available whereas sheet steel was scarce.

The body for the 1800 'Town and Country' saloon – the name Renown came later – was as striking as that of the Roadster, being of a revolutionary razor-edged style developed from up-market pre-war coachbuilding practice. The car still had flowing front wings, running boards, rear-hinged front doors, and separate headlamps – all part of the pre-war ethos – but

Above: A beautifully rebuilt example of the 1800 Roadster with hood erected. On the rear bumper are the tread plates to assist passengers in clambering into the dickey seat.

Left: Rallying in the gentlemanly age – a Triumph Roadster at a checkpoint on a London rally, year unknown. The presence of duffle coats and seamed stockings add to the period flavour.

The razor-edge cars and the press

Road tests in the 1940s and early 1950s were not the searching exposés of today; indeed, it is often hard to winkle out any element of criticism from their bland words; one sometimes forms the impression that the testers were so grateful to get their hands on a car at all that they dared write only platitudes. Thus it is that in the few published tests of the 1800 saloon and Renown you will not gain much insight into any shortcomings – other than that the seats were 'difficult to adjust', and that the column change was only 'good of its type'.

The 1800 comes across as somewhat under-powered, as indeed it was in relation to its weight, the 0–60mph acceleration time being near to 40 seconds, whereas the Renown 2000 could manage an exact half-minute. Seventy-ish seemed about the average top speed, with 50mph cruising happy enough in the 1776cc car, rising to 55mph in the 2000 and even 60mph with the optional overdrive. Representative fuel consumption was around 23mpg. The steering was described as 'light and positive', with the hydraulic brakes 'powerful and pulling up strongly in all conditions, including wet roads,' but otherwise described as 'not worthy of special comment'. The 2000 version in particular was

said to be 'very much a top gear car' – able to pull strongly down to as low as 10mph, and with powerful top-gear hillclimbing ability, something lacking in the 1800. 'Refreshingly accessible' was the description of the engine, thanks to the traditional centre-hinged two-piece bonnet, already by then an anachronism. The one word always used about the styling was 'distinctive' – which could of course be taken either way. The words 'traditional British' and 'quality' also kept coming up in reports on the cars, as did the pleasant airiness of the interior and the excellent visibility given by the large glass area inherent in the razor-edged style. Overall, one gets the impression that testers found the big Triumph saloon unexciting but worthy; in fact, just what the post-war middle classes wanted.

For the Mayflower, again that word 'distinctive' appears in reports – 'quite unlike any other light car,' as *The Autocar* said. The magazine loved the razor-edged look, and made the telling points that it provided for more cabin room in a given length of car than other styles, as well as room to breathe by virtue of an increased volume of air within the boxy shape.

As to how the car went, weighing just under a ton with but 38bhp, it is

not surprising that the 0–60 sprint – if such a word can be used – took 43 seconds, with 30–50mph in top demanding 17 seconds. The car could in favourable conditions be worked up to 65mph, but 60mph was a more realistic maximum. Forty miles in an hour proved possible on the miserable English roads of the day, which was not too bad, with a level cruising speed of 50mph. Not too much was said of hillclimbing ability – with three very widely spaced gear ratios, it must have been either maximum revs in first, or struggling in second. Fuel consumption of 32–35mpg was considered excellent, as was the quality of the column gearchange. 'First-rate' suspension, 'accurate steering' and 'quietness of running' added to the quality feel, as did the well-trimmed interior. The 'self-effacing' engine was said to be capable of pulling the car at 6mph in top gear, should you be so misguided. Taken all round, it is clear that the Mayflower grew on those who tested it the more they drove it – as an all-round package it was considered excellent value at a tax-paid price of £505 in 1950, a sum that not only purchased a modern, top-quality small car, but one that had an indefinable air of character.

married this to an airy square-cut glasshouse.

Frank Callaby was asked by Black to do initial sketches, which were submitted to body manufacturers Mulliners of Birmingham, later to become a Standard-Triumph subsidiary. Meanwhile, Walter Belgrove, finally released from war work, put together his own razor-edged scheme, and eventually an amalgam of the Belgrove and Mulliners proposals was accepted by Black, with Mulliners making the production body, as the envisaged

quantities would be beyond Standard-Triumph's own capacity. As with the Roadster, traditional ash framing with aluminium skinning was used, the bodies being trimmed in leather.

The first production 1800 saloons were on the road in late 1946 and as with the Roadster they received a mixed reception on account of their styling. Sales in car-starved Europe were assured, but reaction to both models in the free market of the US was muted, and neither car had anything like the anticipated export success. Body production methods as

well as material shortages limited numbers built, but nevertheless 2,501 of the 1776cc Standard-engined Roadsters and something over 4,000 of the similarly-engined saloons were constructed.

At the October 1948 London Motor Show the Roadster appeared with the 2088cc Vanguard engine, along with the Vanguard three-speed gearbox and rear axle, these same components finding their way into the saloon a little later, in February 1949. The new cars were known as the Triumph 2000 Roadster and the Triumph 2000

Right: The three-abreast seating of the Triumph 1800 Roadster. In an age of austerity, the Triumph was a high-quality car. Observe the unusual right-hand steering-column gearlever.

Below right: The dickey seats aren't hugely comfortable, especially on bumpy roads, as you are sitting right over the underslung rear axle.

saloon. In the latter's case a further revision took place for the October 1949 motor show when a long-wheelbase (108in) version of the Vanguard box-section chassis replaced the previous tubular frame, the column gearchange simultaneously changing to the left-hand side of the steering wheel. It was only with effect from these 1950-model-year saloons, known as the TDB series, that the name Renown was adopted.

Sadly, the Roadster was dropped altogether in October 1949, after exactly 2,000 of the revised model had been made, of which a mere 184 had been exported. Although no sales success, the Roadster nevertheless helped re-establish the Triumph name. It was a glamorous car at a grey time. Yes, it was more of a boulevard cruiser than a true sports car and, no, the Americans did not want it. But in retrospect it was a worthwhile exercise, and time has proved it a durable vehicle. A surprisingly high proportion survive today, and in good condition cars change hands for five-figure sums. This has in some part been assisted by the use of a 2000 Roadster in the famous 1980s TV detective series *Bergerac* – indeed many today refer to the car simply as the 'Bergerac Triumph'.

Sales of the saloon improved when the larger and more torquey engine arrived, a further 6,501 Renowns being made up to the discontinuing of the TDB series at the start of 1952. In mid-1950 the Renown had become one of the very first cars to be offered with the new Laycock overdrive unit, an option which both increased cruising speed and saved fuel. The final TDC series of Renown saloons had an extra

3in added to their wheelbase, which gave a small amount of extra legroom and a disproportionate amount of weight, as well as ensuring a lack of commonality in body panels with earlier cars. The longer wheelbase had

originally been introduced for the Renown limousine, another of Black's pet projects, and which was really no more than a saloon with the longer wheelbase and a glass division. A mere 189 of these follies were sold in

Driving a 2000 Roadster

When the author was five or six years old, the local doctor acquired a 2000 Roadster, a car that impressed the young Piggott no end – it appeared so low and wide and the possession of a second windscreen in what seemed to be the boot was utterly fascinating, as was the fact that, uniquely, it sported three windscreen wipers. Fifty years on I have now been able to drive such a car, and it comes across as an engagingly stately old cruiser.

Considerable wear in the gear linkage led to a vague change on the car in question but the torque of the Vanguard engine meant the car would pull easily from very low speeds in top. The Triumph does not so much accelerate as gently gather speed until at an indicated 60mph it feels quite fast enough. The cross-ply tyres true to form follow the white lines in the road and cause a certain amount of wandering. Still, by 1949 standards the handling was perfectly acceptable, although the car does not

relish any attempt to rush through corners. The non-servo brakes feel surprisingly powerful and inspire considerable confidence. The wide gaps between the three gear ratios are very apparent, and 45mph is quite adequate in second.

Locating oneself on the slippery leather seat is something of a problem – maybe three-abreast one would be wedged more firmly. The Roadster rides surprisingly comfortably in a rolling sort of way, with few of the creaks and groans usual in open cars, although scuttle shake is only too obvious on hitting a mid-corner bump. Erecting the hood causes serious claustrophobia, and rearward vision becomes a bad joke. Although I did not travel in the dickey seat, I climbed in to satisfy myself that it was possible. The little folding seats in the rear would suffice for a three-mile trip to the pub on a summer evening, but any lengthy journey would become a feat of endurance.

the 1952 model year. By this time post-war car shortages had abated significantly and the razor-edged saloon was looking dated. In 1953 sales slowed to a trickle, leaving fields of unsold Renowns. Black accordingly stopped production temporarily and ordered a major price cut, from £925 to £775 pre-tax. Surprisingly, production of the now seriously old-fashioned Triumph did restart, but only in penny numbers, and the final two Renowns were made on 28 October 1954. They were the last saloons – at least in the UK – to carry the Triumph name for five years, as they had no direct replacement.

With 2,800 of these final TDC-series cars sold, total razor-edged saloon production exceeded 13,000, a mere fraction of the numbers of Vanguards built, but a reasonable success nevertheless, despite the dearth of export sales.

The razor-edged style had one further representative in the Triumph catalogues, for in 1949 a little brother to the Renown emerged. This was the Mayflower, another Sir John Black eccentricity – although one that did ultimately sell quite well.

With only the medium-sized Vanguard and Renown in production by late 1949, it was clear that Standard-Triumph was in danger of missing the small-car market altogether. However, Black had the commercial savvy to realise that his company could not compete at that time with the industry giants in making a cheap small car for the masses – although it tried later. It was for this reason that he saw the Mayflower as being more of a miniature Rolls Royce than a bargain-basement runabout.

The small Triumph was of unitary construction, unlike the Renown, and while the styling was largely the work of Leslie Moore of Mulliners, the actual bodies were built by the makers of the Vanguard shell, Fisher and Ludlow. Both Walter Belgrove and Black himself had some input into the styling, which incorporated a large glass area, built-in headlamps and no running boards, touches which ensured that the Mayflower looked

Above: A well-preserved 1949 TDA-series 2000: it has the 2088cc Vanguard engine but retains the tubular chassis. The flashing indicators are a later addition.

Right: The glassy passenger compartment is evident from the rear; the spare wheel hides in the boot lid.

Opposite: The Standard 1800cc engine in a Roadster. The downdraught Solex carburettor is in evidence.

somewhat more modern than the larger car.

The Mayflower was no sports saloon. Indeed, with only a unique-to-the-model 1247cc sidevalve engine of 38bhp to pull along its considerable weight, how could it be? The aluminium-head engine was developed from that of the pre-war Standard Ten and despite its lack of power it ran sweetly and silently; whilst it would be lucky to stagger up

The Standard Vanguard

The Vanguard is important to the Triumph story not only because its success financed the various Triumph projects, but also because its excellent engine went on, in modified forms, not only to power tractors but also the TR sports cars right up until 1967.

A common misconception is that this engine, with removable water-surrounded cylinder liners, was derived from a design by US manufacturer Continental. In fact, technical director Ted Grinham is on record as citing the 1934–57 Citroën Traction Avant wet-liner engine as his inspiration. As originally designed, it was of 1850cc, but an enlarged 85mm bore brought dimensions up to 2088cc before production began. In this size, it produced 68bhp plus the considerable torque of 110lb ft at a low 2000rpm. Sporting overhead valves, it was fuel efficient too, Vanguards commonly bettering 30mpg despite their weight.

The car that gave its engine to a number of Triumphs, from the Renown to the TR4A of 1967: the Standard Vanguard, in this instance a Phase I with the rear wheel spats not present on the earliest cars and with the fine-slat first-type radiator grille.

Longevity and ease of service were other characteristics, and as well as use in the Renown and Roadster, it soon found its way into Morgan's Plus Four sports car where it gave a great lift to performance.

As the first truly modern post-war British car – just beating the Jowett Javelin to this title – the Vanguard was a major success, selling well in export markets (except of course in the US) and being particularly popular in 'colonial' territories; helping sales, Vanguards were locally assembled in countries such as Australia, India and South Africa. The bulbous, beetle-backed Phase I and Phase IA cars ran until 1953 before being replaced by the Phase II (or Spacemaster in Australia) with its extended boot. In late 1955 the monocoque Phase III arrived, still powered by the same engine. Van, pick-up and estate car versions were also made (the Phase III van and pick-up being Australia-only 'specials'), and the estates were very popular with the services, particularly the RAF. The last manifestation of a long line adopted a six-cylinder, two-litre engine in 1960.

From 1957 the Phase III was available in stripped-out form as the Ensign, initially with a 1670cc version of the Vanguard engine but from May 1962 with a TR-sized 2138cc unit.

A Standard Vanguard drophead coupé – never an official UK model, but a number were built by the Belgian firm Imperia who assembled Standards and Triumphs from kits. This example, however, has right-hand drive.

Right: The saloon dashboard, similar to that of the Roadster, went over to a new five-dial arrangement on the later Renown.

Below right: The inviting-looking rear compartment of Triumph's razor-edged saloon, complete with pull-out Bakelite ashtrays in the armrests.

to 60mph flat-out, it could cruise happily at 50mph. Only a three-speed gearbox was offered (this being a derivative of the Vanguard 'box), although all gears at least had synchromesh; operation was by column lever. Independent front suspension was by wishbones and coil springs, a system which in modified form later appeared on the TRs, and rear springing was by orthodox semi-elliptics, the axle being a modified Vanguard unit, again as later utilised on the TR2, but with a low 5.125-to-1 ratio necessitated by the tiny engine. Full hydraulic braking offered very adequate retardation.

Equipment was good for a small car, and for some markets included leather upholstery and a heater as standard, while metallic paint finishes were available at extra cost.

Announced in October 1949 at the London Motor Show, deliveries, which included CKD kits for local assembly in some overseas markets, did not commence until mid-1950. Sales to non-US markets were brisk, and for the first time since the war, a Standard-Triumph model was relatively easily available on the home market. Americans sadly did not take to the Mayflower, dashing Sir John's hopes of major success there. Unfortunately the small Triumph, deliberately named to appeal in the US, was not really suitable for American conditions. At best it could be considered a contender for the second-car market, or as a quaint little British eccentricity, interesting and stylish, but not a real car: as a serious vehicle for long-distance cruising, it was neither fast nor mechanically robust enough.

The 1950 Motor Show saw the introduction of what can only be considered as another Black folly, the Mayflower drophead. Allegedly

Above: 'The Little Rolls-Royce' – a charming recreated village scene depicts the Triumph Mayflower from the early 1950s. Triumph were early users of metallic paint.

Right: The interior of the Mayflower is plain but well executed. A steering-column gearchange was always used.

conceived as a present to please his wife, Sir John had Mulliners slice the roof off a Mayflower and turn it into a drophead coupé, complete with a heavy hood incorporating traditional pram-irons and the inevitable huge blind spots. Also inevitable was the addition of body stiffening that further increased weight on a car that was underpowered in the first place. Production plans were shelved after just ten examples had been made. Lady Black is reported to have loved her example, however!

By this time there was a clamour from the sales department to fit a more powerful, overhead-valve engine to the Mayflower, but despite the fact that such a conversion already existed – supplied to Morgan for their 4/4 model – it never reached the Mayflower, which continued with virtually no development during its three-and-a-half-year production run.

Rather, the company made the decision in early 1952 to pursue the opposite end of the small car market, and to go after all for volume. Thus began the gestation period of the Standard Eight – one of the most basic of cars ever thrust on the buying public, and one described (perhaps unkindly) as the poor man's Ford Anglia. The Mayflower was duly withdrawn in the autumn of 1953.

In retrospect, transposing razor-edged styling to a small car was a brave attempt at something different and classy, but had ultimately led only up a blind alley. Sales of the Mayflower totalled a round 34,000, just one half of which – 17,605 – were exported. The car was not a flop by any means, but it ended up a long way from the 100,000 US sales Sir John had optimistically envisaged. The Mayflower has proved surprisingly durable and engenders considerable affection amongst enthusiasts, ladies particularly admiring its cute style.

The TRX 'Silver Bullet'

The TRX Roadster was a bizarre aberration, conceived by Sir John Black in 1947 as a potential replacement for the Roadster, but which took ages to finish. Black set Walter Belgrove to design the TRX almost as a flight of fancy: it was to be as modern a car as possible, to the point of being futuristic. The only constraints were that a modified Vanguard chassis had to be employed, together with its drivetrain. Having missed the chance to style the original Roadster, Belgrove grasped the opportunity. Sadly, the result was certainly striking and up-to-date, but too heavy, too complex and too expensive to manufacture economically.

Black had long wanted a true sports car in his company's line-up to take on both Jaguar and MG in the lucrative US market, one with almost limitless potential. The TRX was designed with this in mind, and to that end the car incorporated 'power-everything' – features that it was felt would appeal in the USA, and which were years ahead of their time. Thus a complicated hydraulic and electrical system operated a power hood, powered seats, pop-up headlights, plus power-operated jacks, windows and radio aerial.

The bullet-shaped bodywork incorporated complex curvatures and was made of double-skinned aluminium panelling, difficult to produce and

Belgrove's folly? The TRX Silver Bullet, the futuristic, all-powered Roadster of 1950, a car years before its time yet far too complex to manufacture at anything like a realistic price. This is one of two survivors.

difficult to repair. The unique one-piece bonnet was capable of being opened from either side. The car was beautifully trimmed to the highest standard and was finished in silver metallic paint. A 'B' badge (for 'Belgrove') was set on the front wings, the Triumph globe appearing elsewhere.

The car was unveiled at 1950 London Motor Show, where it caused something of a sensation and elicited a good number of orders and an invitation to appear at the forthcoming Festival of Britain. However, the TRX was nowhere near ready for production. Road-testing soon showed

that here was another boulevard-cruiser, for the car wallowed around and even by the standards of the day could not be said to handle well. It was also barely faster than the 2000 Roadster. The engine had twin SU carburettors and other minor tuning modifications, raising its output to approximately 71bhp, but this was nowhere near enough to produce the sporting performance that Black desired or that the car's looks promised: the TRX was simply too heavy.

Throughout 1951 and into 1952, the TRX was evaluated by various Standard-Triumph directors and marketing men, but detailed costings proved that it could not be built at a realistic price. In addition, the prototype caught fire on two occasions, and much trouble was experienced in getting the various powered systems to work correctly. By mid-1952 it became obvious that the 'Silver Bullet' was not the way to go, and Black ordered work to start on the 20TS sports prototype, the car that ultimately became the TR2. As for the TRX, it was quietly forgotten after just two prototypes plus an uncompleted third car had been made – another fascinating 'might-have-been'.

The interior is suitably ritzy – but sporting it is not.

The Vanguard Sportsman

There never was such a thing as a TR saloon, but there very nearly was – in the shape of the Standard Vanguard Sportsman. Introduced in August 1956, this was a Phase III Vanguard with uprated brakes and suspension, an engine almost to TR3 specification, an optional floor gearchange with overdrive, and a neat Triumph-style grille. The plan had been to badge this crossbreed as a Triumph, and indeed the Triumph globe appears on the grille, but at the last moment the decision was reversed and the car remained a Standard. The Sportsman was surprisingly rapid, being capable of around 95mph, but sadly it did not have handling or braking to match its speed. Perhaps it was just as well that it was not given the Triumph badge. Available for only just over a year, fewer than 1,000 cars are thought to have been built, making them rare indeed today.

Buying Hints

1. The wood framing on a restoration-project Roadster will invariably need replacing at least in part. The vulnerable elements are the sills, the timbers around the door apertures and the lower parts of the door frames, plus the wood around the windscreen.

2. Saloon wood framing is similarly rot-prone, especially around the rear wheelarches. One of the few areas where the frame can be inspected is in the boot area: remove the trim panels in the boot and you can see the timber. Mostly the sight will not be a pretty one. Poorly fitting rear doors are a sign, in any case, that all is not well. Although no replacement timber is available, the Triumph Razoredge Owners' Club can provide drawings.

3. Beware a Roadster that has had a rear-end accident. Most of the strength at the rear comes from the double-skinning of the alloy panelling around the wheelarches. This can be difficult to repair, and a car that has received a bash here may well be full of filler.

4. The Roadster chassis has two sheet-steel stiffeners welded to the longitudinal chassis rails at the front of the car, and these can rust

through; replacement is straightforward. Look also for rust at the point where a flat steel plate is welded to the front transverse tube to serve as the radiator mount, at the back of the car where the main rails dip under the axle, and on the chassis tube adjacent to the headlamp mountings. The outriggers to which the body is mounted should be checked for corrosion, whether on a Roadster or a tubular-chassis saloon.

5. The Vanguard chassis of later saloons is very robust, but look out for rust at the rear end. At the front, the mounting on the crossmember to which the steering idler is attached can fracture, resulting in woolly steering; this mounting is often reinforced in the course of a repair.

6. Regardless of what you might have heard, there is plenty of steel in an 1800/2000/Renown body – and it rusts. Spots to check include the rear of the front wings, the rear wings, the inner wings, the boot floor, and the boot sides. The good news is that the doors are protected by the running boards, and thus tend not to corrode.

7. Engine and gearbox parts for 1800s are hard to find, despite being shared with the Standard Fourteen. Both the Triumph Roadster

Club and the Triumph Razoredge Owners' Club offer excellent support, so keeping a car on the road shouldn't pose a problem, all the same. The brake master cylinders are unique to the Triumph 1800, but fortunately a club specialist can rebuild these. Later cars use the Morris Minor cylinder.

8. The Vanguard-derived elements of the Mayflower's running gear go on for ever, and there is plenty of interchangeability with the TR; in any case, the Triumph Mayflower Club has an excellent spares operation. Brake parts, master cylinder excepted, are common with those used on early Morris Minors.

9. The alloy cylinder head is the only Mayflower weak point, being prone to corrosion; suspect, therefore, a car suffering from overheating and/or water loss.

10. The body of the Mayflower is gratifyingly rust-resistant; sills and wing bottoms will corrode through, however, and all the normal weak spots – behind the headlamps, the bottoms of the doors, and so on – should be checked. Outer sills are available, but otherwise you will have to resort to secondhand panels, which fortunately are to be found through the club.

Driving the Mayflower

The Mayflower is to be driven in accordance with its looks: sedately, in other words. Not that there's a huge amount of choice, as the sidevalve engine and three-speed gearbox limit performance to the genteel side of slow. A happy cruising speed is a nicely refined 45mph, but given a bit of space the upright little saloon will creep up to 50–55mph and then plug along at this rate. Hills slow the Mayflower considerably, but the long-stroke engine's torque means that a downchange isn't always necessary. At least the gearchange is nice and easy, with a firm and precise movement, while synchromesh on first helps wring the best out of the car's modest 38bhp in extreme circumstances.

In its chassis behaviour the Mayflower surprises. With relatively firm suspension, it handles accurately, with none of the front-end softness of an Austin of the period, and without the heroic understeer of its razor-edged big brother the Renown. Helped by quick, smooth and well-weighted steering, it can be cornered at quite a reasonable pace, helped by short-travel brakes that inspire ample confidence. The only flaw is a fair bit of roll, possibly exacerbated by a front track three inches narrower than that at the rear.

All in all, the Mayflower is an unexpectedly charming little device for those who are happy to let the scenery pass at a gentle pace; with an ohv engine and a four-speed gearbox it would have been transformed.

The radiator badge of the Mayflower evokes the origins of the car's name, harking back to the vessel in which the Pilgrim Fathers sailed to America.

Lady Black's pet – one of the ten Mayflower drophead coupés built in 1950, one of which was used by the chairman's wife. Although stylish, its weight and cost militated against this model reaching full production.

The *Herald* *family*

To understand the history of the Triumph Herald range of small cars, introduced in 1959, one must first mention the Standard Eights and Tens that the Herald replaced – and risk a certain amount of

One of the set of initial publicity pictures used for the Herald's press launch. Three fashionable ladies take a picnic to a country house location.

indigestion. The little Standards were the direct follow-on to the Triumph Mayflower, the 803cc Eight appearing in October 1953 and the less spartan 948cc Ten a year later. They are important in the Triumph story, as the Ten's engine and gearbox formed the basis of the Herald's mechanicals.

The Standard Eights and Tens improved rapidly after a somewhat shaky start. After all, basic as they

initially were – and the Eight was so basic that Sir John Black tastelessly referred to it as the 'Belsen line' – the engineering of the cars was sound. They had a modern four-speed synchromesh transmission and an overhead-valve engine, both something beyond Ford at that time, and the handling and brakes were well up to the standards of the day. Indeed, a Standard Ten managed to win the

Right: The car that donated its engine (albeit in enlarged form) to the Herald and the Spitfire. The Standard Eight was a basic car even by the values of the day.

Below: The convertible is a genuine four-seater. Look closely at this photo and you can see the positive camber of the crude swing-axle rear suspension. The lifting handle on the bonnet was only found on the 948cc Heralds (except the 'S') and on 1200s made up until June 1961.

1955 RAC Rally outright, and even Stirling Moss drove a modified example. As well as the four-door saloons, there was a more upmarket Pennant from 1957, and a Companion estate car which continued in production until 1962; the van and pick-up variants, meanwhile, lasted until 1965, thus being the last vehicles in the UK to carry the Standard name. As a range, the Eight/Ten must be judged a success, with well in excess of 200,000 examples being built.

Meanwhile, the Triumph badge was largely restricted to the TR sports car. In the US an ill-fated attempt was made to sell the Standard Ten off the back of the TR2/3 by calling it the Triumph TR10 – yes, really – and the more upmarket Triumph badge had appeared on Standard cars in some other export markets. But no proper new Triumph saloon was available after a proposal to badge a version of the Vanguard Phase III as a Triumph (see previous chapter) had been abandoned at the last moment. Despite this, the decision was taken to use the Triumph name for the new small car.

Herald 948 cc
1959–64

ENGINE:

Capacity	948cc
Bore x stroke	63mm x 76mm
Valve actuation	Pushrod
Compression ratio	8.0:1
Carburettor	Single Solex
Power	35bhp at 4500rpm
Maximum torque	51lb ft at 2750rpm

TRANSMISSION:
Rear-wheel drive; four-speed gearbox

SUSPENSION:
Front: Independent by coil and wishbone; anti-roll bar; telescopic dampers
Rear: Independent by swing axles and transverse leaf spring, location by radius arms; telescopic dampers

STEERING:
Rack-and-pinion

BRAKES:
Front/rear: Hydraulic drum

WHEELS/TYRES:
13in steel disc wheels
Tyres 5.20 x 13

BODYWORK:
Steel panels
Separate chassis

DIMENSIONS:

Length	12ft 9in
Wheelbase	7ft 7½in
Track, front	4ft 0in
Track, rear	4ft 0in
Width	5ft 0in
Height	4ft 4in

KERB WEIGHT: 15.75cwt

PRICE INCLUDING TAX WHEN NEW:
£702, or £737 with coupé engine (April 1960)

NUMBER BUILT:

Saloon (incl 'S')	76,860

Herald Coupé/ Convertible (948 cc)
1959–61

As saloon except:

ENGINE:

Compression ratio	8.5 to 1
Carburettors	Twin SU
Power	45bhp at 6000rpm
Maximum torque	51lb ft at 4200rpm

DIMENSIONS:

Height	4ft 3¼in

KERB WEIGHT:
15.25cwt (coupé)

PERFORMANCE:
(Source: *The Motor*)

Max speed	75.5mph
0–60mph	25.5sec
30–50mph in top	15.9sec
50–70mph in top	30.6sec

PRICE INCLUDING TAX WHEN NEW:
£731 coupé; £766 convertible (April 1960)

NUMBER BUILT:

Coupé	15,153
Convertible	8,262

Herald 1200
1961–70

As 948cc except:

ENGINE:

Capacity	1147cc
Bore x stroke	69.3mm x 76mm
Power	39bhp at 4500rpm
Maximum torque	61lb ft at 2250rpm

BRAKES:
Front: Discs optional on all models from October 1961

WHEELS/TYRES:
Estate: tyres 5.60 x 13in

KERB WEIGHT:
15.4cwt (saloon)

PERFORMANCE:
(Source: *The Motor*)

Max speed	75.4mph
0–60mph	23.9sec
30–50mph in top	13.7sec

PRICE INCLUDING TAX WHEN NEW:
£579 saloon; £604 coupé; £642 convertible; £662 estate (December 1962)

NUMBER BUILT:

Saloon	201,142
Coupé	5,319
Convertible	43,295
Estate	39,819 incl Courier van

Herald 12/50 saloon
1963–67

As 1200 saloon except:

ENGINE:

Compression ratio	8.5 to 1
Power	51bhp at 5200rpm
Maximum torque	63lb ft at 2600rpm

BRAKES:
Front: Disc

KERB WEIGHT:
16.6cwt

PERFORMANCE:
(Source: *Autocar*)

Max speed	77.5mph
0–60mph	25.2sec
30–50mph in top	14.9sec
50–70mph in top	25.8sec

PRICE INCLUDING TAX WHEN NEW:
£635 (August 1963)

NUMBER BUILT:
53,267

Herald 13/60
1967–71

As Herald 1200 except:

ENGINE:

Bore x stroke	73.7mm x 76mm
Capacity	1296cc
Compression ratio	8.5 to 1
Carburettor	Single Zenith-Stromberg
Power	61 bhp at 5000rpm
Maximum torque	73lb ft at 3000rpm

BRAKES:
Front: Disc

DIMENSIONS:

Track, front	4ft 1in

KERB WEIGHT:
16.4cwt (saloon)

PERFORMANCE:
(Source: *Motor*)

Max speed	82.1mph
0–60mph	16.6sec
30–50mph in top	10.8sec
50–70mph in top	17.1sec

PRICE INCLUDING TAX WHEN NEW:
£728 saloon; £785 convertible; £805 estate (April 1968)

NUMBER BUILT:

Saloon	38,886
Sunroof saloon	1,547
Estate	15,467
Convertible	11,772
CKD	14,978

Vitesse 1600
1962–66

As Herald except:

ENGINE:
Six cylinders in line, cast-iron block and head
Capacity	1596cc
Bore x stroke	66.75mm x 76mm
Compression ratio	8.75:1
Carburettors	Twin Solex
Power	70bhp at 5000rpm
Maximum torque	92lb ft at 2800rpm

BRAKES:
Front: Disc
Rear: Drum

WHEELS/TYRES:
Tyres 5.60 x 13in

DIMENSIONS:
Length	12ft 9in
Track, front	4ft 1in
Track, rear	4ft 0in
Width	5ft 0in
Height	4ft 4½in

KERB WEIGHT:
18.1cwt (saloon)

PERFORMANCE:
(Source: *Autocar*)
Max speed	87mph
0–60mph	17.8sec
30–50mph in top	10.0sec
50–70mph in top	14.2sec

PRICE INCLUDING TAX WHEN NEW:
£735 saloon (January 1963)

NUMBER BUILT:
Saloon	22,814
Convertible	8,447

Vitesse 2-Litre
1966–68

As Vitesse 1600 except:

ENGINE:
Capacity	1998cc
Bore x stroke	74.7mm x 76mm
Compression ratio	9.5 to 1
Carburettors	Twin Zenith-Stromberg
Power	95bhp at 5000rpm
Maximum torque	117lb ft at 3000rpm

KERB WEIGHT:
18.3cwt (saloon)

PERFORMANCE:
(Source: *Motor*)
Max speed	98.3mph
0–60mph	12.4sec
30–50mph in top	7.3sec
50–70mph in top	9.2sec

PRICE INCLUDING TAX WHEN NEW:
£839 saloon; £883 convertible (September 1967)

NUMBER BUILT:
Saloon	7,328
Convertible	3,502

Vitesse 2-Litre MkII
1968–71

As 2-litre Vitesse MkI except:

ENGINE:
Compression ratio	9.25:1
Power	104bhp at 5300rpm
Maximum torque	117lb ft at 3100rpm

SUSPENSION:
Rear: Independent by transverse leaf spring with lower wishbones, Rotoflex couplings, location by radius arms; lever-arm dampers

WHEELS/TYRES:
Tyres 155 x 13in

DIMENSIONS:
Track, rear	4ft 0½in

KERB WEIGHT:
18.9cwt (saloon)

PERFORMANCE:
(Source: *Motor*)
Max speed	101mph
0–60mph	11.3sec
30–50mph in top	7.6sec
50–70mph in top	8.3sec

PRICE INCLUDING TAX WHEN NEW:
£972 saloon without overdrive (February 1969)

NUMBER BUILT:
Saloon	5,649
Convertible	3,472

By 1956, with a new management team at Standard-Triumph following the enforced departure of Black and the resignation of Walter Belgrove, the time was right for some fresh thinking about the next-generation small car, codenamed Zobo. It had already been settled that the car would have a separate chassis, a reversal of the universal trend towards monocoque bodies. The incorporation of a chassis frame was the idea of new director of engineering Harry Webster. It would make for easy assembly of the car when supplied in kit form for overseas markets, something that the company was keen to pursue; it would facilitate offering different styles of body on the one basic chassis; finally it would perhaps most importantly make the building of the bodies in the UK easier, for Standard was having big problems with bodywork suppliers. Fisher and Ludlow had been taken over by rival

BMC and were thus presumed to be lost to the company as body builders, while Pressed Steel did not have sufficient capacity to take on the Zobo work. Whoever was to manufacture the body, there was an equally fundamental problem: none of the various styling proposals produced in-house really gelled. In desperation the directors looked abroad – and where better than to Italy? At this point there enters the story Giovanni Michelotti, the diminutive Italian who had such an effect on the style of Triumph cars for more than a decade. His first project for Standard-Triumph as a consultant had been a proposed revamp of the TR3 in early 1957, and the company was sufficiently impressed to pay him a retainer to secure his future services.

In mid-1957 Michelotti spent some weeks endeavouring to instil some style into the home-grown proposals for Zobo, but even he could make little

of it. Finally, in September 1957, Webster suggested that Michelotti come up with something entirely of his own. Webster later recalled that Michelotti sketched in outline what became the Herald coupé in no more than five minutes, as he watched. This design looked so right that eighth-scale drawings were produced overnight for Webster to take back to Coventry, just in time to prevent serious money being committed to one of the alternative – and unsatisfactory – designs.

Not only had Michelotti broken the impasse, but via his associates at the Vignale coachbuilding company he assured Triumph that a prototype completed bodyshell could be in Coventry in barely eight weeks. And indeed it was, causing great excitement. In addition to the coupé, a full four-seat saloon and an estate car were also commissioned.

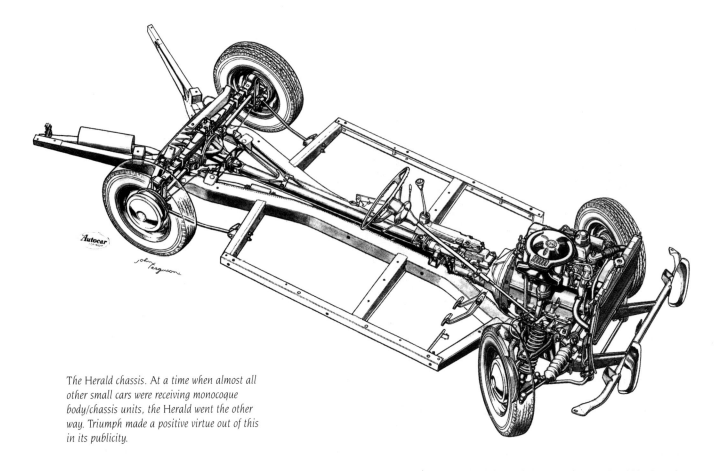

The Herald chassis. At a time when almost all other small cars were receiving monocoque body/chassis units, the Herald went the other way. Triumph made a positive virtue out of this in its publicity.

The Brabham Herald-Climax

In 1960 Jack Brabham was Formula One World Champion, his name a household word. Impressed with the little Herald, but thinking, like others, that what it badly needed was more power, Brabham had his Surrey-based engineering works drop the 1216cc Coventry-Climax single-overhead-camshaft FWE engine into an otherwise standard Herald coupé. The engine was in somewhat detuned roadgoing form, as used in the Lotus Elite of the period. With twin SUs it gave 83bhp at 6500rpm, and was notoriously economical.

Brabham had created one of the first of the 1960s cross-breed sports saloons, the Herald Climax predating both the Mini-Cooper and Lotus-Cortina by some time.

To fit the engine, which weighed less than the standard unit, an 8in clutch with a special bellhousing was used to mate it to the normal Herald gearbox. Its extra length necessitated an electric fan being fitted ahead of the uprated radiator.

As regards braking, hard Mintex M20 linings were fitted all round, for the Herald's disc set-up had not yet arrived. Quite incredibly, absolutely nothing was done to improve the car's handling or its rear suspension according to the 1960 report in *Autosport* magazine, and nor did this occasion any particular comment. The tester managed over 102mph flat-out, with a standing-start quarter mile in 17.6 seconds, 0–60mph in 10.8 seconds, and a fuel consumption of better than 27mpg overall.

The Herald-Climax was judged quite some vehicle – 'a most delightful little car, and there are no snags at all', was the conclusion. The Triumph could be driven at 15mph in top gear, such was its flexibility, and the car's totally standard outward appearance left amazed faces everywhere when the terrific acceleration was used, including some allegedly very angry sports-car drivers. To have one's own Herald thus converted by the World Champion cost £395 all-in, which still did not bring the price of a complete converted car up to the cost of a new TR, against which it was just as fast. It is thought that a total of 16 such cars were built, mainly coupés, of which just a couple are believed to have survived.

Left: The two-tone interior of an early 948cc Herald. As a coupé it has extra instrumentation, as well as twin carburettors. The dashboard is of black-painted compressed fibreboard, with a painted metal glovebox lid; those wanting something less low-rent could order an accessory wood-capping conversion. You could also pay extra for leather seat facings, and even obtain the saloon with a twin-SU coupé engine.

Below: The Herald's crisp modern styling marked a departure from Standard-Triumph's ponderous previous efforts. The coupé has the original one-piece unribbed roof that gave way to a ribbed two-piece design in June 1960.

The prototype coupé was registered at the turn of 1958 and then began the problems of how to get the body made in quantity. This was ultimately solved in a novel way, by having the body structure bolted together, assembly being at Triumph's Canley plant. This allowed various body components to be manufactured by different firms in different places. Mulliners, to become in April 1958 a wholly-owned subsidiary of Standard-Triumph, was responsible for the majority of the pressings, with some being made by its offshoot, Forward Radiator. Pressed Steel was also involved, and the pressings for the one-piece forward-hinging bonnet and front wings were sourced in Liverpool from Hall Engineering, which would also soon become part of the company's empire. While today's enthusiasts should be very grateful to Harry Webster and his team for selecting this method of construction, as body repair using bolted-on rather than welded-on panels is considerably

easier, a disadvantage at the time was that all the separate sections had to be very accurately pressed so they fitted correctly. Sad to relate, this wasn't the case on early production cars, leading to serious water leaks which gave the company a multitude of warranty claims.

Zobo was finally named the Herald, after Alick Dick's yacht, and it seemed that Standard-Triumph had a little winner on its hands. The well-tried 948cc Standard Ten engine, although somewhat lacking in torque, revved willingly and had proved both economical and reliable in service, as

The 1200 Herald convertible looks especially good in powder blue, a commonly chosen finish. It proved a particularly popular car for the girl-about-town and occupied the ground inhabited by the Mini cabriolet today.

had its associated four-speed gearbox, now treated to a short-throw remote-control mechanism. Accessibility of the power plant was unrivalled once the bonnet was pivoted forward; even the front suspension and steering were wholly visible. On the saloon the engine was used in Standard Pennant form, providing 35bhp on a single Solex carburettor. The coupé, however, had twin SU carburettors, better manifolding and other adjustments, increasing power to 45bhp, with the same 51lb ft of torque being produced higher up the rev range.

In two major respects the Herald stood apart from the competition. Firstly – and much was made of this in the early advertising – its rack-and-pinion steering sported a turning circle of just 25ft, a full 10ft less than most

small cars could boast: the Herald could do a complete U-turn in an average street, albeit at the cost of serious front-tyre wear. Secondly, it was the first low-cost British car in large-scale production to be equipped with independent rear suspension, now taken for granted, but then a kind of Holy Grail. The system was somewhat suspect, comprising swing axles with a transverse leaf spring, located by radius arms and telescopic dampers. When a Herald was driven sportingly the problems arrived, and already the prototype Heralds had been given a front anti-roll bar to tame their wayward handling. The swing axles allowed the rear wheels to progress rapidly to extreme positive camber under hard cornering, decreasing rear tyre contact with the road. This led to a sudden loss of grip,

7777 NX

Above: Wire wheels were never an option on the Herald, but they were available as an aftermarket conversion. They certainly suit this second-type coupé.

Right: The classic wooden Herald dashboard – retained on the 1200 to the end – arrived with the 1147cc engine. It was used unchanged on the 1200 coupé – which thus lost its two auxiliary dials – and, as here, on the early Vitesses.

with potentially dire results. If you re-set the rear spring to give negative camber this helped a lot, but Standard-Triumph itself never implemented any cure to the on-the-limit handling problems of the Herald. Still, the system was cheap, and having independent rear suspension did prove a major selling point.

The new Herald was viewed on its introduction in April 1959 as a modern, bright, airy and well thought-out car with some innovatory engineering. At £702 for the base saloon, with the coupé only £29 more, it was a premium-priced product, when a two-door Morris Minor de luxe cost only £619, and this up-market image was further helped by a range of cheerful new colours, many of them duo-tone. Another respect in which the new Triumph was ahead of the

The estate car version of the Herald 1200 is a particularly useful vehicle, and has excellent visibility through the long side windows and one-piece tailgate. The Courier van was less successful, and was dropped in 1964. (Jon Pressnell collection)

game was that it was introduced as having no greasing points; however, rapid front suspension wear soon led to grease nipples being fitted. The Mini had yet to arrive, the Morris Minor was ten years old, and Ford was still selling side-valve cars with three-speed gearboxes. Sales took off like the proverbial rocket, and a waiting list soon built up.

Although the Herald was the main breadwinner for Standard-Triumph in the 1959–60 period, the company's financial position was deteriorating. This was partly because of the costs involved in meeting Herald warranty claims, but principally because of the cost of buying out various supplying firms, plus the expense of the new assembly hall being built at Canley and the generally weakening economic climate of the period. Of the six major car-building groups in the UK, Standard-Triumph was by some way in

the least robust health. However, this did not directly affect the introduction of further Herald variants. March 1960 brought the smart four-seater convertible, which with the Morris Minor was one of the only two low-cost true four-seater open cars on the market. The twin-carburettor engine was fitted, but the extra weight meant that the 948cc Herald convertible was hardly fast. The hood was easy to erect, though, and for a period the car was very much the thing for the smart girl-about-town.

The launch of the Mini and the ohv Ford 105E Anglia led Triumph to bring out the pared-down Herald 'S' saloon in February 1961 – this being sold at the competitive price of £664 including tax. What was really needed, however, was more power. Harry Webster finally devised a way of enlarging the 948cc engine to 1147cc, and the 39bhp Herald 1200 was born. By this time, in the spring of 1961, the initial quality problems had been overcome, and the expanding Herald range was selling steadily. The 1200 engine produced only 5bhp more but much more valuable was the 20 per cent increase in torque. The old twin-

carburettor engine was dropped, all 1200s having a single Solex carburettor. A higher rear axle ratio, giving more relaxed cruising, was one of the other ancillary benefits, and meant that fuel consumption for the 1200 was no greater than for the smaller engine.

A month after the launch of the 1200 in April 1961 came the Herald estate car, a really useful dual-purpose vehicle with an exceptionally large glass area. By January 1962 the estate had spawned the 5cwt Courier van as Standard-Triumph tried to get in on the lucrative light commercial market. Never a big seller, the Courier lasted only until late 1964, and surprisingly it ran alongside the 7cwt Standard Ten vans and pick-ups.

An important innovation arriving in October 1961 was front disc brakes, at first as a £15 optional extra but eventually becoming standard on some models. Meanwhile the cheapskate 'S' model with its 948cc engine was kept in limited production until January 1964 for fleet customers.

Major upheaval occurred in Standard-Triumph's world at the end of 1960 when the financial crisis

Left: The Herald 12/50 saloon features a fabric sunroof as standard as well as a revised front grille.

Below: The 13/60 makes use of the Vitesse bonnet, but with larger single headlamps.

The Herald and Vitesse in competition

Unlikely competition cars they may seem to us today, but nevertheless both the Herald and Vitesse did appear in international competition in their heyday. During its first two seasons the sporty little Herald coupé was one of the cars to have for aspiring rally men – and also, because of its amazingly small turning circle, for devotees of the then fashionable round-the-pylons type of driving test. Tuning modifications abounded, and at amateur and local level the Herald, especially the coupé, did well. But it also shone as an international rally car fielded by the works competition department under Ken Richardson, a man more used to preparing TR3s.

Perhaps the Herald's most ardent supporter was 'Tiny' Lewis, who had his own Herald coupé, registered 'TL 5'. This car was works-supported, and to all intents was a works entry. Its first major appearance was in the June 1959 Alpine Rally, and Lewis and his co-driver Tony Nash finished ninth overall. For the new and unproven Herald, this was a pretty impressive result, seeing as it was pitted against 3-litre cars driven by the world's top rally-drivers, and it encouraged the factory to drop its reticence and field Herald coupés in its own name.

For the 1959 RAC Rally three cars were entered, for Peter Bolton, Cyril Corbishley and Keith Ballisat, alongside Lewis in 'TL 5'. Three of the four finished, Triumph coming second in the team-prize awards. This led to a full-scale assault on the 1960 Monte Carlo Rally, with five Herald coupés entered by the works: three retired and the best finisher was Cyril Corbishley at 25th overall. However,

The Herald coupé was soon appearing in rallies, and with some success, especially in the hands of 'Tiny' Lewis. Here he is seen during the 1960 RAC Rally, about to attack the cones on the Wolvey skidpan. The roof-mounted spotlight was de rigueur in those days.

Lewis, by now driving a full works car, achieved first in class in the 1960 Tulip Rally.

Despite this success, the dire financial situation in 1960-61 ensured that there were very few other works entries around this time, although privateers campaigned the Herald with enthusiasm and some success. None did better than Geoff Mabbs, who managed to win the 1961 Tulip Rally outright, using his own Herald coupé. A bizarre handicap system assisted, as did 'Tiny' Lewis retiring his own car to give Mabbs a clear run, but an outright win was an outright win, and the publicity department made much of this, probably the Herald's finest hour. It was also the last appearance of the Herald in the works team, activities being temporarily halted by the Leyland takeover.

A change of heart by the new management in early 1962 led to the competition department being revived under Graham Robson, initially concentrating its efforts on the new TR4s. But November's RAC Rally saw Vic Elford out in a works 1600 Vitesse. This car was '407 VC', a development vehicle fitted with an experimental triple-SU version of the 1600 engine which produced 95bhp. Twin long-range fuel tanks were fitted to aid weight distribution and wide-rim wheels from the Courier van were used: apparently the handling with the extra weight in the tail was surprisingly good. Elford proved remarkably fast, setting some stage times in the top ten of the 250-car entry, but the gearbox gave up at the halfway stage, putting him out.

In January 1963 a team of three Vitesse 1600 saloons was prepared for a determined attempt on the Monte Carlo Rally. The three powder-blue-and-white cars were consecutively registered 6001 VC,

6002 VC and 6003 VC. Top drivers Vic Elford, Mike Sutcliffe and John Sprinzel were engaged, the latter driving a standard car in the Group 1 category. The other two cars were modified Group 2 cars, although only cylinder-head tuning was carried out – the triple-SU set-up being ineligible. A primitive anti-lock braking arrangement, working only on the rear wheels, was fitted to all three cars.

That January of 1963 produced dreadful weather all over Europe, but all three Vitesses managed to finish, Elford doing particularly well and coming in third in class and 24th overall. The problem was that the Vitesse as sold simply did not have enough power to make a top rally car and management refused to make a production version of the triple-SU engine available so that this could be homologated. Vic Elford took 6003 VC, uprated to 95bhp, on the Manx Rally in mid-1963, and was at one point leading the whole field until a differential failure put him out.

This same car was used by Elford for a do-or-die attempt on the Liège-Rome-Liège rally in September. Authority to develop the car came from Sir Donald Stokes himself after Elford had convinced him he could win outright. For this, the final appearance of the works Vitesse in international rallying, 6003 VC was fully modified. A tuned 110bhp 2-litre engine was used, together with a TR4 clutch, gearbox, overdrive and differential. Much strengthening was incorporated and it was felt that the car could indeed last the distance on the roughest and toughest event in the rally calendar. Indeed Elford, with co-driver Terry Hunter, was going well and in third place when after the halfway point in the event the car suddenly and without warning caught fire, ending up a complete write-off. All the crew could do was to watch as the Triumph Vitesse's rallying career went up in smoke.

With the arrival of the 13/60, the estate – and the convertible – were only available in this form. This example is on display at a Paris motor show.

deepened to such an extent that a takeover in early 1961 by Lancashire lorry and bus builders Leyland Motors was the only way out. Leyland was able to inject much-needed cash into Triumph, thereby financing new-model development and up-to-the-minute production. Without Leyland, there is little doubt that the Triumph story would have ended at about this point, so the takeover can only be viewed as a good thing, whatever one may think of the subsequent British Leyland débâcle.

April 1963 saw yet another Herald variant, the upmarket 12/50 saloon. This model had the unique feature of a standard full-length fabric sunroof, together with a tuned 1200 engine producing 51bhp and 63lb ft of torque. A new range of colours also helped sales, and before long many Heralds sold in the UK were to this specification. The 1200 saloon, convertible, coupé, and estate cars continued, of course, receiving a 46bhp engine in November 1964. By late 1964 sales of the coupé had dwindled to such a point that it was withdrawn, along with the Courier van; the rest of the range sold better than

ever under Leyland leadership, and the 1964 model year was to be the Herald's best year, with 52,000 cars sold worldwide.

At the 1967 Motor Show a revised Herald called the 13/60 was introduced, using a 61bhp single-carb version of the Spitfire MkIII's 1296cc power unit; with a surprisingly good torque figure of 73lb ft at 3000rpm, this allowed a further rise in axle ratio. At the same time a Vitesse-type bonnet was fitted, albeit with only single headlamps, while upgraded seating and a better-stocked dashboard kept the Herald up with the competition. The 1200 saloon continued, but only in saloon form.

With the Herald range now eight and a half years old, sales were inevitably in decline. The first model to be deleted was the 1200, in May 1970, followed by the 13/60 saloon in December that year, the convertible and estate hanging on until May 1971. In retrospect it is surprising that the

Right: The wood dashboard was retained on the 13/60, but with twin dials – meaning the arrival of a water-temperature gauge – and recessed switchgear.

Below: The 1600 Vitesse as introduced in 1962, shown here in convertible form. Although the car was obtainable in single-tone finishes, the majority had the contrasting side flash as seen here.

Herald continued so long, but then the much more modern 1300 front-wheel-drive saloon which had been running alongside it since 1965 was substantially more expensive.

A significant Herald spin-off arrived in May 1962. This was the sporting Vitesse, reviving an old Triumph name. In the early 1930s there had been a brief vogue for small-capacity six-cylinder engines, but these had soon disappeared, and the conventional

wisdom was that a 'six' was of at least 2 litres in capacity. With the Vitesse, however, Triumph returned to the 'small six', producing a 1596cc version of the 1998cc in-line unit then powering the Standard Vanguard and which would soon be seen in the new Triumph 2000. The engine was in essence the old Standard Eight/Ten 'four' with two additional cylinders, and on twin Solex carburettors it produced 70bhp and an impressive 92lb ft of torque – good

enough for a 90mph maximum speed. It was mated to a close-ratio version of the Herald gearbox, and a most useful overdrive option was available, which allowed for 20mph per 1000rpm in overdrive top – unusually high gearing for a small car in 1962.

Available as a saloon or convertible, the Vitesse was given a new bonnet incorporating 'Chinese eye' slanting double headlamps, and was frequently finished with a contrasting side flash.

Left: The rear pockets are a handy Herald feature also found on the Vitesse; this is a very early 1600 example.

Below: The interior of the Vitesse as it was before it gained the four-dial arrangement, with rev-counter, in September 1963. The simple vinyl trim is given a lift by the wood door cappings.

The polished wooden dashboard of the 1200 was used, at first unchanged but from September 1963 with a four-dial instrument cluster incorporating a rev-counter.

The bad news remained the handling. The extra weight at the front promoted understeer, which changed to sudden oversteer when the swing-axle rear suspension jacked up under hard cornering – for although spring and damper rates had been adjusted,

the new car still had the basic Herald independent rear originally designed to cope with just 35bhp. The car needed careful handling, and came in for some criticism in road tests. Still, 9in front discs ensured that the Vitesse stopped well enough, and at a price of £735, or £784 for the convertible, it was something of a bargain, and had the advantage of being available, uniquely in its class, as a four-seater convertible.

Despite the continued rumblings about the inadequacies of its rear suspension, the Vitesse sold well for four years, and in October 1966 was made into something still more rapid and sporting by the fitment of a 95bhp 2-litre engine. New seating, improved GT6-type disc brakes, an all-synchromesh gearbox and an uprated diaphragm clutch also arrived. The IRS was only slightly modified in an attempt to make it cope, and road

The steering wheel on a 2-litre would normally be a plastic-rimmed wire-spoke design, but this wood-rim Moto-Lita surely adds to the driving pleasure.

Driving the Herald and Vitesse

The various members of the Herald family offer differing driving experiences but with certain common characteristics. These include a pleasant driving position, excellent visibility, and agreeable interior presentation in all but the rather low-rent early cars. Be warned, though, that the bolt-together construction can result in plenty of squeaks and rattles in a neglected example.

Starting with the Herald, the 948cc cars have an engine that is as sweet as its small displacement would suggest, but in a relatively heavy car the performance errs towards the gutless. The 1147cc cars are sprightlier, with better torque, and the 12/50 is reasonably lively. The 13/60 is undoubtedly the cream of the crop, though, and is really quite zippy; in common with all the Heralds, however, it is relatively low-geared, and can get out of breath on motorways. Allied to a smooth hydraulic clutch, the gearchange is easy, light and reasonably quick, although remember that there's no synchromesh on first. If the change is sloppy, re-bushing the remote will make a big difference.

Quick and well-weighted, the steering helps get the best out of the Herald. As for the car's cornering

behaviour, experienced Herald-ists say the problems are over-stated. If you keep the power on through corners you will get round without the car biting back; hit the brakes mid-corner, though, and the rear will come round. Quick reflexes will catch it, but better to be aware of this trait, and drive accordingly. As for the ride quality, despite its four-wheel independent suspension the Herald has relatively firm suspension that gives a jiggly ride.

The Vitesse scores with that lovely six-cylinder engine, sweeter but less torquey in 1600 form, less smooth but more muscular in 2-litre guise. Non-Rotoflex cars have the same cornering characteristics as the Herald, but with a greater tendency to understeer. Play with the throttle and the extra power means you can break the tail away in a helpful way, but you must know what you're doing. The MkII tames the rear most effectively, and you won't be caught out if you lift off mid-corner.

Accept the car's shortcomings, and either drive around them or modify the suspension, and you'll find a Herald or Vitesse agreeable and practical transport – and remember that you can mix-and-match components across the range to tailor the car to your tastes.

testers – by the mid-1960s more ready to reveal a car's faults – muttered about rear-wheel tuck-under and sudden-death handling. Fortunately, tuning specialists such as SAH were by then marketing de-cambering conversions for the rear suspension, such modifications producing a marked improvement.

None of this is to imply that the 2-litre Vitesse was an unsafe car in normal driving. However, if driven to the limit of its new-found performance, especially by the unskilled, there could be a rear-end handling problem. Triumph was aware of this, but the cost of an improved

set-up supposedly militated against its introduction. But in 1966, the GT6 coupé was also announced, and as a lighter car with the same power it had even more wayward handling, for which it attracted a significantly bad press. It was realised that something would have to be conjured up to tame these powerful Triumphs.

The engineering department thus produced an ingenious solution whereby most of the Herald's suspension was retained, but a lower wishbone was incorporated to limit camber change of the rear wheels. Driveshaft articulation at the outer end was accommodated by a large,

rubber-doughnut Rotoflex coupling, the inner end having a conventional universal joint. Radius arms for location were still used, as was the transverse leaf spring. This cost-effective answer worked well on the road, and was introduced on the Vitesse 2-litre MkII and GT6 MkII in October 1968, but it never found its way onto any of the lesser Herald-range cars, nor onto the Spitfire. Amazing as it may seem now, this rapid two-litre car was still being sold new in 1968 with cross-ply tyres – now there's brave for you...

Also with the MkII Vitesse came a new grille, a revised dashboard, and a

Above: This period advertising image plays up the sporting character of the Vitesse: the car had strong performance for its day.

Left: The MkII version of the 2-litre Vitesse is seen here in convertible form, a highly desirable package both then and now. The MkII sports this revised front grille and the then fashionable fake-Rostyle wheel trims. Invisible but important are the rear suspension modifications.

Buying Hints

1. The chassis frame can rot anywhere, but is usually worse towards the rear, as oil leaks from the engine can protect the front. The outriggers and body-to-chassis mounting brackets are particularly susceptible, and poor door fit may be caused by a sagging chassis. The main chassis rails are strong, but if they have deteriorated a repair will be expensive. Suspension mounting points front and rear should be thoroughly checked. Fortunately, a good number of survivors will have had renewed or extensively restored chassis frames by now.

2. Main body rotting points are as follows: sidelight housings and the lower part of bonnet, wheelarches, boot floor and spare-wheel well, the valances under the bumpers, the bottoms of the doors, and under the rear seat.

3. Engines are well-proven, reliable and inexpensive to rebuild. Valve guides can wear, leading to smokiness, and the timing chain can rattle, but this is not usually serious. A well-built engine should comfortably last 100,000 miles.

4. Vitesse engines are prone to wearing their crankshaft thrust washers, this allowing the crank to shift when the clutch is depressed. Although fixing this is not an engine-out job, it could still be expensive.

5. Gearboxes are strong, but weak synchromesh is an inevitable sign of age, both of the component itself and its design. Despite its short throw, gear selection can be vague, and first and reverse are very close together.

6. Steering and suspension items are again strong, reliable and cheap to replace – in fact Heralds (and to a lesser extent Vitesses) are one of the simplest and cheapest of classics both to run and to maintain.

7. The later 2-litre Vitesses have much improved rear suspension, but the Rotoflex rubber doughnut couplings only last 25,000–30,000 miles and are not cheap or particularly easy to replace. Vibration in the driveline upon acceleration is usually worn universal joints; these, like the differential, have a much harder time when coupled to a 2-litre engine.

8. Brakes will be front discs on most cars and present few problems.

9. The driveability of any of the Herald range can be easily improved by slotting in a 1500 Spitfire engine. With this done the car is much more usable on today's roads, this conversion having virtually no downside. Less ambitiously, a 1300 engine can equally be used in 948cc/1147cc models – but do make sure in all these cases that suspension and brakes are upgraded to match.

10. There are still plenty of cars to choose from, and the later the car the more equipment, as one would expect. Note that convertibles are a lot dearer than saloons, the stylish Herald coupé is much rarer and quite sought-after, and the Courier van is virtually extinct. The Herald estate is a good-value classic and a useful load-carrier. All things considered, the Herald family make excellent daily-use vehicles, as virtually all spares are available. They are also cars which are still good value.

retuned engine giving 104bhp, almost exactly three times the output of the original Herald – small wonder that the suspension had needed improvement. In its rejuvenated form, the MkII Vitesse was something of a 'pocket rocket', achieving 0–60 mph times of just over ten seconds. This prompted Triumph to advertise it as 'faster than eleven leading sports cars', a smug Vitesse owner being shown in front of a number of disgruntled two-seater drivers alongside their MGBs and Alpines. But the fundamental design was nearly ten years old, and sales continued to decline.

The Vitesse was marketed in the US solely as a convertible, being pitched as a rapid small car for the young professional who wanted something different, or as a second car for the more wealthy. Called the 'Triumph Sports Six' – as if to emphasise that not all small European cars had puny four-cylinder engines – it was simply too expensive to catch on, and was withdrawn in 1964 after a mere 679 sales in the States.

During 13 years of production a grand total of 576,979 Heralds and Vitesses was manufactured – no small achievement considering the company's position at the bottom of the big league, and a success in any terms. Many were assembled overseas, for Standard-Triumph had long been keen on exporting

completely knocked down (CKD) kits for local construction. As well as the large company-owned assembly facility at Malines in Belgium, cars were built in Southern Ireland, South Africa, Australia and South America. In addition, production in India – under the Standard name – latterly included a four-door derivative, and even, very briefly, a four-door estate. When BL disengaged from India in 1970, the Standard Motor Company in Madras (now called Chennai) developed its own version of the four-door Herald, with a restyled rear and a coil-sprung live back axle; called the Standard Gazel, this was made from 1971 until 1977.

Above: The Indian-built Standard Gazel has four doors, a restyled tail and a live rear axle on coil springs. (Standard Motor Club)

Left: In MkII form the Vitesse dashboard has recessed switches, necessitating the auxiliary dials to be paired on the right of the panel.

The *Triumph 2000 family*

In its heyday in the early fifties, Standard's Vanguard had been a hugely successful car, both at home and abroad. But although the 1955 American-inspired monocoque Phase III had breathed new life into the model, by the end of the decade the Vanguard was looking distinctly dated.

Standard-Triumph was acutely aware of this, and had been working on a replacement since 1957. Codenamed Zebu, this used a separate chassis and had independent rear suspension by semi-trailing arms and coil springs, and a rear transaxle to improve weight distribution. It was intended to have a

Triumph 2000 MkI
1963–69

ENGINE:
Six cylinders in line, cast-iron block and head
Capacity	1998cc
Bore x stroke	74.7mm x 76mm
Valve actuation	Pushrod
Compression ratio	8.5:1
Carburettors	Twin Zenith-Stromberg
Power	90bhp at 5000rpm
Maximum torque	117lb ft at 2900rpm

TRANSMISSION:
Four-speed all-synchro; overdrive option

SUSPENSION:
Front: MacPherson strut
Rear: Independent by coil springs and semi-trailing arms; telescopic dampers

STEERING:
Rack-and-pinion

BRAKES:
Front: Disc   *Rear:* Drum
Servo assistance

WHEELS/TYRES:
Steel disc wheels
6.50 x 13in (saloon)
175 x 13in (estate)

BODYWORK:
All-steel monocoque

DIMENSIONS:
Length	14ft 5¾in
Wheelbase	8ft 10in
Track, front	4ft 4in
Track, rear	4ft 2½in
Width	5ft 5in
Height	4ft 8in

KERB WEIGHT
Saloon 22.5cwt; estate 23.9cwt

PERFORMANCE:
(Source: *Motor*)
Max speed	97.6mph
0–60mph	13.6sec
30–50mph in top	7.7sec
50–70mph in top	9.8sec

PRICE INCLUDING TAX WHEN NEW:
£1,094 (March 1964)

NUMBER MADE:
Saloon	113,157
Estate	7,488

Triumph 2.5PI MkI
1968–69

As 2000 MkI except:

ENGINE:
Capacity	2498cc
Bore x stroke	74.7mm x 95mm
Compression ratio	9.5:1
Fuel system	Lucas mechanical injection
Power	132bhp at 5500rpm
Maximum torque	153lb ft at 2000rpm

WHEELS/TYRES:
Tyres 185 x 13in

KERB WEIGHT:
23.6cwt (saloon)

PERFORMANCE:
(Source: *Motor*)
Max speed	107.2mph
0–60mph	9.9sec
30–50mph in top	8.3sec
50–70mph in top	9.8sec

PRICE INCLUDING TAX WHEN NEW:
Saloon £1,481 (February 1969)

NUMBER BUILT:
Saloon 8,658   Estate 371

Triumph 2000/2000TC MkII
1969–77

As for 2000 MkI except:

ENGINE:
Compression ratio	9.25:1 (1969–73)
	8.8:1 (1973–77)
Power	84bhp (DIN) at 5000rpm
	91bhp (DIN) at 4750rpm (2000TC)
Maximum torque	100lb ft at 2900rpm
	110lb ft at 3300rpm (TC)

SUSPENSION:
Front anti-roll bar fitted from 1975

WHEELS/TYRES:
Saloon: 175 x 13in from 1973

DIMENSIONS:
Length	15ft 2½in saloon
	14ft 9¼in estate
Track, front	4ft 4½in
Track, rear	4ft 5in

KERB WEIGHT:
23.5cwt

PERFORMANCE:
(Source: *Motor*)
Max speed	95.7mph
0–60mph	14.1sec
30–50mph in top	10.2sec
50–70mph in top	11.8sec

PRICE INCLUDING TAX WHEN NEW:
£1,626 saloon; £1,921 estate (January 1971)

NUMBER BUILT:
Saloon	92,053
Estate	7,118

Triumph 2.5PI MkII
1969–75

As 2.5PI MkI except dimensions as 2000 MkII saloon and estate

KERB WEIGHT:
23.5cwt (saloon)

PERFORMANCE:
(Source: *Motor*)
Max speed	110.5mph
0–60mph	9.7sec
30–50mph in top	8.6sec
50–70mph in top	9.5sec

PRICE INCLUDING TAX WHEN NEW:
£1,867 saloon; £2,162 estate (January 1971)

NUMBER BUILT:
Saloon	43,353
Estate	4,102

Triumph 2500TC/2500S
1974–77

As 2000 MkII except:

ENGINE:
Capacity	2498cc
Bore x stroke	74.7mm x 95mm
Carburettors	Twin SU
Power	99bhp (DIN) at 4700rpm
	106bhp (DIN) at 4700rpm (1975–77)
Maximum torque	133lb ft at 3000rpm (1974–75)
	139lb ft at 3000rpm (1975–77)

WHEELS/TYRES:
185 x 13in
175 x 14in (2500S)

SUSPENSION:
Front anti-roll bar fitted from 1975

KERB WEIGHT:
23.1cwt (2500S saloon)

PERFORMANCE:
(Source: *Motor*)
Max speed	104.3mph
0–60mph	11.5sec
30–50mph in top	8.1sec
50–70mph in top	9.4sec

PRICE INCLUDING TAX WHEN NEW:
2500TC saloon £3,153; 2500S saloon £3,353; 2500S estate £3,893 (August 1975)

NUMBER BUILT:
Saloon	37,752
Estate	2,601

1500cc or a 2000cc six-cylinder engine, a development of the Standard Ten unit with two cylinders added. The striking four-door body had a reversed-angle rear window as used on the Mercury Turnpike Cruiser, and would have been built by Pressed Steel. The car was meant to be in production by March 1960, but with this schedule soon slipping, everything was thrown up in the air in 1959 when Standard-Triumph was tipped off that another company was poised to come out with two cars having similar styling – this being Ford, with its Anglia and Classic models.

A re-styled rear was considered, as was a wholly-new style by Michelotti, and there was even a grim idea in 1959 to mount a stretched four-door Herald body on the Zebu mechanicals; these, meanwhile, had been revised, and there was now a conventionally-placed gearbox, strut front suspension, and a backbone-type chassis. As the dire financial crisis of 1960 took hold, one further option was considered: building a version of the American Motors Rambler, fitted with the Standard 'six'. Eventually, however, the whole Zebu project was shelved; meanwhile, as a holding move, the 1998cc six-cylinder engine was fitted to the ageing Vanguard to produce the 'Luxury Six'.

When Leyland took over the wreckage of the company in early 1961, things had thus reached the point where there was no longer any Vanguard replacement planned at all and the company was losing £600,000 a month. This staggering sum is equivalent to around £9 million a month today, so small wonder all model development had gone on hold. Something had to be done, and Leyland authorised work to commence in July 1961 on 'Barb', a crash programme to produce an almost wholly new mid-range sporting saloon to be on sale in just two years – a tall order indeed.

Michelotti was invited to come up with a completely new body shape, and by the end of 1961 Pressed Steel was starting the process of tooling up for the body, which was now to be a monocoque, complete with the fashionable four-headlamp look. Carried over from the aborted Zebu were the strut front suspension, rack-and-pinion steering and the semi-trailing IRS, with the latter in the car's final form being mounted on a subframe. The new six-cylinder engine was intended to be used in either 1596cc or 1998cc form, but ultimately the smaller unit was abandoned, having already found a home in the Vitesse. The transmission (with optional overdrive or automatic) was to use a floor change and to feature synchromesh on all four gears as well as a diaphragm clutch. Front disc brakes and rear drums, with power assistance, pulled the car up.

The sales plan was to move more upmarket than the Vanguard, and into sports-saloon territory, hence the individual front reclining seats, full instrumentation and polished-walnut dashboard and door cappings. The long and low look was emphasised by the car's relative narrowness, while a sporting character was hinted at by the long bonnet with its dummy air scoop and the relatively truncated boot. By late 1962 the financial climate had improved, thanks partly to two purchase-tax cuts but mainly to Leyland's severe cost-cutting measures, and all who saw the prototype felt sure that the company was onto a winner. It did not take too much thought to decide that a sports saloon should carry the Triumph name and not become a Vanguard Phase IV. In any case, by the 1960s the word 'Standard' had connotations of austerity: thus a 60-year-old company name was largely laid to rest in 1963 when the last Vanguards and their

Triumph 2000 versus Rover 2000

The 1963 London Motor Show was dominated by these two cars, both unveiled at this event. In retrospect, it can be seen that the Triumph and Rover 2000s were creating a new sector of the market, one that still exists. They fitted the desire of the young(ish) family man to drive a mid-sized, mid-range saloon with sporting pretensions – the BMW 3-series is today's direct successor. They were not seen as 'old men's cars', but rather as the car for the chap in a hurry, the executive who was going places...

Although they were competing head-on, the Rover and Triumph were quite different in character. The Triumph had a smooth six-cylinder engine based on well-tried components; the Rover had an all-new overhead-camshaft 'four' that was marginally more powerful. Both had all-synchromesh gearboxes, but whereas you could have your Triumph with an optional overdrive or automatic transmission, the Rover offered neither. Both too had sophisticated rear suspension, that on the Rover being by the expensive but excellent de Dion system. Four-wheel disc brakes (inboard at the rear) stopped the Rover, but the

Triumph had to make do with front discs only.

Dimensionally the cars were almost identical, but the Rover had arguably the more futuristic styling. Interiors were luxurious on both, with the Rover probably the more so. However, its individually shaped rear seats meant that it was a strict four-seater, whereas one could squeeze five into a Triumph.

Performance was much the same, with the Rover perhaps just having an edge – it would touch 100mph to the Triumph's 95mph – and running costs were all but identical. Where the Triumph did score hugely was on initial cost. Its UK tax-paid price was £1,094 as compared to the Rover's £1,264, making the Rover 15 per cent dearer. That £170 was a lot of money in 1963, and would have swayed many buyers.

In terms of customer perception, the Rover was set just above the Triumph, although up to the arrival of the more sporting 2000, Rover had long had a staid image. Both were however perceived as quality marques, above the Austins and Fords of the world. Another Triumph plus, although it was not available initially, was the estate car version.

Although a handful of Rover 2000 estates were built by outside specialists, such a model never entered production at Solihull.

It is hard, at 40-odd years on, to appreciate the excitement that the arrival of these two pioneer sporting saloons generated. The author, as a car-mad schoolboy, can well recall it. He had an uncle who in early 1964 was torn between the two marques. Should he wait for the Rover at more money, or should he buy the more readily-available Triumph? Indeed, the Rover was, in 1964, much harder to obtain, the relatively small Solihull factory being overwhelmed by the mass of orders, whereas Triumph's vast new Canley assembly hall was able to produce as many 2000s as there were customers.

Road test and press reports tended to favour the innovative Rover, but price and the buyers tended towards the Triumph, which consistently outsold its dearer rival. The truth is that they were both good cars and both succeeded as they deserved. As for the uncle, he bought the Rover, seduced by the thought that here at last was a Rover he could afford!

cheaper relations, the Ensigns, were made, although vans bearing the Standard name were made for some years more. The new car was to be called logically, but rather unadventurously, the Triumph 2000.

That Rover, then still a respected independent company, was also developing an advanced middle-market 2-litre sports saloon was widely known, this being another reason for the new Triumph to be both sporting and well-equipped, to enable it to meet the Rover challenge head-on. Leyland's management was however confident that the Triumph 2000 would be priced more favourably than the Rover, and so it proved to be

(see above). Possession of a six-cylinder engine of both perceived and actual smoothness was also a major Triumph advantage. As more details of the forthcoming Rover 2000 filtered along the industry grapevine, it became clear at Triumph that their saloon would have to have its interior appointments upgraded; as a consequence, some hasty re-specification work was done during 1963 to ensure that the 2000 was not eclipsed by the Rover. Nevertheless, it did just prove possible to meet the target introduction date of October 1963's London Motor Show, although in truth Triumph was not in a position to begin quantity production. The

2000 was unveiled, to much ceremony and razzamatazz, as the first truly new medium-sized saloon from the company for more than a decade. Hopeful customers were promised that series production would commence at the start of 1964, but meanwhile a pilot build of 40 or so cars was lent to potential customers and dealers for extended road trials – Triumph made much of this early PR exercise at the time, but the time frame was too short for any comments to translate into physical improvements on the first production cars. A significant event also taking place at this time was that (Sir) Donald Stokes took overall control of

*Above: A view of the 2.5 PI saloon in its
original guise as introduced in October 1968:
a very rapid and desirable car for the times.*

*Right: The cockpit of the rare Mk1 2.5PI;
white-on-black dials in a black panel arrived
on the 2000 for 1967, thus the only real
difference on the original 2.5PI is the addition
of a leather-rim sports steering wheel.*

Standard-Triumph within the Leyland
empire. He had previously been
director of sales.

The Triumph 2000 was on the whole
very favourably received – indeed, it
sold at a premium for a brief period in
early 1964. Note was taken of the early
customers' comments, and minor
changes to the dashboard and to the
design of the seats were made for the
1965 model year. A little luxury
incorporated at this stage was electric
operation of the screen washers.
During the first part of 1964,
production (in the new assembly hall
at Canley) ran at about 350 units a
week, but before long this built up to
over 500, eventually peaking at more

The Triumph 2000 family in competition

The 2000 family has quite a considerable competition history. An example or two was even raced in the 1960s, but principally the 2000 and later the 2.5 PI were rally cars, and pretty successful ones at that.

Being a competition-minded company, Triumph was well used to employing motor sport as a way of bringing new models to public attention and so it was that a team of three modified 2000s was entered in August 1964 for the gruelling Spa–Sofia–Liège event, successor to the old Liège–Rome–Liège rally. The car's inherent strength made it potentially suitable for rough, long-distance endurance events, but sadly on that first outing all three works 2000s suffered from the same problem at much the same stage of the event: the subframe carrying the rear suspension broke away from the bodyshell due to fatigue cracks, a problem rapidly and successfully dealt with back at Coventry. This happened despite all the cars having reinforced bodyshells.

All had highly-tuned 150bhp engines fitted with triple Weber carburettors, uprated TR4 gearboxes and overdrives, limited-slip differentials, and uprated brakes, plus 15in instead of 13in wheels to increase ground clearance. Those lucky enough to drive them reported that they handled surprisingly well, demonstrating both considerable speed and considerable fuel consumption, the latter down into single figures during rally stages. All were white with a matt-black bonnet and a powder-blue roof.

Four cars were entered as a works team in November 1964's RAC Rally. The 2000s were well in contention during this tough event, three out of the four finishing, with Roy Fidler and Don Grimshaw coming in sixth overall and second in class to an Austin-Healey 3000.

For 1965 a fifth car, with left-hand drive, EHP 78C, was added for Simo Lampinen, and a full international programme was embarked upon. Space precludes giving full details, but the best results for the 2000s included a first in class on the Tulip

Rally for Thuner and Gretener, a fifth overall (first in class) for Fidler and Taylor on the RAC Rally, and a second overall on the Welsh Rally for Lampinen and Davenport. Although not quite an outright winner, the works 2000s had shown themselves very capable and strong rally cars.

In 1966, four new 2000s were prepared, FHP 991C to FHP 994C, but successes were more elusive than in the previous year, although Roy Fidler managed a second overall on the Welsh Rally and a first in class on the Circuit of Ireland. In addition the factory prepared a full-race Gp5 2000 for Bill Bradley to campaign in the British Saloon Car Race Championship. The car proved durable, but was too heavy to be amongst the winners. Bradley continued to race the big Triumph saloons privately for some years.

Best results for the works 2000s in 1967 were a first in class on the Circuit of Ireland plus a sixth overall on the Gulf London Rally, both for Roy Fidler, who was easily the most successful of the big Triumph

Brian Culcheth and co-driver Johnstone Syer press their works 2.5 PI saloon on in the November 1969 RAC Rally. They finished third in their class. The big saloons ran with matt black bonnet panels.

competition drivers. Sadly, the November 1967 RAC Rally was cancelled because of foot and mouth disease, after the factory had built up two 2.5PI prototypes for the event. Incidentally *Motor* magazine managed to road-test a works 2000 in 1966, and despite it having a detuned road camshaft the magazine achieved a 0–100mph acceleration time of 33.9 seconds, albeit at a cost of 12.7mpg.

There were no works 2000s or PIs entered in 1968's events, but in 1969, with the 2.5PI now on sale, several examples were campaigned. As a result of the creation of British Leyland, works Triumphs were henceforth prepared at the former BMC competition department at Abingdon, which caused some consternation at Coventry. Initially a team of MkI cars was put together for November 1969's RAC Rally; although the MkII cars had been announced, they were not yet homologated. In this very snowy event the three PIs all finished, the best being Andrew Cowan's car at eleventh overall and first in class. His team-mates Culcheth and Hopkirk brought their

cars home second and third in class, an excellent effort overall. In fact these 2.5PI Triumphs were no more powerful than the 150bhp 2000s of 1965, but they were a lot more smooth, tractable and reliable.

April 1970 was to be the finest hour for the big Triumph. The long-planned World Cup Rally took place, this event still being reckoned to be the toughest rally ever run. The BL competition department took the event very seriously, persuading Sir Donald Stokes that the 150bhp and 125mph 2.5PI was a winner and obtaining a large budget with which to finance a team of four cars and all their servicing and recce requirements – even aeroplanes were chartered. The bodyshells of the four cars (XJB 302H to XJB 305H) were strengthened but with some aluminium panelling to save weight, while flared arches allowed 15in Minilite alloy wheels to be used, and two spare wheels plus 32 gallons of fuel were carried in a reshaped boot. Finally, the passenger's seat could be made into a bed, for the event was 16,000 miles through 25 countries in six weeks with very little in the way of rest.

The big Triumph's finest hour: 'XJB 305H' is hustled along by Culcheth and Syer during 1970's marathon World Cup Rally, this picture being taken on the San Remo stage. They finished first in class and second overall after a tremendous drive.

The Triumphs did almost all that was asked in that although two retired, Brian Culcheth managed to come second overall with Paddy Hopkirk fourth, truly a tremendous effort in an event where only about 20 per cent of starters finished at all. The 2.5PI had proved itself to be one of the most unbeatable of all long-distance rally cars of the period.

Finally, two months later Culcheth and Johnstone Syer managed to win the Scottish Rally outright. In 1971 the 2.5PIs were still being used in some events, the best result being Culcheth's second overall in Cyprus, but by 1972 it was virtually all over for the big Triumph's international rally career, the final appearance coming in April that year when Culcheth won his class in the East African Safari. Thereafter the team effort moved to the new Triumph Dolomites.

Driving a 2500S

First impressions are of how the large glass area makes the car feel light and airy. The Bri-Nylon seats look and feel dated, however, while personally I have never cared for Triumph's 1970s matt-finished wood dashboard – it somehow always looks fake. Still, the instruments, switches and controls are all well positioned and effective.

On pulling away, the first thing to notice is the notchy feel to the gearchange, but the instant action of the overdrive by its gearlever switch is some compensation. The six-cylinder non-injection engine still has that lovely smooth feel and pulls well, though not outstandingly – I should imagine a good PI feels a lot brisker. It is after all a heavy car for its 106bhp. Acceleration is however perfectly adequate to cope with today's traffic and in overdrive a comfortable cruising speed seems to be 70–80mph.

As is invariably the case, though, it is wind noise that really sets the big

Triumph apart from modern cars. In the past 30 years more progress has been made in suppressing wind and road noise than in any other automotive field, so although a 2500S may well cruise all day at 90mph, to do so would be wearing.

The power steering on the car in question proved accurate and direct. The rear suspension seems soft, though, and causes the car to be a little wallowy – maybe just age or worn dampers – but it would not have prevented me from pressing on had I been in a hurry. The whole car is commendably free from shakes and rattles, and the excellent brakes inspire as much confidence as those on my everyday Audi.

Taken as a whole, this example of the final generation of big Triumph saloons provides an enjoyable, comfortable and reasonably rapid drive. It certainly feels as if everyday use would present no problems – nor be that expensive, for the owner reports 28mpg overall.

relatively inexpensive but swift sports saloon the Triumph 2.5PI was evolved. Fuel injection, at least as far as UK cars were involved, was still a novelty in 1967, but when Lucas made its 'PI' mechanical system available that year, Triumph was the first – and only – mass-production maker to utilise it. A particular reason was to achieve a high power output combined with good drivability. Using triple twin-choke carburettors and a full-race camshaft, up to 150bhp had been coaxed out of the 2-litre units fitted to the works rally 2000s but only at the cost of making the engine totally impractical for normal road use, as well as giving horrendous fuel economy. The very accurate fuel metering inherent in fuel injection allowed a wild camshaft to be used yet low-speed tractability to be retained. It also improved fuel consumption enormously.

In addition, low-speed torque could be further generated by a capacity increase. The only method available to Harry Webster and his engineers was to increase the stroke, for the bores were already at maximum. By doing this, a capacity of 2498cc was achieved, giving a huge boost to torque. Fine-tuning produced a reliable and road-useable 150bhp, and in October 1967 the TR5 received this new engine, making it by far the fastest TR yet. It was probably just as well that the system was launched in a low-production sports car, for there were numerous teething troubles. The Lucas petrol injection could, as time has proved, be made to work very well, but it needed sympathetic and knowledgeable setting-up and tuning.

Once a year of expertise had been gained, Triumph judged the time right to launch the 2.5PI. The engine was detuned to 132bhp, but still produced an excellent 153lb ft of torque at a low 2000rpm. This endowed the PI saloon with terrific acceleration, sub-ten-second 0–60mph times being reported, with 100mph coming up in around half a minute. Small wonder that police forces immediately took note, for here was a Jaguar replacement at only two thirds the cost. Four-speed all-synchromesh

than 850 cars weekly. The Triumph 2000 proved to be a profitable, well respected and long-lived line.

October 1965 saw a most useful addition in the shape of a stylish estate car version – constructed by Carbodies of Coventry, which received part-built saloons onto which it grafted the estate car rear with its one-piece tailgate. The resulting car looked surprisingly attractive, despite this primitive build method.

October 1966 brought more improvements to the 2000, such as restyled seating and a revised and much more efficient ventilation system. However, despite Rover introducing a more potent TC version of its 2000 at this time, Triumph was content to let its car continue with just the 90bhp engine. This was despite rally Triumph 2000s being tuned to produce nearly 150bhp; still, only Triumph knew

what was being planned for the 2000 shell in 1968…

In retrospect, the mid and late 1960s can be seen as the revitalised Triumph company's heyday – under strict but astute management every car was profitable, the range was wide, and a new car with 'Triumph' on the front was considered a quality vehicle. The UK's economy was booming as was that of most of the civilised world – car production and with it exports were climbing inexorably – and everything seemed possible. It was during this period that consideration was given to producing a four-door fastback GT version of the saloon, but tooling costs were too high and the project was shelved.

Those who wanted a really rapid four-door, four-seater saloon had somewhat limited options in the late 1960s, and so in order to offer a

Above: Two PI Triumphs for the price of one. The background car is one of the very rare MkI 2.5PI estate cars whereas the car in the foreground is a 1971–72 MkII saloon. Both sport the correct Rostyle wheel covers.

Left: The re-vamped rear of the MkII 2000 saloon, introduced in October 1969. These wheel covers are found on the 2000, 2000TC and 2500TC.

Left: In contrast, the 2.5PI has leathercloth-covered rear pillars, a ribbed matt-black tail panel, and dummy Rostyle wheeltrims.

Right: The MkII saloons have this much improved dashboard layout with a matt wood finish; as a 2.5PI this car has a five-dial arrangement including a rev-counter, a set-up inherited by the later 2500S. The Bri-nylon seat material was something of an innovation at the time.

Below: On lesser MkIIs the dashboard features two main instruments – plus the MkII's neat multi-function warning-light dial; note also the unusual rotary lighting control on the column shroud. This car sports an automatic gearbox.

transmission with optional overdrive was fitted, overdrive top providing relaxed cruising at 24.5mph per 1000rpm. For the less sporting, an automatic transmission was also available, as also was an estate car from March 1969. This was the first of the really modern high-performance hold-alls and again became a police favourite.

The 2.5PI was an immediate hit, more than 9,000 MkI cars being built, including just 371 2.5PI estates, making this one of the rarest of Triumphs. October 1969 saw the only significant update for the 2000 and 2.5PI, when the MkII arrived, with a front-and-rear Michelotti facelift that was codenamed 'Innsbruck' and added around 8in to overall length. Because of the way it was constructed, the estate car did not benefit from all this extra length, receiving only the restyled front.

A host of improvements included a new cylinder head on the 2000, a wider track, uprated brakes, an alternator in place of the dynamo, a new full-width wood-veneer dashboard with modernised instruments and controls, new heating and ventilation, and redesigned seating. The MkIIs were indeed much

Above: The 2500TC differs externally from the 2000TC only in the presence of a round badge on each rear pillar; the interior fittings of the two cars are identical.

Left: The interior of a 2500S. In its day the MkII 'Innsbruck' cars had one of the most quietly tasteful luxury interiors on the market. (Jon Pressnell collection)

improved, with a particularly well-executed interior, but the 2000 was no faster: despite the new cylinder head, power output did not increase, and indeed actually dropped nominally to 84bhp because a DIN rating was now employed.

As for the 2.5PI, in MkII form it sold more than 43,000 units (plus another 4,102 estates) over the period October 1969 to Spring 1975, a handsome quantity for a relatively expensive and up-market vehicle. The Lucas PI system was never entirely troublefree, however, and was also relatively costly, and after the arrival of the 2500TC in 1974 the 2.5PI

was gradually sidelined. Production was wound down in early 1975 and the last car left the lines in July that year.

Meanwhile, in May 1974 the 2500TC had been introduced to bridge the gap between the 2000 and the 2.5PI. With twin carburettors rather than fuel injection, it disposed of 99bhp (DIN) and was available as a saloon and an estate, with optional overdrive or automatic transmission – although overdrive was soon standardised on manual cars.

As part of the May 1974 range re-jigging all cars received a new black-and-chrome grille and rubber-trimmed bumpers, and then in June 1975

revised induction arrangements boosted power of the 2000 to 91bhp (DIN), with an accompanying hike in torque. The car was now renamed the 2000TC – misleadingly, as the 2000 had always had twin carburettors.

This final round of modifications in June 1975 saw the 2.5PI replaced by a new 2500S variant with the carb-fed 2500 engine but the injection model's better-equipped dashboard and vinyl-trimmed rear pillar, plus Stag-style alloy wheels; additionally, power steering and head restraints were standard. The 2500TC continued, but only as a saloon, and the 2000TC estate was also deleted, henceforth

Buying Hints

1. Like all Triumphs of the 1970s, later cars rust more badly due to poorer and thinner steel. As well as the usual rot-spots (see section on 'Ajax' cars), additional areas to check include the seam between the lower front wing and the valance, and the rear suspension mounting points. To check the latter, lift the rear seat cushion. If the floor is rusty then the pick up points below will be worse. The top spring mounts also rot.

2. Clearing drain holes is important on these cars – they are frequently blocked in poor restorations or in neglected cars, leading to rapid rusting. The sills, which are a major structural component, are particularly prone to this, as are the bottoms of the front wings. The front outriggers also rust due to blocked drain holes, and will need full replacement if they are badly corroded.

3. As the bonnet is front hinged, any frontal impact will misalign it, so check the gaps carefully.

4. The independent rear suspension means that there are a large number of suspension bushes which wear rapidly. They can be replaced with modern polyurethane bushes, with advantages both to life and to the car's handling. The top mounts of the strut front suspension of course need regular review and can weaken considerably. Steering rack bushes and mounts also need regular replacement. Check too the integrity of the mounts for the rear subframe.

5. Always try to buy a car with a good interior: supplies of trim items are poor. The relatively low value of even good cars makes re-trimming an unviable proposition anyway. As with other 1970s Triumphs, pay particular attention to the wood veneers, as these are difficult and expensive to revive.

6. All these six-cylinder engines are prone to the crankshaft thrust-washer problem detailed in the Herald/Vitesse section, but that apart they are very sturdy, reliable and long-lived units, with mileages of 120,000–150,000 miles being common. The 2.5-litre version with its longer-throw crankshaft will need the bottom end attending to somewhat earlier than the short-stroke 2000 unit. The 2000 can blow head gaskets at times as the holding-down studs are somewhat marginal. The PI system on the now rare injection cars is detailed in the TR4-TR6 section.

7. The gearbox is a version of the TR4 unit but with different ratios. The synchromesh can wear rapidly and the change is notchy, but the 'box is basically bulletproof and durable, as is the frequently-fitted overdrive unit – any problems are usually electrical.

8. The differential is strong and very much a standard Triumph item, but the differential subframe bracket tends to split, particularly on later cars. A reinforced item is now available.

9. There are six universal joints in the transmission which can produce alarming clonks if worn. In addition, driveshaft splines wear and produce similar noises. These splines can stick if not properly lubricated, and this will cause the whole rear of the car to twitch when accelerating through a corner.

10. The 2000/2500 Triumphs are solid, sturdy cars with bags of reserve strength, and can go on and on despite neglect. They can still be purchased very cheaply for the most part and yet are a practical proposition for daily use – witness the number one still sees. As a go-to-work classic, indeed, few cars are more suitable (or comfortable) than the big Triumphs, and the estate car must count as the ultimate 'practical classic'. As usual, though, buy the top car you can afford, as the cost of major restoration will far outweigh the finished value.

---

the only estate available being a 2500S. All 'Innsbruck' cars gained a front anti-roll bar at this juncture, and improved manifolding accompanied by bigger SU carburettors. These uprated engines were more powerful and had better torque, with the 2500 models now offering 106bhp (DIN) and maximum torque of 139lb ft at 2750rpm.

The big Triumphs were finally withdrawn in May 1977, in favour of the forthcoming smaller-engined versions of the Rover SD1. In all, 316,653 examples had found homes over the 14-year period, an impressive total for what was never a cheap car. The Rover 2000/3500 family was also in production for the same 14 years, but not much more than half the number were sold as compared to the Triumphs.

Marque loyalties were still potent in the 1970s, and many were those who were unhappy that there were to be no more large Triumphs, for the Stag too ceased production at about this time. With all those years of progressive development behind them and with their upmarket fittings, the final 2500S models really were the pinnacle of the Triumph marque – it is not surprising therefore to find that 30 years later they are still sought after by enthusiasts, particularly the rare estate car version, which is truly a multi-purpose, everyday classic. Indeed, it is surprisingly often that one encounters examples of the Triumph 2000 family still in everyday use.

Top: A Mark II 2000 estate in its element. Despite the unlengthened tail, the design does not look unbalanced. (Jon Pressnell collection)

Above: An image from the 1976 range catalogue, depicting the last manifestation of the Triumph 2000 theme, namely the 2500S of 1975–77 with its Stag-pattern alloy wheels. These cars have proved enduringly popular within the Triumph fraternity. (Jon Pressnell collection)

Left: The estate version of the 2500S retains the presentation of the 2.5PI. (Jon Pressnell collection)

The front-wheel-drive *Triumphs*

The Triumph 1300 as introduced in late 1965, with its revolutionary (for the company) front-wheel drive. It used space efficiently and was agreeably compact, but suffered from a rather dumpy look. Later cars derived from the 1300 avoided this by being lengthened both front and rear.

The history of the small/medium Triumph saloons of the late 1960s and 1970s is complex, particularly as seemingly identical cars can be either front-wheel-drive or rear-wheel-drive. There are also renamings to add to the difficulty. The often overlooked and now quite rare fwd cars were made between October 1965 and October 1973. In their day they were surprisingly successful, with

more than 214,000 built. They are also historically significant as being the only front-wheel-drive cars produced by Triumph.

By the early 1960s, when the need for an eventual replacement for the Herald range was much occupying minds, BMC had broken the small-car mould with its fwd transverse-engined Mini, and was poised to announce its hugely successful 1100. Triumph had no wish to be left behind, and it was but a short step for the project for a new Herald (codenamed Ajax) to be given a front-drive configuration. Ajax was also to be a monocoque, as by 1963 the body supply problem that had determined the Herald's separate-chassis construction had been solved; the new bodyshells would be built in Triumph's Liverpool facility.

Harry Webster was in overall charge, and he resolved to use a conventional fore/aft engine position rather than going transverse. For compactness the transmission was to sit closely behind the engine, as opposed to in the sump, as in the Mini/1100. The layout finally adopted put the all-synchro gearbox below and just behind the engine with the final drive forward just below the oil sump. A neat and compact layout, the only real disadvantage was that more under-bonnet height was needed to accommodate the power pack. Having had no direct previous experience of front-wheel-drive passenger cars, Harry Webster later confirmed that Triumph had secretly purchased a Morris 1100, dismantled its mechanicals and substituted the Ajax power unit and transmission so that testing could be performed unobserved.

The engine itself was to be a development of the trusty Herald unit, bored out to 1296cc – the first time that this capacity had been used, although it would later appear in the Herald and the Spitfire. An eight-port cylinder head was a direct spin-off from the Le Mans Spitfires of 1964, and with a single carburettor 61bhp and 73lb ft of torque were delivered. The design as approved in 1963 provided for the power unit and transmission to sit on a subframe bolted to the monocoque body. The subframe also located wishbones top and bottom for the front suspension, with a combined spring and damper

Triumph 1300
1965–70

ENGINE:
Four cylinders in line, cast-iron block and head
Capacity   1296cc
Bore x stroke   73.7mm x 76mm
Valve actuation   Pushrod
Compression ratio   8.5:1
Carburettor   Single Zenith-Stromberg
Power   61bhp at 5000rpm
Maximum torque   73lb ft at 3000rpm

TRANSMISSION:
Front-wheel drive; four-speed all-synchromesh gearbox

SUSPENSION:
Front: Independent by strut and twin wishbones
Rear: Independent by coil springs and semi-trailing arms; telescopic dampers

STEERING:
Rack-and-pinion

BRAKES:
Front: Disc
Rear: Drum

WHEELS/TYRES:
Steel disc wheels
Tyres 5.60 x 13in

BODYWORK:
Four-door saloon; all-steel monocoque

DIMENSIONS:
Length   12ft 11in
Wheelbase   8ft 0½in
Track, front   4ft 5in
Track, rear   4ft 6in
Width   5ft 1¾in
Height   4ft 6in

KERB WEIGHT:
17.5cwt

PERFORMANCE:
(Source: *Motor*)
Max speed   83.0mph
0–60mph   19.0sec
30–50mph in top   12.2sec
50–70mph in top   18.7sec

PRICE INCLUDING TAX WHEN NEW:
£835 (October 1967)

NUMBER BUILT: 113,008

Triumph 1300 TC
1967–70

As Triumph 1300 except:

ENGINE:
Compression ratio   9.0:1
Carburettors   Twin SU
Power   75bhp at 6000rpm
Maximum torque   75lb ft at 4000rpm

BRAKES:
Servo assistance standard

PERFORMANCE:
(Source: *Motor*)
Max speed   89.4mph
0–60mph   15.4sec
30–50mph in top   12.2sec
50–70mph in top   16.0sec

PRICE INCLUDING TAX WHEN NEW:
£874 (October 1967)

NUMBER BUILT: 35,342

Triumph 1500
1970–73

As Triumph 1300 except:

ENGINE:
Capacity   1493cc
Bore x stroke   73.7mm x 87.5mm
Compression ratio   8.5:1
   9.0:1 from October 1971
Carburettor   Single SU
Power   61bhp (DIN) at 5000rpm
   65bhp (DIN) at 5000rpm from October 1971
Maximum torque   81lb ft at 2700rpm
   80lb ft at 3000rpm from October 1971

SUSPENSION:
Rear: dead axle on coil springs, location by radius arms; anti-roll bar; telescopic dampers

BRAKES:
Servo assistance

DIMENSIONS:
Length   13ft 6in
Track, front   4ft 5½in
Track, rear   4ft 2½in
Width   5 ft 1½in

KERB WEIGHT:
18.6cwt

PERFORMANCE:
(Source: *Motor*)
Max speed   87.6mph
0–60mph   16.5sec
30–50mph in top   10.9sec
50–70mph in top   14.3sec

PRICE INCLUDING TAX WHEN NEW:
£1,136 (January 1971)

NUMBER BUILT: 66,353

The four-wheel-drive Rallycross 1300

This intriguing competition car was built in 1967/68 as the result of a collaboration between Ray Henderson of the Triumph competition department (then being run down by BL in favour of Abingdon) and Harry Webster, director of engineering at Triumph. At that time four-wheel drive was specifically banned in rallying, but the new sport of rallycross was one where within reason no holds were barred. It was also enjoying popularity in the UK as it was regularly televised and hence could bring the Triumph name before a new audience. The rallycross 1300 used a modified form of the transmission employed in the Pony 4x4 vehicle (see page 67) mated to a 2000-type final drive and an independently-sprung rear end via a conventional propshaft. Unlike modern four-wheel-drive systems, there was no centre differential, which led to a slight mismatch in the front and rear wheel speeds at times, although on loose surfaces this did not seem to matter. A control allowed the driver to disconnect the rear drive if desired, and proceed only in front-wheel drive. With more than 100bhp, thanks to an engine in full Le Mans Spitfire tune, complete with double twin-choke Weber carburettors, 'LVC 151F' was a formidable machine on loose rallycross-style events, winning several such races outright in the hands of its usual driver, rally ace Brian Culcheth. Apparently it ran at various times both as a 1300 and a 1500, and for serious competition used Minilite alloy wheels.

Unlike some of the Triumph projects which it inherited, the newly-formed BL chose to continue with the 4wd 1300, and the Abingdon competition department eventually took over the running of the car, still largely using Culcheth as its pilot. In this form it continued successfully in 1969, but the idea was never duplicated or further developed, so the car remained yet another of the many Triumph/BL might-have-beens. By the early 1980s, highly-tuned 4wd saloons were dominating rallying: so often Triumph was too early and failed to make use of its excellent innovative engineering skills. Sadly the unique 4wd 1300 was written off in a rallycross accident and never rebuilt.

Culcheth flying high, on his way to winning the 1969 Lydden ralllycross event in the 4wd 1300. (Bill Price)

Right: The complex front-wheel-drive 1300cc power unit of the Triumph 1300. The engine is installed on a subframe in a north/south direction with the gearbox behind it, the drive turning through 180 degrees. There are disc front brakes and the suspension is an unusual twin-wishbone strut set-up. (Jon Pressnell collection)

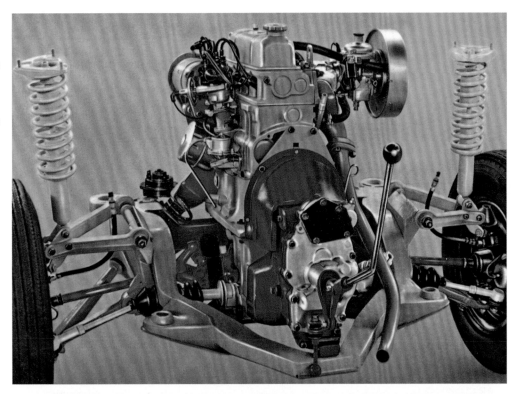

Below: An October 1966 photograph shows a 1300 given a contrasting coloured roof by its enthusiast owner. The Triumph 'globe' motif still features on the hubcaps.

Left: The 1300 – and the fwd 1500 – has an unusual direct-action cranked gearlever. The dashboard is plain but well equipped, and there is a steering wheel adjustable for rake and reach. Folding window winders are an ingenious – if less than convenient – safety feature. (Jon Pressnell collection)

Below: Launch-time photo of the front-drive 1500 – complete with Leyland 'swirling plughole' badges on the hubcaps.

unit sitting above the top wishbone. Rack-and-pinion steering with a surprisingly good lock for a front-wheel-drive car was also provided, as were disc front brakes. At the rear, independent suspension was by means of semi-trailing arms, telescopic dampers and coil springs.

Michelotti received the brief to design the body, his instructions being to produce a car with a short rear overhang, a wheel at each corner, and a strong family likeness to the 2000. His main constraint was the height of the bonnet necessary to cover the tall power unit; despite this, and despite the use of single headlights, he was able to style a car that was unmistakably a blood brother to the big Triumph saloon.

Whilst this work on the supposed Herald replacement continued, the Herald itself showed no sign of losing popularity – in fact the mid-1960s were its best period. It made little sense to dump a winning formula, so the plan became to run the two cars in parallel, distancing the new fwd car from the Herald by furnishing it luxuriously and moving it up a price bracket. Such niceties as thick carpet, a well-equipped dashboard and wood door cappings, plus an adjustable steering column, were included, and the then new Ambla mock-leather was used for the trim. On its introduction the Triumph 1300 cost around £200 more than a Herald, this premium of 35 per cent pitching it into a different market, and probably one more at the older end of the age range. The 1300 was indeed something of a contradiction: with its front-wheel drive it was seen as innovative, yet its style and interior were much more conservative.

Press reaction upon launch at the October 1965 London Motor Show was very favourable – 'the best small car currently available', the *Autocar* report called the 1300. But with only 61bhp to pull nearly a ton of car along, this was no sports saloon, nor were the handling and cornering quite the equal of the BMC cars, thanks to rather dead steering. The car could however be hustled with confidence through fast corners in the wet. Ride was firm but comfortable, and the excellent seats came in for much praise, as did the luxury interior in general. The 1300 was definitely perceived as a quality compact car,

The Triumph Pony

The Triumph fwd engine and transmission unit did eventually see one other commercial use – although not in the UK, for the intriguing Pony was built only in Israel.

The Pony was a small and chunky 4x4 truck, rather akin to a scaled-down Land Rover. It had a ladder chassis with long-travel independent suspension and with all wheels driven, the rear in rather similar fashion to the system later used on the rallycross 1300 saloon. Originally Triumph intended to produce the vehicle in the UK, but for reasons unknown production was deferred several times despite the prototypes being satisfactorily sorted.

Finally, in 1966 the rights and tooling were sold to a company called Autocars in Israel, who put this useful vehicle into series production. The prototypes remained in Coventry where they earned their keep for many years as works hacks shifting stores around. Even had Triumph manufactured the Pony on a production basis, it probably would not have survived the Rover/BL mergers which brought Land-Rover into the corporate fold.

The chunky little Pony 4x4 used fwd 1300 parts; ultimately it went into production in Israel. (Graham Robson collection)

just the right size for many buyers, and it was seen as good value at about the £800 mark. The limited performance produced by the single-carburettor engine came in for some criticism, especially as when extended in the gears it became noisy and harsh. Top speed was around 85mph, but 0–60mph acceleration was pedestrian even by 1965 standards, at 19.5 seconds. However, cruising at 60–65mph the 1300 was 'quiet and relaxed', and this after all was what interested most buyers. Overall fuel consumption averaged 34–35mpg, which was pretty creditable for such a weighty car.

Although overshadowed in later years by the faster Dolomites, the first of the Ajax line undoubtedly attracted

From the rear the 1500 is more elegant than the Manx-tailed 1300.

customers who would not have looked at a Herald. Sales were excellent right from the start, so the mystery is why Leyland-Triumph did not immediately develop the line. Instead, the 1300 stayed in production almost unchanged for a full five years until August 1970, the only relief being the introduction in October 1967 of a much-needed twin-carburettor version, the 1300TC. As well as the carbs, this model benefited from a higher compression ratio, a reprofiled camshaft, and a servo for the brakes. At £42 more than the standard offering, it was well worth the extra, which bought you 75bhp and 75lb ft of torque, enough to bring the 0–60mph time down to a respectable 15.4 seconds. At this time Triumph's product planners wanted to produce a cheapened version of the 1300 with a shorter boot, coded Manx, but this

was abandoned when cost savings proved insufficient.

Both 1300 and 1300TC models were replaced by the fwd 1500 of August 1970, a rather strange crossbred beast that is today even more overlooked than the 1300, and is not to be confused with the 1500TC and Dolomite 1500s which came a little later and which had rear-wheel drive. The 1500 had bodyshell revisions which included a longer nose and a slightly longer tail (and hence greater boot space), these together adding 7in to the length. Under the skin, however, there was a significant change: in order to share parts with the rear-drive Toledo (as described in the next chapter), the 1500 went over to a dead rear axle, with an optional rear anti-roll bar. As well as saving money, the change was intended to eliminate the 1300's proneness to lift-off oversteer.

Buying Hints

1. Rust is the greatest enemy on this entire family of small Triumph saloons. Check first the front inner wings, the panels behind the headlamps under the bonnet, and the exterior around the headlamps. Then move on to edges of the sills, the bases of the A-posts, the screen pillars, the wheelarches, and the door frames and bottoms. The trailing edge of the boot lid, the boot floor, and the rear edge of the roof are also vulnerable. Less visible points to check include the front bulkhead, the front footwells, the front valance, the front subframe mounting points, and the battery tray.

2. The earlier the car, the sounder it often is – later mid-to-late-1970s vehicles seem to have been built from poorer quality steel, and it shows. Most panels are obtainable one way or another, but there are often supply difficulties.

3. The interiors were of good quality and if reasonably treated will have survived well, but the wooden door cappings split and peel. Trim can be very hard to find.

4. The Herald-derived 1300/1500 engines are tough and simple but can be oil-starved when started from cold. A modern canister filter with a non-return valve is a good cure. Overheating can be a problem, and the temperature gauge should be watched. Valve guides can wear, leading to smokiness, and valvegear can be noisy, but parts are readily available as so much is common with the Spitfire/Herald ranges.

5. Transmission parts for fwd cars are becoming hard to find. Driveshaft couplings are prone to cracking and require frequent replacement. On fwd cars the starter ring gear is exposed, which can cause the starter to stick. Play in the gear linkage is endemic, by the way.

The engine was a further stretch of the Herald unit, this time to 1493cc, by means of an increase in stroke. This produced a useful increase in torque (to 81lb ft) but did almost nothing for power which stayed at 61bhp, albeit now measured on the DIN scale. In October 1971, minor engine revisions conjured up 65bhp, but even this was hardly going to set the road alight in almost a ton of car. What was becoming increasingly apparent at Triumph even before the 1500 was launched was that British Leyland saw the Ausin-Morris line as carrying the front-wheel-drive flag, which rather left the Triumph front-drivers as also-rans. It could have all been so different if Triumph's engineers had really put energy into developing the 1300 concept, for the original car of 1965 was an excellent start. As it was, the Triumphs can be seen as something of a blind alley, particularly the 1500 of 1970–1973.

In the autumn of 1973 when the 1500 model was withdrawn, to be replaced by an almost identical car but with rear-wheel drive, no doubt some eyebrows were raised in the motor industry at what would seem to be a retrogressive change. At least it made production-engineering sense.

But despite this, the eight-year run of the fwd 1300/1500 must be counted a success; indeed, there was a period when the 1300 was Triumph's best-seller. Homes were found for 113,008, plus a further 35,342 examples of the 1300TC. Even the 1500 managed a total of 66,353 units in its three-year life. Sadly, despite their being a well-built, quality small car, relatively few examples of Triumph's flirtation with front-wheel drive survive today.

The dashboard and the interior trim are in the same style as on the MkII 2000 and 2.5PI; slender door cappings distinguish the 1500 and 1500TC from the later Dolomite 1500HL. (Jon Pressnell collection)

From *Toledo to Dolomite*

The rear-wheel-drive Toledo two-door saloon of 1970. Unadorned and somewhat basic, it took the place of the Herald as Triumph's bottom-of-range vehicle.

The first indication that Triumph was reversing its adoption of front-wheel drive was the appearance of the rear-drive Triumph Toledo in August 1970, alongside the front-wheel-drive 1500. Superficially the two vehicles appeared similar, yet they differed considerably under the skin, with the Toledo very much the poor relation.

Introduced only as a two-door saloon, the Toledo was intended to

Toledo
1970–76

ENGINE:
Four cylinders in line, cast-iron block and head
Capacity 1296cc
Bore x stroke 73.7mm x 76mm
Valve actuation Pushrod
Compression ratio 8.5:1
Carburettor Single SU
Power 58bhp at 5300rpm
Maximum torque 70lb ft 3000rpm

TRANSMISSION:
Rear-wheel drive; four-speed all-synchromesh

SUSPENSION:
Front: Independent by strut and wishbones
Rear: Live rear axle with coil springs, location by radius arms; telescopic dampers

STEERING:
Rack-and-pinion

BRAKES:
Front: Drum; disc from October 1972
Rear: Drum
Servo assistance from October 1972

WHEELS/TYRES:
Steel disc wheels
Tyres 5.20 x 13in (5.60 x 13in on four-door); later 155 x 13in radial

BODYWORK:
Two or four-door saloon; all-steel monocoque

DIMENSIONS:
Length 13ft 0½in
Wheelbase 8ft 0½in
Track, front 4ft 5in
Track, rear 4ft 2in
Width 5ft 1¾in
Height 4ft 6in

KERB WEIGHT: 16.5cwt

PERFORMANCE (Source: *Autocar*)
Max speed 83mph
0–60mph 17.6sec
30–50mph in top 13.5sec
50–70mph in top 20.5sec

NUMBER BUILT:
1300-engined 113,294
1500-engined (export) 5,888

PRICE INCLUDING TAX WHEN NEW:
£889 (October 1970)

All Dolomites as Toledo except:

Dolomite 1300
1976–80

SUSPENSION:
Front: Anti-roll bar standard

DIMENSIONS:
Length 13ft 6in
Track, rear 4ft 2½ in

KERB WEIGHT: 19.2cwt

PRICE INCLUDING TAX WHEN NEW:
£2,070 (March 1976)

NUMBER BUILT: 32,031

1500TC/Dolomite 1500
1973–80

ENGINE:
Capacity 1493cc
Bore x stroke 73.7mm x 87.5mm
Compression ratio 8.5:1
Carburettors Twin SU
Power 64bhp at 5000rpm
71bhp at 5500rpm from March 1975
Maximum torque 78lb ft at 3000rpm
84lb ft at 3000rpm from March 1975

TRANSMISSION:
Rear-wheel drive; four-speed gearbox
Optional automatic transmission

SUSPENSION:
Front: Anti-roll bar on Dolomite 1500

STEERING:
Rack-and-pinion

BRAKES:
Front: Disc
Rear: Drum
Servo assistance

WHEELS/TYRES:
Steel disc wheels
Tyres 155 x 13in

KERB WEIGHT:
19.3cwt (Dolomite 1500 HL)

PERFORMANCE:
(Source: *Autocar*)
Max speed 91mph
0–60mph 13.2sec
30–50mph in top 10.1sec
50–70mph in top 12.7sec

PRICE INCLUDING TAX WHEN NEW:
£1,295 (1500TC, November 1973)

NUMBER BUILT:
1500TC 25,549
Dolomite 1500/1500TC 43,255

Dolomite 1850 (HL)
1972–80

ENGINE:
Capacity 1854cc
Bore x stroke 87mm x 78mm
Valve actuation Single overhead cam, chain-driven
Compression ratio 9.0:1
Carburettors Twin Zenith-Stromberg SUs from October 1973
Power 91bhp at 5200rpm
Maximum torque 105lb ft at 3500rpm

TRANSMISSION:
Four-speed all-synchromesh gearbox, overdrive or automatic transmission both optional

SUSPENSION:
Front: Anti-roll bar
Rear: Anti-roll bar from 1976

BRAKES:
Front: Disc
Rear: Drums
Servo assistance

WHEELS/TYRES:
Steel disc wheels
Tyres 155 x 13in

KERB WEIGHT:
19.0cwt

PERFORMANCE:
(Source: *Autocar*)
Max speed 100mph
0–60mph 11.6sec
30–50mph in top 8.2sec
50–70mph in top 9.7sec

PRICE INCLUDING TAX WHEN NEW:
£1,399 (January 1972)

NUMBER BUILT: 79,010

Dolomite Sprint
1973–1980

As Dolomite except:

ENGINE:
Capacity 1998cc
Bore x stroke 90.3mm x 78mm
Valve actuation Single overhead camshaft, chain-driven; 16 valves
Compression ratio 9.5:1
Carburettors Twin SU
Power 127bhp at 5700rpm
Mximum torque 124lb ft at 4500rpm

TRANSMISSION:
Overdrive standard from May 1975

SUSPENSION:
Rear: Anti-roll bar

WHEELS/TYRES:
Alloy wheels
175 x 13in tyres

KERB WEIGHT:
19.8cwt (overdrive)

PERFORMANCE:
(Source: *Autocar*)
Max speed 115mph
0–60mph 8.7sec
30–50mph in top 8.4sec
50–70mph in top 9.8sec

PRICE INCLUDING TAX WHEN NEW:
£1,740 (July 1973)

NUMBER BUILT: 22,941

replace the Herald, and used the 1296cc engine mated to an all-synchromesh gearbox also used in the forthcoming Morris Marina; this gearbox was a development of the GT6 unit. Drive went to a live rear axle suspended on coil springs and located by radius arms and two diagonal links. The 1300's hybrid strut/wishbone front end was retained, as was its rack-and-pinion steering, but braking, rather regressively, was by drums all-round despite the Herald 13/60 having front discs.

The Toledo was a thoroughly straightforward if unexciting product: there was never a 'TC' version, the 58bhp engine continuing right through, although a small number of cars were made for export with the 1500cc engine. At first only a two-door body was offered, but this was joined in October 1971 by a four-door which also added a wraparound rear bumper. A touch of Triumph luxury was provided by a walnut-veneered dashboard, but in other respects the Toledo was pretty basic. In October 1972 servo-assisted disc brakes made a belated appearance, but no other mechanical improvement ever materialised. In April 1975 a new black-and-silver grille arrived, but otherwise Triumph's base model soldiered on unchanged until early 1976. Total Toledo production

Above: This late – and thus 71bhp – 1500TC of 1975 has a side rubbing strip and a door mirror, but is otherwise identical to earlier 1500TCs and to the preceding 1500. (Jon Pressnell collection)

Left: Although the cheapest Triumph saloon, the Toledo still featured a wooden dashboard. The steering wheel looks more dated than the rest of the interior, and the gear lever is strangely offset, possibly a legacy of the old front-wheel-drive layout. (Jon Pressnell collection)

amounted to just over 119,000 units, the majority of which were built at Triumph's new but ill-fated 'Liverpool No. 2' plant at Speke, it being the first model to be wholly assembled there.

Meanwhile, in October 1973 the 1500 gained a TC label, signalling not only the arrival of a twin-carb 64bhp engine but also an important engineering change: it became a conventional rear-wheel-drive car using the Toledo drivetrain, albeit with a higher rear axle ratio. This change in configuration allowed automatic transmission to be offered as an option. The interior appointments were unchanged, and thus one class up from the Toledo, as was the price, which was £1,668 in 1974 against £1,370 for the lesser car. Even after an upgrade to 71bhp in February 1975,

Above: The four-door version of the Toledo.

Right: To judge from its 1970/71 registration, this must be a pre-production 1850 Dolomite, for the model did not appear until January 1972. For the time it was a well-equipped and rapid car, and soon became extremely popular.

performance was hardly sparkling, but was judged perfectly acceptable at the time. The 1500TC accounted for 25,549 units in its two and a half year production period.

In March 1976 Triumph put some order into its Ajax range by bringing all models together under the Dolomite name, with all cars using the same

1500/Dolomite long-tail body. The new Dolomite 1500HL shared the 1850cc Dolomite's internal and external presentation, whereas the Dolomite 1300, replacing the Toledo, kept the simpler Toledo dashboard and trim and had a body lacking the matt-black detailing of the other cars in the range. Further to this, a basic Toledo-

Dolomites in competition

Despite its unpromising looks, the Dolomite Sprint became not only a modestly successful international rally vehicle but also a highly competitive racing saloon. To hear this story in detail the author refers readers to Graham Robson's authoritative book *The Works Triumphs* (Haynes).

By the early 1970s the whole of British Leyland's competition programme was being run by BL Special Tuning, based at the MG works in Abingdon, and it was they who developed the Sprint as a rally car. The 1854cc Dolomite was never rallied seriously, although works driver Brian Culcheth did try out a couple of mildly uprated cars.

The advent of the prototype Sprints in 1972 led to the Dolomite first being properly considered as a rally contender, Culcheth taking 'CKV 2K', one of the prototypes, to a second in class and nineteenth overall in June 1972's Scottish Rally. Financial problems led to there being no works Triumphs rallied in 1973, but for 1974 the Sprint was campaigned in earnest both in rallying by Special Tuning and in saloon car racing by Ralph Broad's Broadspeed concern. Broad soon had the engines giving 175bhp at a heady 8200rpm, later improved to 200bhp as prepared by Don Moore with full-house modifications and running on twin-choke Webers. The racing Sprints were very effectively driven by Tony Dron, Roger Bell, and Andy Rouse, achieving fifth overall in the 1974 Spa 24-hour race and third overall in the Tourist Trophy as well as many successes in shorter events – culminating in Leyland winning the manufacturer's championship that year. In 1975 Rouse won the British Saloon Car Championship outright in a Group One Sprint, while in 1976 he managed second in his class. The sight of the Broadspeed Dolomite Sprints three-wheeling it around the curves is one not easily forgotten by those, including the writer, who saw it. Even as late as 1978, in its fifth season, the Broadspeed Sprint was still competitive enough to win races and in the hands of Tony Dron it won the Class B Saloon Championship outright. Broadspeed eventually coaxed 235bhp out of the Sprint when the car was able to run in Group Two specification – an amazing achievement.

In top-level rallying there were also successes. Here Brian Culcheth was the team's number one driver, with Tony Pond coming along in 1976. In 1974 the rally Sprints suffered a number of reliability problems, steering, brakes, and cooling faults all causing retirements, but by 1975 Abingdon had sorted the cars, allowing Culcheth to finish an excellent second overall on the Tour of Britain rally (a feat which he repeated in 1976) and then first in class on the RAC Rally. The Broadspeed-prepared engines were reported to give a reliable 160bhp in rally form.

Although during its four-year international rally career the Dolomite Sprint never quite won a major event outright, it was frequently first in its class and after the 1974 season's difficulties had been overcome it proved extremely reliable, usually lasting better than its TR7 stablemates upon which Abingdon was concentrating by 1976. It was basically too heavy and too under-braked to ever to be able to beat the Escorts on speed, but it could and did outlast them on occasion. The Sprint's real forte was tarmac events – the greater the proportion of hard surfaces in an event, the better its chances. Had BL's financial position been stronger in the mid 1970s, leading to the sort of cash that Ford employed becoming available, then who knows what the race and rally Sprints might have achieved. There were even attempts to develop the 16-valve engine into a competitive Formula Three engine, but although it could produce the power, sustained reliability was always a problem. Had the Sprint-engined TR7 gone into full production rather than the V8 version, it may well have been that Triumph's ingenious 16-valve engine would have received yet more development – who knows?

Tony Dron lets one of the very successful works racing Dolomite Sprints show its paces in the mid-1970s. Gordon Spice follows in a Ford Capri. The Dolomite looks remarkably standard from the outside.

In a dark colour the Dolomite's matt-black trimmings are less obtrusive.

spec 1500 model was introduced, while all three 1300/1500 models gained the 1850cc Dolomite's front anti-roll bar and the 1500s became available with optional overdrive.

As for the original 1854cc Dolomite of January 1972, in its day it was both a class-leading and a successful car, while in later Sprint form it was a truly sporting one. The heart of the new car was its engine, a modern five-main-bearing four-cylinder design with a chain-driven, single overhead camshaft and an aluminium cylinder head. It became known as the 'slant-four', as it was designed to be installed canted over at a 45-degree angle to reduce overall height and also to be in effect half a V8.

The engine's origins go back to 1963 when Triumph was reviewing future requirements and settled upon an overhead-cam 'four' of between 1200cc and 2000cc with a related V8 of double the capacity. At that same period Saab was considering how to

replace its ageing two-stroke triples, and via engine designer Harry Ricardo the Swedish company was put in touch with Triumph. It was eventually agreed that Triumph would build its new engine for Saab in 1709cc form for the forthcoming 99 model, and thereafter use it in a new Triumph model, the Dolomite. The engine thus first appeared in the Saab 99, sales of which began in August 1968. Development costs were shared by the two companies, Triumph tooling up to produce up to 40,000 such engines for Saab. From the start the engine was arranged so that it could be employed in either fwd or rwd cars, the Saab being front-wheel-drive. At the time of the engine's design, Triumph too had thought that it would appear in a fwd car of their own, but this was not to be, the front-wheel-drive 1500 being dropped the year after the Dolomite arrived. By 1972 Saab had set up its own plant to build its own untimately very different 'slant-four', leaving all

the engine production available for the Dolomite.

In truth, there was very little new in the Dolomite: it was just a fusion of existing Triumph components with the Saab engine, put together to make an attractive small sporting saloon. An adapted 1500 body was used, with modified Toledo rear-wheel-drive underpinnings, there being anti-roll bars front and rear and a higher 3.63 to 1 axle ratio, along with raised internal gearing and noticeably closer ratios for the Marina/Toledo four-speed gearbox. Overdrive became an option from March 1973, giving a nicely long-legged gait, while automatic transmission was available from the start.

In 1854cc form the engine produced 91bhp at 5200rpm, with 105lb ft of torque at 3500rpm, sufficient for a sporting performance,

The Panther Rio

The Panther Rio was not without a certain logic: the fuel crisis had punched a hole in sales of Panther's pastiche 1930s cars, and there wasn't much wrong with the Dolomites other than their old-fashioned bodies. Why not, therefore, amalgamate Panther luxury coachwork with Triumph underpinnings, and create a miniature would-be Rolls-Royce for such straitened times? This was exactly what Panther chief Bob Jankel

achieved, elegantly re-skinning the Dolomite with sharp-lined aluminium panels and fronting the car with a vaguely Rolls-like Palladian grille flanked by Ford Granada headlamps. Announced in September 1975 as the 1854cc Rio and the Sprint-based Rio Especiale, the new little Panther had a plush leather interior and a Dolomite dashboard with leather trimmings and high-grade veneering. The price, naturally,

was commensurate with such hand-crafted quality, and at four pounds shy of £9000 the Especial cost three times the price of a Dolomite Sprint; perhaps not surprisingly, only 38 Rios were made, the last in 1977.

The Panther Rio was a re-skinned and beautifully re-trimmed Dolomite, available in either 1850 or Sprint (Especiale) form. Only 38 were made.

albeit with less rapid 0–60 acceleration than the recently deceased 2-litre Vitesse. Initially twin Stromberg carburettors were fitted, but SUs replaced these in late 1973.

One of the Dolomite's chief selling points was its luxury interior, largely inherited from the 1500, and which included walnut door cappings and dashboard, thick carpets and the latest reclining Bri-Nylon seats – this being an era when many cars were still having to make do with vinyl. The driver's seat was height-adjustable, with a fully-adjustable steering wheel. Also standard were inertia-reel seat belts, a heated rear window and full Smiths instrumentation including a

rev-counter. The whole tenor of the car was that of a beautifully-fitted, compact executive saloon with some sporting pretensions, and it was very much what the market was looking for in 1972, especially at £1,399 tax-paid, which appeared something of a bargain given the equipment provided. In standard form the Dolomite would just top 100mph, cover 0–60mph in a shade over 11 seconds, and return 30mpg – small wonder that it sold extremely well right from its introduction in January 1972. Triumph were soon producing 500 examples per week and could have sold more had cars been available. In the March 1976 range re-jig the original 1854cc

Dolomite became the 1850HL, with only the most minor of equipment changes, and it continued in production with all the other Dolomites until the range was discontinued in November 1980. During its nine years of manufacture, 79,010 of the '1850' were made, and a number are still in daily use.

The exciting Dolomite Sprint arrived in 1973. By this time the compact sports saloon market had really taken off, both in the UK and continental Europe, with BMW then – as now – leading the way. Although the Dolomite 1850 was a good value-for-money player in this league, something faster and more overtly

Above: The facelifted Dolomite 1850HL saloon is shown here, photographed in September 1976; the TR7-style black plastic hubcaps don't do the car any favours, but at least the bib spoiler (not present on the physically identical 1500HL) helps high-speed stability.

Right: When the Toledo and 1500 were folded into the Dolomite range a long-tailed but Toledo-trimmed Dolomite 1500 became available alongside the more plush Dolomite 1500HL. This brown colour is typical of Toledos and lesser Dolomites.

Driving a Dolomite Sprint

It is hard to credit that this model is now over 35 years old, for here is a truly modern classic – modern that is, in terms of dynamic ability.

One starts by getting the driving position correct, and the Dolomite is an early example of a car with fully-adjustable seats and steering wheel. It is quick work to get comfortable and the high driving position means all-round visibility is excellent. The seats are comfortable, and the interior exudes quality in a '70s sort of way, with, as ever, instruments that are a model of clarity and switchgear that is user-friendly and sensible.

The engine is somewhat clattery and agricultural upon starting from cold, but once warm it improves considerably; in fact the more you rev it the smoother it becomes, right up to 6000rpm or more. Truly it is the

heart of the car and one only wonders why BL continued with the 1854cc eight-valve model once the Sprint came along, particularly as both give the same 28–30 mpg.

The gearchange still has that notchy feel so often mentioned by road-testers; the overdrive operation is instantaneous, as indeed it should be. However, even with overdrive engaged, the car still feels undergeared by today's standards, a trait common to virtually all older vehicles. Straight-line acceleration is terrific – faster than my modern Audi. The car pulls really well, and yet will if asked lug along at low speed as well, the mark of a truly versatile engine. A cruising speed of 80–85mph feels just about right, the only thing spoiling this relaxed progress being the intrusion of the

wind noise inevitably generated by the quarterlights.

In all aspects of performance the Sprint can more than keep up with modern traffic. The handling on 70-profile tyres feels secure although you could certainly lose the tail quite quickly on wet roads in second gear, but then that's part of the fun of a high performance, rear-wheel-drive car. Straight-line stability is good, and the brakes feel as good as those on the average modern vehicle.

As a four-door saloon with a decent boot, the Dolomite is a really practical car, and one in which it should prove easy to cover 400-plus miles in a day in reasonable comfort. With that splendid high-revving yet torquey engine, the Sprint truly is a great sporting saloon – and one not to be underestimated.

Three Dolomites pose together, a Mimosa Yellow Sprint, a Sprint in British Leyland racing colours and, in the middle, one of the very rare Panther Rio luxury conversions of the Dolomite Sprint, as described earlier: all the 'hard points' of the Dolomite structure are unchanged.

Above: The Dolomite Sprint engine shows how it is canted over at 45 degrees. The spark plugs are well buried, and the twin SU carburettors are mounted on very long inlet tracts.

Below: The rear view of the Sprint was the view most drivers saw in 1973, for it was one of the fastest saloons on the road. The vinyl roof, yellow and black 'Sprint' badges and alloy wheels show up well.

Buying Hints

1. Bodies are essentially as the fwd cars, so the same points apply; equally, remarks on the Herald and 1300/1500 apply to the engines of Toledos, rwd 1500s and 1300/1500 Dolomites.

2. The 1850 and Sprint units are more sophisticated engines with more to go wrong. As when new, overheating has always been the prime problem, this leading to warped alloy cylinder heads and a lot of expense. Correct anti-freeze levels and use of corrosion inhibitors is essential – and beware of the thermostat having been removed to disguise any cooling difficulties. The 1850 is prone to timing-chain rattle, but the duplex chain on the Sprint

avoids this. Both engines require regular oil changes and will not tolerate prolonged abuse. Again, oil filters without non-return valves cause problems on start-up by starving the crankshaft and bearings of oil. Oil leaks are common on both engines.

3. Transmission in all cases suffers from weak synchromesh, the larger Dolomites being also quite prone to jumping out of gear. If overdrive is fitted, it tends to be very reliable, with a low oil level or electrical problems tending to be the usual cause of non-functioning. Rear axles are available, but that of the 1850 Dolomite is a smaller lighter-duty unit than that of the Sprint. Beware of 1850 Dolomites that are

masquerading as Sprints – often the incorrect axle is a giveaway.

4. Steering is usually sound, but suspension bushes wear rapidly; most are easily and cheaply renewed. Sprints often have lateral movement in their rear-axle locating bushes, which causes poor handling; again these are easily renewed. Brakes tend to be reliable, although the front discs on a hard-driven Sprint are not up to the job.

5. As these cars, even the Sprints, are still not worth serious money, the top advice is to buy the best car one can afford, for the costs of restoring a doggy body alone will far outweigh whatever the finished car is worth.

sporting was required to tackle the German cars head-on. In addition, Ford's rally-developed sporting Escorts were selling well, even if they were a lot more basic than Triumph's offering. As a result Triumph engineers, led by Spen King, Ray Bates and Jim Parkinson, devised an ingenious 16-valve head for the 'slant-

four' engine. Four valves per cylinder may be commonplace today, but in 1973 this was very much racing-car territory. The valves were inclined in the classic pent-roofed cylinder head, but instead of the complication of twin overhead camshafts to operate them, Triumph used a single eight-lobe overhead camshaft operating via

inverted tappets on the inlet valves and with long rockers to open the exhaust valves – a clever solution that offered all the efficiency of 16 valves without the cost of twin camshafts. As it was envisaged that the car might be raced, the cubic capacity was increased to 1998cc to take best advantage of the 2-litre class limit, the increase in bore resulting in a very oversquare engine of 78mm stroke by 90.3mm bore.

Twin 1¾in SU carburettors were used with highly efficient manifolds, and in this form, on a 9.5-to-1 compression ratio, the Sprint engine gave 127bhp, 40 per cent more power than the standard Dolomite could muster. What

Left: The nicely finished and fully equipped interior of the Sprint, demonstrating Triumph's usual matt-finished wood. The overdrive switch is cleverly incorporated in the gear knob.

Opposite: This head-on view of a 1975/6 Sprint shows the black spoiler always fitted under the bumper. It was more than cosmetic, being vital to prevent high speed front-end lift and wander at speeds of over 100mph.

The ingenious 16-valve cylinder head, designed for the Dolomite Sprint, in which all the valves are operated by a single camshaft. The illustration carries an embargo date of 19 June 1973, the date of the Sprint's release.

was even more impressive was that better breathing meant that the Sprint used less fuel at similar speeds than its smaller sibling – a viscous-coupled cooling fan no doubt helped here. Note that Triumph avoided fuel injection for this sporting engine, a tacit acceptance of the problems of the Lucas PI system in the TRs, perhaps?

It was clear that the standard transmission would not survive this large power increase and consequently a gearbox with TR6/Stag internals was devised. Similarly, a TR6 differential was used. Overdrive was an option at first, becoming standard in 1975, and surprisingly for an

overtly sporting car, automatic transmission was offered. Brakes were of course uprated, with a larger servo operating 8¾in front discs and 9in rear drums; whereas the basic car made do with 13in steel wheels carrying skinny 155-section tyres, the Sprint ran on 175-section low-profile rubber mounted on attractive 5½in alloy wheels.

Little needed to be done to the car's interior, for the normal Dolomite had a very adequate specification. Externally, however, the Sprint was unmistakable, being given a fashionable black vinyl roof together with coachlines and appropriate badgework. One very necessary addition was a front spoiler to avoid front-end lift at the 120mph of which the car proved capable. Again, as was the fashion, a range of very bright colours was used, in common with Triumph's two-seaters – indeed, the first 2000 Sprints were produced

in bright Mimosa Yellow, which with the black roofs looked striking to say the least.

The arrival of the very rapid Sprint in June 1973 caused a sensation in motoring circles; here at last was a British BMW-beater, faster yet much cheaper, and a great deal was made of this in the initial publicity. The Sprint arrived at the tax-paid price of £1,869, whereas the BMW 2002 was around £1,000 more yet no faster – a huge differential that should have ensured the Dolomite Sprint's success, provided of course Triumph could maintain build quality, which was always a problem in the British Leyland era.

Press reports agreed that the 16-valve Dolomite combined the performance of the sporting Fords with top-quality comfort, agreeable appointments and relative silence. The torque was such that a Sprint could potter along at 1000rpm in top gear

Sitting lower, on wide alloy wheels, and with a standard bib-spoiler, the Sprint makes the best fist it can of disguising its old-fashioned bodywork.

and then accelerate to 6500rpm and 120mph all without the driver touching the gearlever – quite some achievement. It usually took around 9.0 seconds to reach 60mph, with 0–100mph clocked in well under half a minute – sports-car territory indeed. Testers enjoyed the close-ratio gearbox, but the notchy change was still said to be inferior to that of the Fords. Wheelspin was easy to provoke, leading some to call for a limited-slip differential. The damping was stiffer than on the normal Dolomite, which improved the already good handling; cornering power was well up to par, aided by the fatter tyres and the well-located rear axle. The spoiler had stopped all trace of wander, and the car was said to feel both safe and secure at speed. Altogether the Sprint was considered a splendid package and, initially at least, it sold just as fast as Triumph could make it; a total of 22,941 were built in the 1973–1980

period, the majority at the earlier end of this timespan.

The Dolomite was the principal model that carried Triumph through the 1970s, a period of financial and industrial turbulence that led to its direct replacement being cancelled altogether. Known under the code SD2, this was in essence a scaled-down version of the Rover SD1 with a hatchback body and the 2-litre eight-valve version of the 'slant-four' engine as used in the TR7. The running gear was largely TR7, and a number of SD2 prototypes were authorised by 1975. However the Austin-Morris division of BL was also in need of a new mid-range car, and realising that such in-house competition was nonsensical, it was decided to amalgamate the two projects. Before much progress could be made on this would-be Triumph-Morris (known as TM1), further consolidation saw it abandoned in favour of LM10/LM11,

eventually to emerge as the Maestro/Montego duo. Had it become a Triumph Dolomite MkII, the SD2 would have reached production in late 1978 and might have carried the Triumph name longer into the 1980s than proved to be the case. But as with so much in the British motor industry at this period, it was not to be.

The Dolomite thus continued until November 1980, looking progressively more and more old-fashioned. Even that marvellous 16-valve engine was never further developed nor used in any other model save a handful of TR7s. It died quietly, a victim of corporate rationalisation and financial problems, effectively being replaced by the 1981 Acclaim, a Triumph-badged Honda.

The 'sidescreen' TRs

The first TR – the unique 20TS prototype shown on the Standard-Triumph stand at the October 1952 London Motor Show. The bob-tailed rear end did not survive the redesign, but the front and central sections were carried over to the TR2 with only minor modifications.

In recent years the handy description 'sidescreen' TR has grown up to differentiate the TR2/3/3A/3B series of 1953–1962 from their later TR4-6 brethren. These later cars all have winding glass windows, whereas the earlier TRs rely on primitive sidescreens to keep out the weather, hence the terminology.

Arguably Triumph's most successful range of cars and certainly its most widely known, the TR series had its beginnings in the very early 1950s. It was born of Sir John Black's passionate desire to beat Jaguar and MG at their own game and flood the North American market with cheap yet fast sports cars to earn much-needed dollars for Britain. The 1800 Roadster had been a leisurely tourer at best, and one which certainly failed to excite the US market. The second attempt, the TRX 'Silver Bullet', was equally far from the cheap, cheerful and fast two-seater that the market awaited. Nor was it quite third time lucky, for the 1952 Triumph sports prototype needed major revision before becoming the winning TR2 of 1953. Still, they got there in the end, something for which today's enthusiasts must be duly grateful.

At the start of 1952 Standard-Triumph was back at square one in the sports car stakes following the shelving of the TRX roadster. As a shortcut, Black had tried to purchase the small but successful Morgan company, which had for some years used Standard engines. Fortunately for the history of both Triumph and Morgan, he was rebuffed. There was, however, another sports car running around the Midlands in the early 1950s that used the Vanguard engine. This was a one-off special with a basic two-seater body, called Buttercup on account of its yellow paint. It had been constructed by Ken Rawlings, an employee of PJ Evans, the Birmingham Standard-Triumph dealers, and had proved very successful in trials, driving tests, and on the road. There is now no doubt that Standard's directors had seen this car – indeed Black had ridden in it – and they were much influenced by it when the idea of a Vanguard-powered

TR2
1953–55

ENGINE:
Four cylinders in line, cast-iron block and head

Capacity	1991cc
Bore x stroke	83mm x 92mm
Valve actuation	Pushrod
Compression ratio	8.5:1
Carburettors	Twin 1½in SU
Power	90bhp at 4800rpm
Maximum torque	117lb ft at 3000rpm

TRANSMISSION:
Rear-wheel drive; four-speed gearbox, optional overdrive (top only to January 1955, then on second, third and top gears)

SUSPENSION:
Front: Independent by coil and wishbone; telescopic dampers
Rear: Live axle on semi-elliptic springs; lever-arm dampers

STEERING:
Cam-and-peg

BRAKES:
Front: 10in drum
Rear: 9in drum (later 10in)

WHEELS/TYRES:
Steel disc or wire wheels
Tyres 5.50 x 15in

BODYWORK:
Two-seater sports; separate chassis, steel panels

DIMENSIONS:

Length	12ft 7in
Wheelbase	7ft 4in
Track, front	3ft 9in
Track, rear	3ft 9½in
Width	4ft 7½in
Height, hood up	4ft 2in

KERB WEIGHT:
18.75cwt

PERFORMANCE:
(Source: *The Autocar*)

Max speed	103.5mph
0–60mph	11.9sec
30–50mph in top	9.3sec
50–70mph in top	10.4sec

PRICE INCLUDING TAX WHEN NEW:
£844 (January 1954)

NUMBER BUILT: 8,628

TR3
1955–57

As TR2 except:

ENGINE:

Carburettors	Twin 1¾in SU
Power	95bhp at 5000rpm, later 100bhp at 5000rpm

BRAKES:
Front: Discs (11in) from October 1956

KERB WEIGHT:
20cwt

PERFORMANCE:
(Source: *The Autocar*)

Max speed	102mph
0–60mph	12.5sec
30–50mph in top	10.2sec
50–70mph in top	12.5sec

PRICE INCLUDING TAX WHEN NEW:
£1073 with hardtop (January 1957)

NUMBER BUILT: 13,377

TR3A
1957–62

As TR3 except:

ENGINE:
From late 1958 optional 2138cc engine, with 9.1:1 compression ratio, 100bhp at 4600rpm 127lb ft at 3350 rpm

BRAKES:
Rear: Drums reduced in size to 9in x 1¾in from June 1959

PRICE INCLUDING TAX WHEN NEW:
£991 (May 1959)

NUMBER BUILT: 58,236

TR3B
March–December 1962

As TR3A except:

ENGINE:
(Later cars in 'TCF' chassis series)

Capacity	2138cc
Bore x stroke	86mm x 92mm
Compression ratio	9.0:1
Power	100bhp at 4600rpm
Maximum torque	127lb ft at 3350rpm

TRANSMISSION:
All-synchromesh TR4 gearbox

NUMBER BUILT: 3,334

two-seater came up. There was no need to buy the rights to Buttercup, for it was built largely from Standard-Triumph's own parts bin and the company could clearly do something similar – and so it did.

The original plan had been to base the new sports car on the chassis of the obsolete Standard Nine, a good number of these frames having been found in store, and the prototype seems indeed to have been built around elements of one of these chassis, in line with Black's brief to employ as many existing company-made components as possible. This was not only to keep costs down but also to save time – already his dollar-earning sports car was years late.

However, limited money was available for a new body design. The instructions given to chief body designer Walter Belgrove were to come up with a modern yet simple design that incorporated elements of both current and pre-war thinking, the latter as evidenced by the car's bob-tail with its exposed spare wheel.

The idea was to produce initially maybe 20 of these cars a week, principally as a way of reviving Triumph's pre-war sporting image. If this went well, then volume production and export would follow. Through its indecently rushed development period from early 1952 until its unveiling at the Motor Show in October, the car was known simply as the Triumph Sports, and codenamed 20TS. Although sometimes today referred to as the 'TR1', this term is incorrect.

In addition to the proven Vanguard engine, fitted with twin SU carburettors (in which form it produced 75bhp), the 20TS also used a modified four-speed version of the Vanguard gearbox – with, of course, a floor lever in place of the Vanguard column change. The rear axle was taken from the Mayflower but with a 3.89-to-1 ratio. This, together with 15in steel disc wheels, provided a gearing of 19mph per 1000rpm in top, which the torquey engine could easily pull. Mayflower coil-and-wishbone suspension, suitably beefed up, was employed at the front, this having telescopic dampers set within the coils. The rear layout could not have been simpler, in that semi-elliptical springs alone located the rear axle, which passed over the main chassis rails. Lever-arm dampers did their best to add some semblance of control to what was always an alarmingly basic layout. Cam-and-peg steering was used, the steering box being mounted right at the front of the cruciform-braced chassis.

The TR2 Francorchamps Coupé

In early 1954 the Belgian firm of Imperia began importing TR2s in CKD (completely knocked down) kit form for local assembly. It had been importing other Standard-Triumph models as CKD kits for some years, the principal reason being that tax and tariff barriers could thus be avoided. Imperia was not just content to assemble TR2s: it designed an elegant fixed-head coupé named the TR2 Francorchamps, after the racing circuit of that name near the Belgian town of Spa. It had lengthened doors with winding glass windows, and excellent all-round visibility was ensured by rear quarter windows and a large rear window, in conjunction with a Perspex roof panel. Unfortunately this made the cabin get very warm in the summer, while the enclosed cabin magnified the mechanical and exhaust noise inherent in the TR2. The car was retrimmed in more upmarket materials and offered in a range of subtle metallic colours: it looked expensive and it was expensive,

sufficiently so that only 22 examples were ever built, all left-hand drive and in both long-door and short-door form. Still, it was a brave attempt to provide something different and deserved to succeed. Interestingly the Coventry factory itself never made any attempt at turning the 'sidescreen' TR into a fixed-head coupé.

This silver-grey Francorchamps, complete with transparent opening/removable roof panel, was displayed at the 1955 Brussels Show, at a price equivalent to £1,000; the bolt-on wire wheels seem a questionable detail.

Above: A prototype TR2, with the original long doors. The sidescreens are also simpler than on later cars. The front badge and grille were changed for production TR2s. Below: This later TR2 has the shorter doors – and in this case runs on wide-rim wire wheels.

The Swallow Doretti

'A TR2 in a party frock' was how some wit once described the Doretti, an upmarket, aluminium-skinned sports car based on TR mechanicals. It was built by the Swallow Coachbuilding Company of Walsall, Staffordshire, and utilised a strong tubular chassis supplied by another subsidiary of Swallow's parent company, Tube Investments Limited.

The TR2 engine, gearbox, axle and suspension were fitted largely unaltered. Despite the fact that the wheelbase was 7in longer than that of the TR2, the main consequence of which was in effect to put the engine further back in the chassis, the Doretti was somewhat cramped inside and less practical than its parent: the boot did not hold as much and there was less space behind the seats. The Doretti was also ½cwt heavier, and slightly slower than the TR, although undeniably prettier – perhaps some compensation for its higher price.

Most crossed to the USA, not least to Cal-Sales in California, headed by the lady after whom the car was named, Dorothy Deen, 'Doretti' being an Italian version of the name Dorothy. Sir John Black was personally involved in the setting-up of the Doretti project, with Deen's father Arthur Andersen, and it was whilst passengering Ken Richardson in the first Doretti that Black was injured in a crash outside his own factory gates in November 1953. This happening started a chain of events that rapidly culminated in Black being ousted by his board of directors at the start of 1954.

In all, 274 cars were made between October 1953 and February 1955, production apparently ceasing as a result of pressure from other sports-car makers whom TI supplied with steel – and who resented the company making a rival to their own cars.

A picturesque line-up of a Swallow Doretti, a TR2 fitted with an ugly roll-over bar, and a glassfibre-bodied Peerless.

Left: The TR2 engine bay – 1½in SU carburettors were used on this model; as an earlier 'long-door' example, this car has the original internal cable-release bonnet locks. The rocker cover is correctly painted black – only later cars had chromed covers.

Opposite: A TR2 in high-speed trim; a metal tonneau and rear spats improve aerodynamics, as does removal of the front bumper and addition of a stick-on numberplate. Although this car is a re-creation, similar aerodynamic aids were available from the factory in period.

Belgrove's body was simple and rugged-looking, featuring cutaway doors to add a sporty touch. Compound curves had to be avoided to save expense, which meant the 20TS had something of a slab-sided look. A wide-opening bonnet gave excellent engine access, although the same could not be said for the radiator, which hid under the front panel. This front panel incorporated an open-mouthed air intake which while efficient at cooling was not to everyone's taste aesthetically. The truncated rear made the car look unbalanced, with too much front end and not enough rear, and meant that the only carrying space was behind the seats. Full instrumentation and a pair of bucket seats demonstrated the car's sporting status, with weather equipment consisting of a 'kit-of-parts' hood and detachable sidescreens. The windscreen was bowed slightly to counteract wind pressure.

The whole car was something of the proverbial 'curate's egg', being good in parts, although it was generally agreed that the rear end was not satisfactory. As the car had been completed in such a rush, there had barely been time even to road-test it before the show, so it was very much an unknown quantity, and certainly

Assembly abroad

Imperia assembled quite a number of TR2s and TR3s for sale in various continental countries. By 1958 however, Standard-Triumph had decided to open its own assembly plant in Belgium at Malines and took the job over, continuing to build TRs (inter alia) until the 1971 model year.

Another CKD kit assembler was South Africa, where something over 1,000 TR3s and TR3As were built locally, all right-hand-drive of course. The strange thing was that one could have either a locally-assembled TR or order one built in Coventry – illogical but true.

Around 100 early TR3s were assembled in Australia in 1956, but for some reason (maybe tariff changes?) only this one batch was made, all other cars coming ready-built from the UK.

Local assembly of TRs also took place in the Irish Republic and according to some reports in Mexico – although I have not been able to confirm this. CKD cars often appeared in non-standard colour schemes – not surprisingly, as the bodies left Coventry only in primer. There may well have been other differences on account of local sourcing of certain materials.

had received no serious development. Indeed, the 20TS was a long way from being ready for public sale: only the one prototype existed, a second partly-built car never being completed.

The fact was that the 1952 London show had been stolen by a competitor, Donald Healey's beautiful new Hundred. Although significantly dearer than the Triumph, the Healey had at

least shown itself capable of 110mph in road tests, and was much more developed and nearer to being a production proposition. Clearly the 20TS would need more work, and just how much became obvious at a press day held shortly afterwards.

Although quite sprightly in a straight line, the Triumph's handling and cornering were deeply suspect, the problem being soon diagnosed as

The Peerless and Warwick GT

Announced in late 1957, the Peerless was a 2+2 glassfibre-bodied saloon of incredibly low build, manufactured by a small concern in Slough, Buckinghamshire. An advanced tubular spaceframe was used, there was an expensive de Dion rear suspension, and a standard TR3 engine, gearbox (with optional

Several Peerlesses were raced with some moderate success – one even competed at Le Mans. Here an example is seen in March 1959 at what looks suspiciously like the Goodwood chicane.

overdrive) and differential were used. TR instruments and many other items from Standard's corporate parts bin also surfaced on the car, which had some pretensions to being a luxurious Grand Tourer.

Despite being a four-seater of sorts, the Peerless was lighter than the TR, and was also more streamlined and as a result had a higher top speed of 110–112mph, and acceleration that was at least as good. Handling was also superior, owing to the de Dion rear end. But as was almost inevitable with a small

and undercapitalised manufacturer, the Peerless suffered from lack of development and quality control. Not least there was a lack of rigidity, causing noise and rattles, these being accentuated by the firm ride. Faults acceptable in a cheap kit-car were less so when the Peerless cost £1,500, or half as much again as a TR.

Although it was a brave attempt at producing an inexpensive GT car, the Peerless was doomed to failure, and the concern was wound up in 1960 after around 300 cars had been made. However, as so often with limited-production enthusiasts' cars, a second attempt was made, the Warwick GT arising from the Peerless ashes that same year. The body was updated, with the line of the fins continuing up into the roof, and with a one-piece hinged front, but essentially it was the formula as previously. However, the body was both lighter and stronger and contained a lot of extra soundproofing, which added greatly to refinement. Cost was unsurprisingly greater, too, and only 40 or so Warwicks were made – including a handful with Buick V8 engines – before manufacture ceased in 1962.

flexing of the chassis. Braking was not up to the 90mph performance either. One of those who was invited to try the 20TS at this time was Ken Richardson, a former BRM test driver and development engineer. He was a man known to Sir John Black, and a man whose opinion Black respected. Richardson was not only a good judge of sports cars but he was also forthright in his views – and in his opinion the 20TS was a mobile disaster, the proverbial accident waiting to happen, and certainly not a vehicle fit to be sold to the general public. He told Black and director of engineering Ted Grinham as much after his short drive, and

was astounded to be offered on the spot the job of sorting the car out and turning it into what it should have been.

The company's best engineers were to be put on the project with Richardson and nothing was to be ruled out. Extra development money was made available, but one thing that Black insisted upon was speed. He wanted the revised car at the Geneva Motor Show in the first week of March 1953. As it was already November, that left chief chassis engineer Harry Webster, Ken Richardson and the team a bare 16 weeks to create the silk purse from the sow's ear. Long hours including many all-night sessions were

worked that winter, but the job was done on time. A whole new tail section including an opening boot and separate spare wheel storage was grafted on, greatly improving the previously awkward proportions, while the front was left much as Belgrove had originally designed it. The offending chassis frame was redesigned and stiffened up considerably by the addition of gussets, heavier-section cross-tubing, extra body mounts, and general strengthening. Front brakes increased to 10in diameter and the rear axle ratio was raised to 3.7-to-1, with close-ratio gears being provided in addition.

However it was in making the

The Triumph Italia 2000

A TR3A with a bespoke body, the handsome Italia, built from 1959 to 1962, was certainly the most upmarket of the TR3 derivatives.

Designed by Giovanni Michelotti, the bodies were built by Vignale in Turin onto TR3A (latterly TR3B) chassis shipped from Coventry. The car was a fixed-head coupé with room in the rear for small children, and the up-market interior featured bucket seats and a restyled dash for the regular TR dials. Top-quality carpeting and smoked Perspex sun visors completed the luxurious cockpit, which was usually trimmed in leather. Although nominally optional, it seems that wire wheels and overdrive were invariably present, as was a fresh-air heater.

Viewed from the front the Italia had something of the miniature Ferrari about it and from the side there were echoes of the future TR4. Unique bumpers were fitted, as were lighting units by Carello. These are the sort of items that are so hard to find today should they be missing on a car being restored. Windscreens too have been all but impossible to source over the years.

As can be imagined, the Italia was expensive, although no list price was ever quoted in the UK, where it was not officially marketed. The best estimate of numbers built is 329, virtually all left-hand-drive although a handful of right-hand-drive examples were made, including the prototype. A majority of the cars were sold in Europe, but at least 16 made it to the States, where some examples hung around in showrooms for years awaiting buyers. Even at the time there were no spare body panels available, and it is said that US customers had to sign a disclaimer to confirm that they were aware of this before purchase of the car.

Performance of the Italia was on a par with the TR3A, the aerodynamic shape counteracting the extra weight.

The exciting and beautiful Michelotti/Vignale TR Italia – under the Italian body is a standard TR3A chassis and mechanicals. The model was never officially sold in the UK, though a handful of right-hand-drive examples were built. From the rear the Italia's stylistic links with the later TR4 are evident.

As with the Peerless, top speed was somewhat better: Triumph recorded a 109mph maximum speed and a 0–60mph time of 14.3 seconds. The Italia is such a beautiful shape that one marvels at why Triumph did not take it over from Michelotti and make the car in quantity. In fact this was considered, but never occurred – probably on account of Standard-Triumph's poor finances. As it is so rare today, the Italia is one of the most coveted of all the TRs; it deserves to have succeeded better than was the case.

TR dials are housed in a smartly modern dashboard.

Vanguard engine bulletproof at sustained high speeds where Richardson had most effect. The prototype of what was now called the TR2 was taken to the Motor Industry Research Association test track near Nuneaton on many occasions that winter, Richardson being under orders to circulate at 100mph until something broke – a brutal but effective régime. Several of the engine's components withered under such treatment, for whilst the Vanguard engine was perfectly suitable for its designed purpose, it was not produced with continuous operation at or near maximum rpm in mind. After two months of such testing, the much strengthened and improved 'four' produced a reliable 90bhp, enough for over 100mph, with better fuel consumption as a result of the engine's higher efficiency.

By late February 1953, Triumph's development boys knew they had an excellent car on their hands, based on their experience of the first prototype, and the proposed selling price of £555 before tax seemed certain to make it the world's cheapest 100mph car. Black was particularly enthusiastic, and authorised full-scale production as soon as possible. Triumph's new car received an excellent reception at the Geneva show, but what was needed was some really headline-grabbing publicity – not only in the motoring press, but such as would make the front pages of the national dailies. Black had always had an eye for publicity stunts, and he'd noticed that both Jaguar and Sunbeam had captured headlines by taking their sports cars over to Belgium and attempting high-speed records on Belgium's new motorways – no such roads existing in Britain, of course. Richardson was summoned and asked whether the TR could beat the Sunbeam Alpine's recent 120mph speed. He was as confident as he could be that it could: as he told the

author in 1994, he had already had the second prototype, MVC 575, up to 120mph in clandestine early morning testing on the Bicester straight in Oxfordshire.

To achieve these sort of speeds from an unblown 2-litre road car more than 50 years ago required a lot of streamlining, and so MVC 575 was given a full undershield, a metal tonneau cover, rear wheel-spats and a single aeroscreen. The engine was in standard form, but had been very carefully assembled and tuned. Acting on Richardson's confidence, Black had arrangements made in May 1953 to transport the car, RAC observers and the world's motoring press to Jabbeke, a small town near Bruges. Here the Belgian authorities were happy to close their new motorway to normal traffic for accurately-timed record runs.

The story of Richardson's high-speed exploits at the venue has passed into Triumph folklore: the car achieved the amazing two-way speed of almost 125mph. Initially there was disappointment as only 104mph was recorded, but it transpired that a plug had come adrift – so 104 mph on three cylinders wasn't too bad! Restored to health, the car proceeded to perform as predicted, Black was pleased, the press were impressed, and international headline news was made. Low drag and low frontal area were the secrets; indeed, Richardson sat on a cushion on the floor to keep himself

out of the airstream as far as possible. But even with hood, full windscreen and sidescreens in place, MVC 575 still managed a flying mile at 114mph. After this exemplary demonstration, suddenly everyone wanted to buy the revised Triumph Sports.

A new brochure was issued, but tooling delays meant that it would be late July before the first two production TR2s emerged, and thereafter only a handful of cars were constructed each week, resulting in a total of just 300 made by the end of 1953. It was not to be until early 1954 that series production really accelerated and the car became generally available. Some 1953 cars went to dealerships for demonstration purposes but the majority went for export, over 40 different countries receiving single examples. The US of course received the major share, for that had always been the car's intended market.

Coinciding with better availability in 1954 came an unexpected but vital boost to the TR's credibility: private entrant Johnny Wallwork won the March RAC Rally outright in his TR2, with TRs also finishing second and fifth. Suddenly the Triumph was taken seriously by the sporting fraternity, and became the car to have for aspiring rallymen – and club racers too, for it soon proved its speed on the circuit. It was an inexpensive, do-everything sort of car. You could go to work in it, go

A nicely restored 'sidescreen' TR cockpit, in this case belonging to a TR2. The space behind the seats is very useful and shrank on later cars.

shopping in it, go on holiday in it, race it or rally it, and all on better than 30mpg – small wonder that it rapidly became a hot ticket. Compared to its deadly rival the Austin-Healey 100, the TR was significantly cheaper to buy, significantly cheaper to run, and yet just as fast. It also had a nicer gearbox and could carry more luggage. In comparison with BMC's other sports

offering, the MG TF, the TR was so far ahead in every respect it was almost embarrassing. At its 1954 price of £844 including Purchase Tax, Triumph's sports car was terrific value. It could also be made even more fit for purpose by the addition of a range of extras, such as overdrive, wire wheels, a heater, and – from late 1954 – a neat hardtop.

In 1954 the factory capitalised on the TR2's potential by setting up a competition department under Richardson. Production was up to nearly 100 cars a week, all of which found ready buyers, and by October 1954 a full 4,000 had been built. At that time the first visible modification was made, when the depth of the doors was shortened to stop them hitting kerbs when opened. This has led in modern times to TR2s becoming known accordingly as either 'long-door' or 'short-door' cars. At the same time the car also received an improved hood with two quarter windows for better visibility.

As a result of competition experience, many mechanical improvements were made in the 27-month life of the TR2, but the concept was so right from the start

Above and left: The 1955–57 TR3 has a cellular grille at the front of the air intake. That and the badgework are the only easy external ways to tell it from the TR2. The 'Triumph' letters are an incorrect addition on the red car.

The 'sidescreen' TR in rallying

The TR2 was set on the road to rally success by the outright victory of Manchester garage proprietor Johnny Wallwork in 1954's RAC Rally; TRs also came second and fifth as well as winning the ladies prize. By the end of 1954 Triumph had established a competition department led by Ken Richardson. A team prize for the TR2s in the 1954 Alpine Rally was an impressive achievement, as was Richardson himself gaining a first in class (fifth overall) in 1955's gruelling Liège–Rome–Liège.

It was 1956 that saw what was probably the TR's greatest rally success when in the Alpine Rally TR3s won the manufacturer's team prize and no fewer than five Alpine cups, unprecedented for a single model. September 1956 saw further success when a Belgian crew came second in class and fifth overall in the Liège–Rome–Liège: the TR was running in the under-2000cc class, but was pitched against larger-engined cars such as Mercedes and Jaguars.

In 1957 a team of three TR3s all finished the Liège in the top ten, giving Triumph the team prize, actual finishing positions being third, fifth and ninth overall. For 1958, after a hiatus caused by the Suez crisis, four TR3A models were campaigned.

Maurice Gatsonides, who had driven TRs since 1954, managed the team's best-ever result in the Monte Carlo Rally by winning his class, but Paddy Hopkirk achieved an outright win in the Circuit of Ireland, with Desmond Titterington finishing second in VRW 221. Ron Gouldbourn came first in his class in the 1958 Tulip Rally and further notable finishes included a first-in-class in the Alpine for Keith Ballisat, a fifth overall in the Liège for 'Gatso' and a first-in-class in the same event for one of the cars driven by the British Army Motoring Association team.

In 1959 and 1960 Standard-Triumph fielded a squad of four new bright-red TR3As. In the former year several first-in-class positions were achieved, including the Circuit of Ireland (Wallwork), the Tulip (Ballisat), the Acropolis Rally (Annie Soisbault), and the Alpine (de Lageneste). Indeed, Ballisat managed second overall in the Tulip Rally against larger-engined opposition including the new works Austin-Healey 3000s. The best result in 1960 was in the Tulip Rally, when TR3As finished first, second, third and fourth in their class, the car coming first being that of privateer David Seigle-Morris. This led to his being given a works drive in the Alpine

Rally, where he again finished first in class.

Standard-Triumph's financial crisis was restricting activities by late 1960, but the heyday of the TR3A as an international rally car had passed. The Healeys were becoming faster and more developed, whereas the TRs were in effect standing still. It had always been a management decision that the TR be rallied in virtually 'as built' form, and almost no engine tuning went on, the cars relying on their ruggedness and reliability to see them through – which it did until the opposition caught up and eventually overtook them.

However, as a clubman's rally car the 'sidescreen' TR reigned supreme from 1954 to 1961, right to the time when major rallies ceased to be all-tarmac events and took to forestry tracks – allowing modified saloons with superior ground clearance to prevail.

June 1954 and the first TR works team is displayed outside the company's Banner Lane plant prior to departing for the Alpine Rally, where the team prize was won. At left is Richardson's co-driver Kit Heathcote. On the right is sales director Lyndon Mills, with Ken Richardson himself in the centre. Note the Lucas 'flamethrower' additional lamps plus twin external horns.

that even the earliest cars proved durable, reliable and fast. The motoring press wrote ecstatic test reports telling tales of unbelievably good fuel consumption figures at high speeds – 'verging on the fantastic' as one magazine reported. Indeed, a TR2 won the Mobil Economy Run with a figure of 71mpg in 1955. As sold, TR2s proved capable of 105–107mph, 0–60mph in around 11.5 seconds and 0–100mph in around 40 seconds. These were excellent figures, especially in relation to cost – you could spend three times as much on a sports car in 1955 and get very little more. Throughout 1955 further minor improvements were made and sales climbed, albeit more slowly than the previous year. Larger rear brakes and an overdrive which now operated on second and third gears as well as on top were significant bonuses, but overall the TR2 remained very much as designed. By October 1955, 8,628 examples had been made, 64 per cent for export.

For the 1955 London Motor Show the car received a new cellular front grille to fill the front air intake, and found itself named the TR3. However, this was something of a marketing exercise, as for the 1956 season the TR3 differed very little from the late TR2s. Wing beading and hinges ceased to be painted – useful recognition features – but other than the grille, appearance hardly altered.

Under the bonnet was a revised cylinder head based on the works team's 1955 Le Mans race experience. Also new were twin 1¾in SU carburettors to replace the previous 1½in units. These changes allowed the company to quote a claimed 100bhp, but on the road the difference was undetectable: all the larger carburettors seemed to do was to increase fuel consumption.

By 1956, the TR really was catching on seriously in the States, helped by some excellent competition results at all levels and very competitive pricing. A new range of colours also assisted, as did the optional provision of child seating in the rear. The really big news for the TR3 did not arrive until September 1956, when the TR became the world's second large-scale production car (after the Citroën DS) to feature disc brakes, something that many racing cars of the time did not have. Along with these came a stronger Vanguard-based rear axle plus a further new design of cylinder head, the so-called 'high-port' head. This helped the larger carburettors to do their job, and the TR engine now cranked out a genuine 100bhp. Following these engine revisions, the mechanical specification of the TR remained virtually the same right up to the end of TR3A production in 1962. In its 24-month production period the TR3 notched up 13,377 sales, about 70 per cent of which were disc-braked

cars. Nearly 90 per cent of all TR3s made were exported, the great majority to North America, and it was because of the importance of this market that the car's only major styling change occurred in October 1957.

In the US the car-buying public was used to annual styling changes, something alien to the UK. Triumph's US dealers felt that 1957's TR3 looked too much like 1953's TR2, and thus they demanded a frontal revision plus a number of other cosmetic and practical changes. The revised car was still officially known as the TR3, but everyone outside the factory soon knew it as the TR3A, a nomenclature that the factory eventually retrospectively adopted. It now had a full-width grille, while new headlight pods were mounted further rearwards and there was a more substantial front bumper. For the first time the TR received locking external door and boot handles, plus improved sliding sidescreens and separate amber rear indicators, and there were seats of a new more padded design. A number of other minor alterations completed the revamp, and before long the 2138cc engine was offered as an option. There were even factory experiments with automatic transmission and a simple form of independent rear suspension, but these came to nothing. The '3A' arrived in the US in October 1957, but was only released in Britain and elsewhere in January 1958.

Following the revisions, the US market really expanded, and this 1957–1960 period proved to be the heyday of the 'sidescreen' TR. Eventually, more than 58,000 TR3As were built, and for a time in 1959, 100 cars were coming out of Canley each day, more cars than Sir John Black had originally envisaged would be built in a month. Of these, an incredible 90 per cent were crossing the Atlantic, with only around 7 per cent of all TRs being built with right-hand drive. Truly the car had become the export success that Sir John Black had always wanted.

The 'sidescreen' TR in racing

In the mid-1950s a lightly modified TR could give a good account of itself in racing as much as in rallying. Not long after Wallwork won the 1954 RAC Rally in his TR2, another private owner, Bobby Dickson, entered the Le Mans 24-hour race in his TR2, OKV 777, co-driven by Edgar Wadsworth. This car had some covert factory support, the works being reluctant to enter the car itself just in case it failed. Happily it did not, finishing fifteenth overall and circulating totally reliably for the 24 hours at an average speed of 75mph and using fuel at the incredibly parsimonious rate of 34mpg, this despite many hours of 100mph motoring. Truly it was the most fuel-efficient as well as the most standard car in the whole race.

A month before this convincing high-speed demonstration the very first works TR, OVC 276, had been entered in the Mille Miglia road-race around Italy, piloted by Gatsonides, with Ken Richardson as his co-driver. The duo started more in hope than in expectation, for no TR had ever attempted even one hour of flat-out racing before, let alone 12 or more such hours. There was very little back-up, no support cars as such, and negligible experience of top-level competition-car preparation to call on back at the Coventry works. It was only really Richardson himself who had ever had direct racing experience, during his time with BRM. Despite all these negative factors, OVC 276 not only completed the arduous Mille Miglia course but managed to finish at twenty-seventh overall, an excellent result in a field of around 500 entrants.

Richardson prepared a report on the car's performance afterwards and was happy to relate that there had not been a single mechanical problem. Incidentally the TR2 was to standard catalogue specification although it had been stripped and very carefully re-assembled. Running on aeroscreens, it proved capable of holding 115mph in overdrive top on Italy's long straight roads.

The Le Mans and Mille Miglia results demonstrated that a very standard TR could make an excellent clubman's racing car, and before the 1954 season was out dozens, if not hundreds, of privately-owned TRs were appearing in races not only in Europe but in the States. It was surely one of the cheapest ways to go racing in the mid-1950s. True, on the crossply tyres of the time the TR developed a reputation for a somewhat wayward rear end, a few even turning over in racing, but it provided a huge amount of pleasure for its pilots, several drivers who later became famous starting out in TRs, Jim Clark included.

Fortified by the Le Mans success, the embryonic works competition department fielded OKV 777 as an official entry in September 1954's Tourist Trophy race in Ulster. Five other private TRs joined it, and Triumph not only won the manufacturer's team prize, but gained second in the team prize as

In 1960 Triumph commissioned four cars from Italian tuning wizard Conrero, for 1961's Le Mans. But in the end only one was made, and that did not appear until 1962. Built around a tubular spaceframe, the sleek coupé used the 'Sabrina' twin-cam on twin-choke Webers, producing a reliable 165bhp with plenty of torque. But the Leyland take-over put paid to Triumph's 1962 Le Mans aspirations and the car was redundant before it had turned a wheel in anger. Once allegedly clocked at 146mph on the M1, the Conrero – which happily survives to this day – would have been the fastest Triumph ever and could well have won the 2-litre class at Le Mans.

well – a further convincing demonstration of high-speed reliability.

For 1955 the factory concentrated all its racing efforts on Le Mans, three cars being entered, registered consecutively PKV 374, PKV 375 and PKV 376. All had slightly modified engines with larger carburettors and revised cylinder heads. They also ran with prototype disc brakes, two cars having Girling front discs with rear drums but one car (PKV 376) sporting four-wheel Dunlop discs as used on the Austin-Healey 100S and the D-type Jaguar. Yet again the TR's legendary reliability was to the fore, all three cars finishing strongly without any serious mechanical difficulty. The final positions were fourteenth, fifteenth and nineteenth overall. In September the factory entered a single car in the Ulster TT, but although Richardson and Dickson survived to finish, they could do no better than twenty-second overall.

For some unknown reason the works competition department concentrated entirely on rallying in 1956, the TR3's first season, but in 1957 it fielded a trio of disc-braked TR3s in the prestigious Sebring 12-hour race in Florida. The cars were all veterans of the 1956 Alpine Rally and were actually entered by Triumph's North American importers. They were however in all but name factory entries. Again the TR's long-distance race reliability was demonstrated, two of the cars finishing first and second in their class, a result that was much trumpeted in the US motoring press.

In May 1957 a plan was hatched to win the ladies prize in the Mille Miglia, and accordingly a lone works car (SHP 520) was prepared for Nancy Mitchell. She did well, until after 400 miles a spin into straw bales clogged her radiator and caused overheating and consequent retirement. In 1958, as in 1956, there were no factory racing entries, although large

Le Mans 1959, and the three TR3S cars line up for their only public appearance, sadly to end in failure, with none finishing. The twin-cam engines, chassis and some other parts were recycled into the following year's TRS cars.

numbers of TRs were appearing in amateur hands on the circuits of the world.

In 1959 a more serious attempt on Le Mans was planned. Triumph felt that success in this race was the most valuable publicity of all and it was prepared to put down cash to achieve it, by means of the expensive development of a twin-cam racing engine. This was fitted to three very special cars known as the TR3S. The 'Sabrina' engine, described in the next chapter, was mounted in a TR3 chassis lengthened by 6in and clothed in a heavy-duty glassfibre body looking superficially like that of the TR3A. A cut-down windscreen was used with a rudimentary hood and wraparound sidescreens to comply with regulations. Four-wheel disc brakes ensured that the TR3S stopped as well as it went.

In practice 135mph proved possible on the long straights, which should have been enough to make the car a serious contender in the 2-litre class. However, major vibration problems caused the fans to disintegrate, holing the radiators on

two cars. Although the fan was rapidly removed from the third car, vibration damage had occurred to the engine, causing oil-pump drive failure. It had however lasted for 22 of the 24 hours. Richardson had argued all along that the cars needed no fans, but he was overruled, the result being an expensive débâcle and the company's only failure to finish at Le Mans. These three cars never raced again, being swiftly dismantled back at Coventry with many components being recycled into 1960s TRS racers (see next chapter), although the body and chassis of one car did survive.

On the amateur front, 'sidescreen' TRs continued to be competitive and were raced and developed well into the 1960s; indeed, Reg Woodcock continued to race his very rapid TR3 right through the 1970s and 1980s with considerable success.

The TR3 'Beta'

By the start of 1960 plans for the Michelotti-designed TR4 were well advanced, but suddenly the decision to proceed with this project was called into question for the usual 1960 reason, the company's acute cash crisis. As a much cheaper alternative it was proposed that new life be breathed into the TR3A by re-engineering it to accept the TR4's rack-and-pinion steering, wider-track chassis and 2138cc engine. This in turn meant increasing the body width and to this end a TR3A body was modified with a new grille and more bulbous wings to cover the 3in wider track: the car looked like a TR3A on steroids, the changes certainly beefing-up the Triumph's appearance. The car was known within the factory as the 'TR3 Beta' – not to be confused with the 1962 TR3B, which was the reintroduced TR3A for the US market.

There were even plans to offer the Beta with a detuned, roadgoing version of the twin-cam 'Sabrina' engine, which would have produced a formidable machine. In the event this did not occur and the two prototype Betas had normal pushrod engines.

It is probably fortunate for

enthusiasts of later TRs that wiser counsels prevailed and the TR4 was allowed to continue, thus ensuring that the TR3 Beta failed to reach production. The 'sidescreen' car was looking pretty dated by 1960 and even the pumped-up Beta would have struggled to find customers: times were changing and customers wanted comfort in their sports cars...except

those die-hards in the US who insisted on the TR3A being reintroduced two years later!

A possible TR3A replacement was 1960's TR3 Beta, but only prototypes were built as the decision to proceed with the TR4 was taken. With its bulbous wings and wider track, it looks like a TR3A on steroids.

So many TRs were built that in late 1959 the body tooling had had to be renewed, leading to some very minor revisions.

In retrospect, it can be seen that having got the formula correct by 1957/58, Triumph was content to rest on its laurels, a rash move which allowed the opposition to catch up both in performance and value-for-money. During the period many behind-the-scenes debates raged as to the likely style of an eventual replacement, but the TR3A itself received almost no further development. Through 1959 none of this seemed to matter, but suddenly in the summer of 1960 the TR market collapsed. The factory still produced vast numbers of cars, but they were

filling fields around Coventry rather than the entry lists of rallies. To be fair to Triumph management, a worldwide recession was partly to blame, but complacency also played a big part. Not only did 1960's TR3A look very much like 1953's TR2 – from the driving seat you would be hard put to tell which you were in – but it went no faster and yet used more fuel. Indeed, so similar was it that none of the main UK motoring magazines even bothered to road-test the TR3A throughout its four-year currency. One of the new Leyland management's first actions was virtually to halt TR3A production for many months until stocks of unsold cars had been shifted. Only 408 TR3As were built in 1961, with a further seven cars in 1962: compare

this to 21,186 TRs constructed in 1959, and you will see just how drastic things had become. The 'sidescreen' TR was (and is) an excellent car, but inept management and financial cramp allowed the lead it had enjoyed in the mid-1950s to be frittered away, and nearly culminated in disaster – there almost wasn't a TR4 at all...

To all this there is a bizarre sequel in the form of the TR3B. By early 1962 the TR4 was finally in production, the vast majority of early cars going to US buyers. Also by then the unsold stocks of TR3As had finally been eliminated, so no 'sidescreen' car was available – why should it be, when the new and modern TR4 could be bought instead? Nevertheless, US dealers were reporting that some potential

Right: A nicely restored TR3A shows off the main concession to modernity made by this model, orange flashing rear indicators.

Bottom: Head on, the wide 'dollar grin' of the TR3A front is obvious; although US buyers liked the update, it proved very much worse at keeping the engine cool than the earlier front design. Later TR3As have the front medallion in blue and white as opposed to the previous black and red.

customers still wanted to buy a new TR3A: they did not want the extra cost, weight and complication of the winding-window TR4, for all its greater comfort. One suspects that these buyers were from the more competition-minded, wind-in-the-hair brigade, but there were indeed a number of them – more than 3,000, as it transpired. Pressure from the US dealerships was such that Triumph was compelled to put the TR3A back into production in March 1962, calling it the TR3B. The first 500 or so cars were exactly as the last TR3As, but the subsequent TR3Bs had TR4 all-synchromesh gearboxes and 2138cc engines. Although there were one or two other detail differences, to all intents the TR3B was a reborn TR3A. It was made until December 1962, a total of 3,334 being produced, virtually all for North America. Some of these were in chassis form and were bodied as Triumph Italias (see box). Triumph was really reluctant to reintroduce the old warhorse, particularly as the production space at Canley had been given over to TR4 assembly by 1962. Still, as the US market was so vital, it did as suggested although the building of the TR3Bs was performed by Forward Radiator, a Standard-Triumph subsidiary, rather than at the Canley plant. Only a limited range of colours and optional equipment was available on these final cars, some of which did not find homes until late in 1963.

Taken overall, the 'sidescreen' TR was a great success, both as a car and in commercial terms – a grand total of 83,656 cars were made over its nine and half year life, and a gratifying number of these, perhaps as many as a quarter, still survive today.

Driving the TR2/3/3A

It is very difficult for the non-expert to tell when sitting in the driving seat whether one is in an early TR2 or a late TR3A nearly ten years younger. Nor do the cars behave very differently on the road. Unless one is driving so hard as to fade the drum brakes of a TR2 or early TR3, the later disc-braked equipped cars show no advantage, and while TR3s and TR3As have a nominal 100bhp engine as compared to the 90bhp of the TR2 this totally fails to show up on the road; as a result, all three models can be treated as one.

The first thing that will strike the novice 'sidescreen' TR driver is how low the cut-away doors are, leading to a feeling of vulnerability that soon passes; keeping the sidescreens in position cures this anyway. Instruments are beautifully clear and just where they should be, in front of the driver. Controls and switchgear owe nothing to ergonomics but are simple enough to use. Brakes are non-servo, even the front disc set-up, and as a result are somewhat heavy, but they have plenty of stopping power if one is firm, and even the all-drum system will not fade in normal driving. The fly-off handbrake with its signal-box type lever is one of the most powerful in the business and puts that of many modern cars to shame.

The bucket seats were good in their day but inevitably seem primitive and uncomfortable now although the writer has undertaken 400-plus mile journeys in a day with only minor discomfort. Weather equipment is somewhat primitive but will keep 95 per cent of the rain and wind out. But that's not what a 'sidescreen' TR is all about – many owners drive the cars top-down all the time. The optional steel hardtop stiffens the car considerably but magnifies all the various mechanical noises and is prone to

drumming, so unless one is historic rallying they are not really a good idea. Luggage space was always a strong point and makes cars such as the MGA look like a sick joke. One can get amazing amounts of stuff behind the seats – even more if the optional rear bench is not fitted – and the boot too is a good size for a sports car. The spare wheel has its own compartment so one does not need to disturb the boot contents to extract it.

The second trait to be noticed will be the heaviness of the steering at low speed, particularly made so by modern radial-ply tyres. The steering lightens up considerably once speed increases but it always retains some vagueness. A great many cars have had a rack and pinion system fitted, and this really can transform the car – at the cost of loss of originality.

The steering is almost certainly the worst dynamic aspect of the 'sidescreen' TR whereas the gearbox is probably the best. Despite the lack of synchromesh on first gear, it is a delightful 'box with a very short and positive-throw change. Indeed, in my experience it is nicer than the notchier and more obstructive TR4/4A gearbox.

Upon starting the rather agricultural 'four' – with a good old-fashioned starter button – the traditional TR roar should be present. The torquey engine will pull strongly from cold and once warm will accelerate cleanly in any gear from 800rpm – 15–100mph in top gear is possible, should one be so minded. If fitted, the optional overdrive will be a delight, with an instant clutch-less change both in and out – and it operates on second, third and fourth except on the earliest TR2s, which have overdrive on top gear only. That makes seven gears in total, or more than on the latest Porsches. Overdrive second, which will propel

the car to over 60mph, is especially useful for overtaking a line of meandering traffic, for the TR despite its years is still more than capable of keeping up with modern vehicles. If the engine has been persuaded, as many have, to give 130bhp or so, it can be a very rapid cross-country car. Cruising on motorways at 90mph presents no problems other than illegality and wind noise, which can rapidly get wearing. The TR will go on all day, however, for reliability is in its nature: the driver will be fatigued long before the car.

A lot of nonsense has been written over the years concerning the TR's supposedly wayward handling. Yes, on original crossplies or first-generation Michelin X radials there can be handling problems, but equipped with modern 165 radials the cars will corner securely and undramatically just so long as they are not expected to emulate hot-hatch front-wheel-drive projectiles. If an anti-roll bar and Koni front dampers are added, as on my own TR3, the Triumph will keep up with most cars on twisty roads although to be fair it needs respecting in the wet.

A good 'sidescreen' TR will run straight and true, needing very little steering correction, and as long as due allowance is made for its age it will cover the ground as well as most cars 40-plus years its junior. Economy too is excellent, my car returning 32mpg on the larger 1¾in inch SU carburettors. TR2s on the 1½inch items should do even better. My Austin-Healey 100 goes no faster than my TR3 yet struggles to better 25mpg. Is the TR a practical proposition for daily use? Dynamically, a definite 'yes'. As regards creature comforts the answer is 'possibly', depending upon one's temperament. Just don't expect your wife or girlfriend to enjoy it on a wet night…

Buying Hints

1. The earliest TRs are more than 50 years old. So if you bear in mind that their designed life was probably 10-12 years, to say they are on borrowed time is to put it mildly. There was little body protection when new, and nor were water and mud traps designed out as they are in modern cars. Fortunately there is a very strong chassis, the front of which is usually covered in engine oil and so stays corrosion-free. At the rear, where it turns up slightly under the axle, is a notorious rust point, as are the four tubular body supports under the doors. These will almost certainly have been replaced. Both rear cross-tubes can rot out, and this is important to check, as one of them carries the rear of the rear spring mountings. All these points are repairable, many with the body in situ. Complete new chassis frames are now available.

2. Still on the chassis, beware misaligned front suspension, caused by kerbing at some time – this is very common.

3. The rear damper mountings can fracture. Rear springs can usually only be changed with the body off, as the front pivot pin is normally irretrievably seized.

4. The body can rot everywhere, even the inner wings. About the only panels that seem immune are the bonnet and the door of the spare-wheel compartment. Floorpans are particularly prone, as are the A-posts and the inner rear panels. Quarter panels behind the doors corrode, as do both inner and outer sills and the boot floor. Pay particular attention to the inside walls of the spare-wheel compartment. The bottoms of the front wings always corrode, because of blocked drain channels, as does the battery tray.

5. Virtually every panel can be purchased, and fitting is relatively straightforward, as many are bolt-on. The flip side is that the door gaps and boot gaps should be even, but this is notoriously hard to get right on rebuilt cars, as is the fit of the bonnet. The 'approximate' dimensions of some repro panels do not help.

6. The front suspension consists of a multitude of parts, relying on a number of joints, wishbones, a vertical link and a brass bottom trunnion which wears rapidly if not lubricated. To rebuild it is straightforward for the home mechanic, albeit time-consuming. It takes around a day each side, so if done professionally this can be very expensive.

7. The antiquated cam-and-peg steering box is prone to wear and tight spots. A rebuild is expensive, hence a lot of cars nowadays have rack-and-pinion conversions.

8. The four-cylinder engine is famous for reliability and if well serviced can do 100,000–150,000 miles, although rocker gear can wear badly and tappets will always be noisy. Oil pressure should be 60–70psi at 2500rpm hot, ie at 60mph in o/d top.

9. The only serious failing is occasional crankshaft breakage. This seems to be wholly a matter of luck and occurs at random, often at low engine speeds. Amazingly the car is still drivable even with the crank broken, although the engine will naturally enough be rough and noisy. In 35 years of driving these cars the author has never had a crank break, but it can and does happen.

10. Many engines are silted-up and hence prone to overheating. This is especially so on the TR3A, with its less efficient front air ducting. Make sure the fibreboard deflector behind the grille is in situ.

11. Brakes are conventional and straightforward, and even the early drum set-up should give no difficulties.

12. Gearboxes are strong, but synchromesh can be weak on second; a tendency to jump out of second or third on the overrun is common and should be checked. Ignore any buzzing sounds from the gear lever on hard acceleration – they all do it.

13. Wiper racks and wheelboxes wear, the latter being hard to reach with the very basic heater unit in place.

14. Starter motors of the original type are prone to problems – replacement by a modern 'hi-torque' type cures this, at the expense of loss of originality.

15. All interior trim can be bought new or reconditioned, but original seats are very hard to find if missing, as are instruments. The capillary temperature gauge is notorious for breaking; if it is missing, finding a replacement could be a nightmare.

16. Weather equipment is all available, though replacement sidescreens never approach the quality or durability of the originals.

17. Pay attention to optional equipment, as some TRs on the market offer a great deal more than others: a basics-only car can be worth far less, the presence of overdrive, for example, adding nearly £1,000 to a car's value. So search carefully and be prepared to spend for a good example. You'll be rewarded by a car that is terrific fun to drive as well as being terrific value for money.

The TR4 *and* TR4A

This intriguing prototype began life with a standard body, as a test-bed for the six-cylinder engine, before being sent to Michelotti as a base for facelifting exercises, culminating in the style here, with flip-up headlamps; behind is a TR4A.

Plans for the replacement of the 'sidescreen' TR date back to 1956, the idea being to introduce a new TR4 in mid-1959. Triumph had begun its long association with the Italian stylist Michelotti in 1957, although he was not actually under contract for a further year. One of his first briefs was to build an up-to-date and luxurious body on a TR3 chassis, and this was unveiled at the 1957 Geneva Motor Show. Known as the 'TR3 Dream Car', its styling was certainly strikingly fashionable – too much so, in fact, for it would have dated rapidly. Winding

windows and other luxury touches added weight, too, meaning that performance would inevitably have suffered, while the car would also have been costly to produce; thus although it created much interest, the project went no further.

By late 1957 Michelotti was having another shot at a TR3 replacement, with a vehicle codenamed Zest. The beginnings of the TR4 shape could be seen in the profile, but from the front – it being built on a standard TR3 chassis – it looked noticeably narrower. Mechanically, independent rear suspension was envisaged, but this was dropped on cost grounds. Zest was well received, but by early 1958 it had been shelved, as all effort (and most of the development budget) was being directed towards the Herald, a much more important car for Standard's future than the proposed TR4.

In the winter of 1958–59 a revised brief went to Michelotti, who responded by producing the Zoom prototype. This was the period when the twin-cam 'Sabrina' racing engine was being considered in de-tuned form as an option in the TR4, and to accommodate this an increase in wheelbase of 6in was needed. Zoom therefore incorporated this extra length, plus a 4in increase in track and body width over Zest. The car also had rack-and-pinion steering, this finding its way into the production TR4.

Two Zoom prototypes were constructed, each sporting a slightly different front, but with the centre section of the car and windscreen very much as on the TR4. The prototypes ran with both pushrod and 'Sabrina' engines, but before long the usual financial problems meant that all plans to build a twin-cam TR4 were abandoned – at first temporarily but, as it turned out, permanently.

It was at this time, in early 1960, that the same financial crisis saw the company consider instead merely producing a modified TR3A, as related in the last chapter.

It must have been a worrying and confusing time for Triumph engineers and product planners, but fortunately it was resolved in mid-1960 that the TR4 should go ahead as a priority for release in September 1961. Michelotti was thus charged with combining the best parts of both Zoom and Zest onto a chassis that retained the 4in track increase but not the 6in longer wheelbase – with the twin-cam sidelined, this was no longer needed.

Michelotti's first Triumph commission resulted in this bizarre 'TR3 dream car'. His designs for Triumph improved rapidly thereafter – thank goodness, as this design would have dated badly.

TR4

1961–65

ENGINE:
Four cylinders in line, cast-iron block and head

Capacity	2138cc
	(1991cc optional)
Bore x stroke	86mm x 92mm
Valve actuation	Pushrod
Compression ratio	9.0:1
Carburettors	Twin SU
	(later Strombergs)
Power	100bhp at 4600rpm
Maximum torque	127lb ft at 3350rpm

TRANSMISSION:
Four-speed all-synchromesh gearbox, optional overdrive on top three gears

SUSPENSION:
Front: Independent by coil and wishbone; telescopic dampers
Rear: live axle with half elliptic springs; lever arm dampers

STEERING:
Rack-and-pinion

BRAKES:
Front: Disc
Rear: Drum

WHEELS/TYRES:
Steel disc or wire wheels
Tyres 5.90 x 15in

DIMENSIONS:
Length	12ft 9½in
Wheelbase	7ft 4in
Track, front	4ft 1in
Track, rear	4ft 0in
Width	4ft 9½in
Height, hood up	4ft 2in

KERB WEIGHT:
19.5cwt

PERFORMANCE:
(Source: *The Autocar*)
Max speed	102.5mph
0–60mph	10.9sec
30–50mph in top	8.5sec
50–70mph in top	9.4sec

PRICE INCLUDING TAX WHEN NEW:
£1,032 (January 1962)

NUMBER BUILT: 40,253

TR4A

1965–67

As for late TR4 except:

ENGINE:
Power	104bhp net at 4700rpm
Maximum torque	132lb ft at 3000rpm
Carburettors	SU from mid-1966

No 1991cc option

SUSPENSION:
Rear: Independent by coil springs and semi-trailing arms; lever-arm dampers
Optional for US market: semi-elliptic rear springs with live axle; lever-arm dampers

WHEELS/TYRES:
Tyres 6.95 x 15 or 165 x 15 radial-ply

DIMENSIONS:
Track, rear	4ft 0½in

KERB WEIGHT:
21.0cwt

PERFORMANCE:
(Source: *The Autocar*)
Max speed	109mph
0–60mph	11.4sec
30–50mph in top	8.0sec
50–70mph in top	9.2sec

PRICE INCLUDING TAX WHEN NEW:
£968 (May 1965)

NUMBER BUILT: 28,465

The interior of the TR4 has a painted dashboard; the big wheel is still very vintage, as is the beefy fly-off handbrake.

instruments were carried over from the TR3A but the level and quality of trim were on a higher plane. The new body featured a large (for a sports car) boot, and a wide front-hinged bonnet incorporating a power bulge gave excellent access to the engine. Heavyweight chromed full-width bumpers were provided front and rear, solidly mounted to cope with American parking habits. All the myriad TR3A options were still available on the TR4, including overdrive, wire wheels and even aeroscreens – the windscreen having been made detachable for racing. Michelotti had cleverly managed to combine the sportiness and practicality of the 'sidescreen' TRs with modern looks and convenience. Despite extra weight, the TR4 performed at least as well as the TR3A and was just as economical. It was a little more expensive, at a price of £1,032 including Purchase Tax, but it was still terrific value and a queue formed immediately upon its introduction in September 1961, by which time Standard-Triumph was under Leyland control.

Initially the TR4 was only available for export, the great majority of 1961's cars going to the States. No significant numbers reached the UK market until April 1962, this gap being filled by the TR3A remaining on offer – with the TR3B being produced as well in 1962. Having dithered over the TR3A replacement for years, it was apparent that the right decision had finally been made, the TR4 being very successful in sales terms.

The motoring press liked it, too, although criticisms of the very basic rear suspension were beginning to appear. British weekly *The Motor* stated that the TR4 offered 'more performance per pound than any other production sports car,' but went on to say that the car would sell even better if the chassis design could be brought up to the same standard as the rest of the car. The new body was

In fact a car that effectively combined the two prototype designs had already been constructed, in the form of the 1960 Le Mans TRS racing cars.

Michelotti rapidly came up with the finalised TR4 production shape, which in effect was a Zest front and rear with a Zoom centre section, the whole mounted on a TR3A chassis given a wider track by the simple expedient of grafting on side extension plates to space the front suspension fulcrums 4in further apart and widening the rear axle by a similar amount. So similar was the chassis to that of the TR3A that it is said that the first few hundred TR4s actually used modified TR3A components. Mechanically, too, the TR4 differed little from its predecessor. In addition to the rack steering a modified gearbox now had synchromesh on first gear and the previously optional 2138cc engine was

standardised – although competition drivers could still opt for the 1991cc version. These modifications apart, the TR4 was very much a TR3A under the skin of its attractive and stylish all-new Italian bodywork. It was this body that sold the car and which was so timeless that it not only continued in production virtually unchanged for eight years, but still fails to look dated today. A splendid new hardtop (the 'Surrey' top) was optional, this having a removable steel roof and a fixed cast-aluminium wraparound rear window section. As the metal roof could not be carried in the car, a foldaway fabric centre section was also provided.

Creature comforts reflected changing times in the sports-car market, with the arrival of winding windows, along with a standard heater and face-level ventilation. Seats and

described as 'practical, convenient and roomy'. Touring fuel consumption came out at 28.7mpg, top speed at 109–111mph in overdrive, Surrey top in place, and 0–60mph acceleration at 10.9 seconds – with 0–100mph in under 40 seconds. The brakes, with discs on the front, were said to be excellent, despite the lack of servo assistance.

In April 1962 US magazine *Car and Driver* managed an amazingly good time of 33 seconds for the 0–100mph sprint; it was most impressed with the

Above: On the road in a TR4; note the pressed-aluminium grille and the absence of the TR4A's chrome side strip with integral sidelights and repeater-flashers.

Right: The spacious cockpit has plenty of room for luggage – or small children – behind the TR3A-style front seats of the earlier TR4s.

The GTR4 Dové

In 1963 Triumph dealer LF Dove of Wimbledon set about providing something different on the TR4 chassis – a TR that the sporting motorist with a growing family could use as his only car. That such a market existed was amply demonstrated in 1965 when the MGB GT arrived. But sadly Dove's version failed to capture the public's imagination. Maybe it was just too early? It was certainly too expensive at £300 (or 30 per cent) more than the price of a TR4 with the factory hardtop, but had Triumph taken over the design, the cost could have been dramatically reduced.

The coachbuilding firm of Harrington was contracted to produce the car, which was called the GTR4 Dové, the acute accent supposedly giving the name a French air. A fully-built TR4 had its boot, rear deck, rear bulkhead and petrol tank removed, and then a full-length glassfibre roof incorporating a lift-up tailgate was grafted in place. A flat 15-gallon petrol tank sat in the spare wheel well, with the spare perched on top. The new roof allowed a folding rear bench seat to be provided, and gave 32in of headroom, enough for growing children but inadequate for all but the most diminutive of adults; with the seat folded, however, there was a surprisingly long luggage platform.

Well executed and well trimmed, the Dové was a genuine attempt to make the TR into a 2+2 GT and deserved to have succeeded. Sadly, weight increased by 4cwt over that of a TR4 roadster. This brought the inevitable fuel consumption and acceleration penalties, although top speed was up slightly, on account of the better aerodynamics; no wonder Dove offered tuned engines by Laystall or S.A.H. Ltd among the options available for the car.

Triumph thought sufficiently of the quality of the conversion to allow full factory warranty on new Dovés. In all, 50–80 cars were built –

The rear view of the GTR4 Dové, the 2+2 coupé version of the TR4 as marketed by Dove's of Wimbledon. The lift-up tailgate can be clearly seen. Do not be fooled by the later 'P' registration – this is a 1963/64 car.

including some conversions carried out on customers' existing cars. Although most were TR4s, between three and five were TR4As, and it seems there was a single TR5 converted. Dovés are quite sought-after today, following a period in the 1970s and 1980s when some were misguidedly converted back into roadsters. Around 25 or so are believed to survive.

---

torque of the 2138cc engine, stating that one could floor the throttle at below 800rpm in any gear and still achieve a smooth and rapid departure. The interior trim was 'superior to that found in many cars of considerably higher price and pretence,' and the testers enthused over all the TR4's practical little details. At a basic price of $2,849 for the soft-top or $2,999 for the hard-top, they felt that the TR4 offered a lot for the money. The only serious criticism was inevitably concerning the rear suspension. 'One cannot help

wondering how a long-standing fault of the TR3 was permitted to live on in the TR4,' wrote the magazine of the limited vertical movement of the underslung rear axle.

What *Car and Driver* didn't know was that Triumph simply could not have afforded to improve the TR4 rear suspension – it had only managed to produce the car at all by the skin of its teeth and with a healthy injection of Leyland cash. The company was acutely aware of the TR's suspension shortcomings and aimed to cure the problem as soon as possible;

nevertheless it was to be more than three years before the TR4A arrived, with independent rear suspension – and ironically the US market then demanded (and got) continued availability of a rigid-axle version.

During its 40-month production few major modifications were made to the TR4: the mechanical parts were already proven by eight years in service during which the TR had acquired a legendary reputation for reliability. In mid-1962 the TR3A-style seats were changed for a somewhat more modern design, and in mid-1963

On the TR4 the rigid rear axle is located solely by simple but effective semi-elliptic springs. The main chassis rails pass under the rear axle, this underslung configuration limiting vertical movement. The chassis is in its essentials identical to that of earlier TRs.

the SU carburettors were deleted in favour of Strombergs, although this change was more to do with motor industry politics than engineering. Additionally, the front disc brakes were uprated and the starting handle was finally put out to grass, while during its final few months the somewhat austere painted dashboard was deleted in favour of polished walnut. This last change was only for the North American market, other buyers having to wait until the TR4A arrived. Finally discontinued in January 1965, 40,254 TR4s were built, only about 2,500 of which remained in the UK. As expected, the States accounted for around 80 per cent of production.

By the mid-1960s most progressive motor manufacturers were offering vehicles with independent rear suspension. As Triumph's basic small car, the 1959-launched Herald, had always been fitted with IRS, the company could hardly deny the buyers of its top sports car this refinement any longer. The trouble was that a complete redesign of the chassis was needed to provide the attachment points and clearance that semi-trailing-arm IRS required. The revised chassis ended up with a rear section shaped something like a bell, with two massive cast aluminium suspension arms pivoting on the lower edge of the 'bell' and a large transverse bridgepiece forming the top mount for the coil springs, which acted directly on the top of the suspension arms. The differential was bolted to the chassis via rubber mountings, universally-jointed driveshafts taking the power to the rear wheels. Unlike the cheaper Herald swing-axle IRS, the TR4A type had the merit of keeping the rear wheels roughly parallel irrespective of load, although there was a certain amount of rear-end squat under power, especially on the 150bhp TR5 of 1967. Bodily the TR4A

of early 1965 was virtually identical to the TR4. A revised grille with horizontal slats was used, and there were substantial sidelight/indicator units mounted on the wings and integrated in the new chrome strips embellishing the wings.

The walnut dashboard arrived for all markets and upgraded and more comfortable seats appeared, as did sunvisors. A retrograde step, however, was the re-siting of the handbrake lever on the top of the propshaft tunnel. This meant it no longer rubbed the driver's leg on rhd cars, but the

leverage available was greatly reduced – it simply did not work as well. A much improved hood of the full convertible rather than the kit-of-parts type appeared too – and not before time.

Mechanically, revisions to the camshaft, manifolding and exhaust system conjured a further 5bhp from the engine, the design of which was by then nearly 20 years old. Later in the TR4A's run SU carburettors reappeared, replacing the Strombergs. Inevitably the TR4A put on weight, so performance remained stubbornly no

The Twin-cam 'Sabrina' engine and the TRS

Triumph's near-legendary twin-cam engine was nicknamed 'Sabrina' after a television starlet of the day renowned for her bust, the engine's camshaft end-covers bearing a distinct similarity to the chest of the lady in question. The engine was intended primarily to help Triumph win the 2-litre class and the team prize at Le Mans, this being something of an obsession with Standard-Triumph chairman Alick Dick, who dug deep to find the considerable development money. It was also envisaged that the power unit would be used in a limited-edition roadgoing TR; sadly, despite several prototypes being made, this never materialised.

Harry Webster, David Eley and their team began design and development during 1957–1958. The engine proved powerful enough, giving 150–160bhp with the possibility of more, but it was bulky, tall and expensive to construct. Indeed, producing it in quantity would have been a very awkward operation, for in effect it was a five-layered sandwich. It was also over-engineered

for the job in hand, being built to cope with up to 200bhp.

At the top of the sandwich was the classic aluminium inclined-valve, twin-cam head with hemispherical combustion chambers, and with the camshafts being driven by chain and sprocket. Next down was the cast-iron cylinder block, then an upper crankcase casting, a lower crankcase casting and finally at the bottom a cast-aluminium sump, the whole lot being clamped together by very lengthy bolts. Cubic capacity was 1985cc, the engine being over-square, with a 90mm bore and a short 78mm stroke – allowing a rev limit of 6500rpm or possibly more. Despite being bulkier than the pushrod TR engine, the 'Sabrina' actually weighed slightly less, thanks to the extensive use of aluminium. As originally fitted in the 1959 TR3S cars, the engine used a pair of special DU6 twin-choke SU carburettors, but later it received two twin-choke Webers.

That the cars using the engine failed in 1959's Le Mans was no direct fault of the engine, which

This TRS finished 18th in 1960's Le Mans; two other such cars also successfully completed the event. Opposite top: Lucas 'bullet' lights apart, the TRS is very TR4-like from the rear.

proved strong and reliable right from the start. This was amply demonstrated in 1960 and 1961 where in each case all the twin-cam TRs completed the full 24 hours of racing. The TR3S cars were described in the previous chapter, but the 1960 and 1961 Le Mans events were contested by four new models, three entrants plus a spare car. Registered consecutively as 926 HP, 927 HP, 928 HP and 929 HP, they had entirely new glassfibre bodies based largely on the Michelotti shape for the forthcoming TR4, but with perhaps more Zoom than Zest in them. Mechanically they were very similar to the 1959 cars, and in fact used some recycled parts from these – although not surprisingly the errant cooling fans that had caused trouble were duly abandoned.

A change in regulations meant that

these TRS racers had to run with taller windscreens, which inevitably made them slower than the 1959 cars, the best speed clocked being 128mph. This it should be noted was just 3mph more than Richardson had achieved seven years earlier in a pushrod-engined TR2 at Jabbeke. The TRS was also very heavy, weighing more than a TR3A despite its being built for racing. In the 1960 race a problem occurred with soft valve seats that had not shown up previously; this afflicted all three engines and caused them to lose a lot of power. However, the drivers managed to nurse the cars through the race, all three managing to finish. Sadly the team prize eluded them, for the slower speeds demanded to preserve the engines meant that they failed to complete sufficient miles to qualify.

In 1961, however, Alick Dick's dream was realised. The same cars running to virtually the same specification proved totally reliable, and were able to circulate around ten seconds a lap quicker, the fastest of

the three managing to cover 2,273 miles in the 24 hours. All three finished well, in ninth, eleventh and fifteenth positions, the car in ninth place being the highest-placed British car. That was sufficient to win the manufacturers' team prize, along with other awards. It was Triumph's greatest success ever on the race track, but was alas rewarded a few days later by Leyland withdrawing all financial support from competitions

and closing Ken Richardson's department.

The twin-cam engine's fate was sealed by this decision. There was still talk of offering it in an upmarket TR4, and one such car (ERW 738C) was built – and was once owned by the author. Around 25 or so of these intriguing engines were made, of which a few survive. Also surviving are all four of the TRS Le Mans cars, although none is currently in the UK.

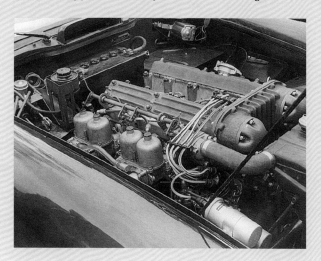

The twin-cam 'Sabrina' engine. The camshaft end-covers which gave the unit its nickname – after busty starlet Sabrina – can clearly be seen. Note the very rare DU6 twin-choke SU carburettors.

better than previously: indeed, it was no better than the 1953 TR2 in terms of acceleration and top speed, and inferior as regards fuel consumption. This point was not lost on the motoring press, who felt the TR could clearly do with more power – a lot more – to put it back to the leading position it had held ten years earlier. One thing that those trying the car did agree upon was the efficiency of the new rear suspension, roadholding being judged much superior to that of the TR4, plus much greater levels of comfort. These bonuses were not without cost, the price of the basic TR4A rising to £968 including Purchase Tax. Today, however, the extra complication of the IRS has meant that many prefer the simplicity and harder ride of the TR2-4 rear end, certainly for historic rallying and other serious motoring.

An interesting sidelight on this is that in the US the distributor for the north-eastern states decided it would rather save money and not have the IRS, and persuaded Triumph to build a bizarre crossbreed TR4A which had conventional semi-elliptic rear springs

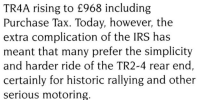

Above: Classically red, this TR4A has the hard top rear window in place; note how the grille differs from that of the TR4.

Left: The TR4A had a polished wooden dashboard to add a touch of class, although the last TR4s sold to the USA also had this feature. Note the advanced (for the time) airflow ventilation grilles, something that Ford claimed to have invented – three years after Triumph started using them.

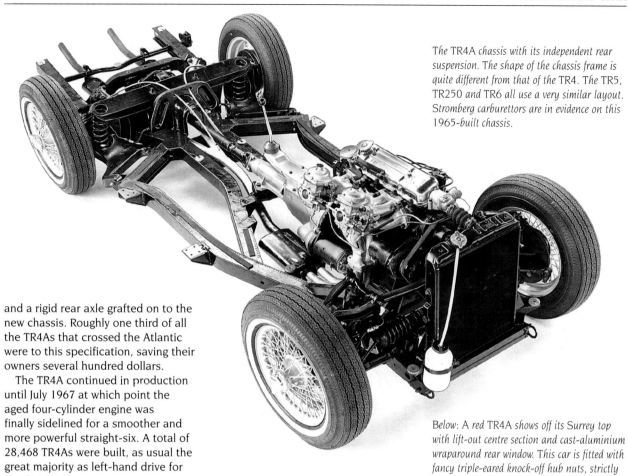

The TR4A chassis with its independent rear suspension. The shape of the chassis frame is quite different from that of the TR4. The TR5, TR250 and TR6 all use a very similar layout. Stromberg carburettors are in evidence on this 1965-built chassis.

and a rigid rear axle grafted on to the new chassis. Roughly one third of all the TR4As that crossed the Atlantic were to this specification, saving their owners several hundred dollars.

The TR4A continued in production until July 1967 at which point the aged four-cylinder engine was finally sidelined for a smoother and more powerful straight-six. A total of 28,468 TR4As were built, as usual the great majority as left-hand drive for North America.

Below: A red TR4A shows off its Surrey top with lift-out centre section and cast-aluminium wraparound rear window. This car is fitted with fancy triple-eared knock-off hub nuts, strictly non-standard.

The TR4/4A in competition

The heyday of the TR in amateur racing and rallying was in the mid and late 1950s with the 'sidescreen' cars. That is not to say, though, that TR4s weren't raced or rallied: they were, although by the time of the TR4A the car had become uncompetitively slow.

People such as Sid Hurrell of SAH, Neil Dangerfield, and Kas Kastner in the US, developed the TR4 for racing, it appearing both in aeroscreen and hardtop forms. Kastner in particular was able to coax serious bhp out of the pushrod engine – as much in fact as the twin-cam 'Sabrina' engine was producing, though possibly with somewhat less reliability. The works never directly raced the TR4/4A models, although the company's US subsidiary did give assistance to private teams on occasions, in particular at the 1963 Sebring 12-hour race where TR4s took a class win.

In rallying the TR4 was still popular with amateur drivers although not as much as its predecessor had been – the nature of rallying was changing, with the new generation of souped-up saloons gaining ground at the expense of traditional two-seat sports cars. However, this did not dissuade Leyland, as Triumph's new masters, from forming a TR4 rally team early in 1962. The competition department, summarily closed six months earlier, was re-opened under the aegis of Graham Robson and was equipped with four new pale blue hardtop TR4s registered 3 VC, 4 VC, 5 VC, and 6 VC – cars that have become very well known over the years.

The plan was to enter these in major international rallies where durability and reliability were more important than outright speed, for the TR4 was heavy in relation to its power. The 'VC' cars were carefully built and received much additional strengthening in addition to tuned engines producing around 135bhp. Several well-known and up-and-coming drivers were engaged, and in 1962 some impressive

results were achieved. These included Mike Sutcliffe finishing first in class and fourth overall in the Alpine Rally and the TR4s coming home second, third and fourth in class in the Tulip Rally. In 1963, an identical result was achieved in the Tulip but otherwise the best that could be managed was a third in class in November 1963's RAC Rally. The team was plagued that year by a succession of bad luck and mechanical failures, but in any case the TR, with its limited ground clearance and lack of power, was becoming outclassed at international level. Accordingly, at the start of 1964 three of the four TR4s were sent over to Canada to contest the Shell 4000 Rally – where they managed to win the GT-category team prize.

The cars thereafter remained in North America for many years, the works team at home turning its

The TR4 was raced within months of its introduction – here we see Neil Dangerfield at the wheel of the SAH Accessories TR4 during 1962. SAH was the leading supplier of Triumph tuning equipment at this time.

attention to the Spitfire for racing and to Vitesses and 2000 saloons for rallying. It would be more than ten years before a TR would be part of a works competition team again.

The TR4A was only raced seriously in North America, where Bob Tullius and his Group 44 team campaigned a very rapid 150bhp racer that could exceed 130mph. TR4As prepared by Kastner to a similar specification also did well in the 1966 Sebring races, finishing first, second and third in class.

A works replica TR4 rally car belonging to Evan Mackenzie raises the dust – only the registration number gives it away.

Buying Hints

1. The TR4 is virtually a TR3A with a different body, so almost all the comments on the mechanicals made in the previous chapter apply equally to TR4s. TheTR4/4A gearbox does however have a synchromesh bottom gear. Listen here for a noisy gearbox, which could mean a worn layshaft – expensive!

2. Cars with independent rear suspension have a different chassis, but all the previous comments apply here too, with the addition that a detailed inspection of the differential mounting area and the chassis mounting points for the rear trailing arms is necessary. Rust in these mounts is common, potentially dangerous, and involves expensive repairs. The transverse bridge-piece above the differential can also rust, as can the top mounting point for the springs. The integrity of the rear part of the chassis is particularly vital on these IRS cars and the later the car, the more corrosion-prone the chassis.

3. Beware of bent chassis, particularly as a result of frontal collision damage.

4. Front suspension is very similar to the TR2/3/3A type but for the rack-and-pinion steering, which has proved reliable in service. Rack mounting points and steering-column universal joints need watching all the same.

5. The independent rear suspension has its own difficulties such as rear hub and carrier wear, worn driveshafts and universal joints, sloppy bushes, and general clonks from the rear. A full IRS rebuild is not cheap, and special tools are required to remove the rear hubs. The differential suffers from oil leaks.

6. The cars are susceptible to body rust virtually everywhere. Although almost all panels can be purchased, a full body rebuild is not to be undertaken lightly, or with a thin wallet. Additional rust spots include

the front edge of the bonnet, the spare-wheel well, the front bulkhead, the windscreen frame, the rear inner wings, the inner sides of the B-posts, around the headlights, and both front and rear valances. Assume that there could be rust absolutely anywhere on the body.

7. Panel and door gaps were never brilliant even when the cars were new, but excessive gaps will usually point to trouble and indicate badly executed repairs or a cheap rebuild. To rebuild one of these bodies properly is both expensive and time consuming.

8. All trim is available and is relatively inexpensive. Missing or incorrect instruments and switchgear can be hard to replace, though. A particular point to watch is the wiper wheel boxes, which wear out and are very difficult to reach for repair. All weather equipment is readily available and at least one does not have to worry about sidescreens.

Even hood-up, the TR4A has a broad-shouldered elegance. The 'IRS' badge trumpets the presence of the semi-trailing arm rear suspension.

The TR5, TR250 and TR6

One of the rarer colours on the TR5 is this attractive blue. Wire wheels as seen here look a lot more appealing than the rather dated Rostyle wheel trims.

By 1967 the TR4A, despite its independent rear suspension, was becoming outdated. Although the body design was only six years old, the performance had simply failed to keep abreast of the opposition let alone ahead of it, and performance was ultimately what a sports car was all about. The TR4A was no faster than the TR2 of 14 years earlier, an unsustainable situation. A moderate increase in the TR's performance was no longer the answer, it was decided: a major leap was needed, to vault ahead of the opposition. In 1967 120mph had the same cachet as 100mph had had in 1953 and 120mph was what was now required to put the TR back at the head of the mass-production sports-

TR5 PI
1967–68

ENGINE:
Six cylinders in line, cast-iron block and head

Capacity	2498cc
Bore x stroke	74.7mm x 95mm
Valve actuation	Pushrod
Compression ratio	9.5:1
Fuel system	Lucas mechanical injection
Power	150bhp at 5500rpm
Maximum torque	164lb ft at 3500rpm

TRANSMISSION:
Rear-wheel drive; four-speed all-synchromesh gearbox with optional overdrive

SUSPENSION:
Front: Independent by coil and wishbone; telescopic dampers
Rear: Independent by coil springs and semi-trailing arms; lever-arm dampers

STEERING:
Rack-and-pinion

BRAKES:
Front: Disc
Rear: Drum
Servo assistance

WHEELS/TYRES:
Tyres 165 x 15 radial on 5in rims

BODYWORK:
Two-seater sports; separate chassis and steel panels

DIMENSIONS:

Length	12ft 9½in
Wheelbase	7ft 4in
Track, front	4ft 1¼in
Track, rear	4ft 0¾in
Width	4ft 10in
Height	4ft 2in

KERB WEIGHT:
20.7cwt

PERFORMANCE:
(Source: *Autocar*)

Max speed	120mph
0–60mph	8.8sec
30–50mph in top	7.5sec
50–70mph in top	7.6sec

PRICE WITH TAX WHEN NEW:
£1,268 without overdrive (April 1968)

NUMBER BUILT:
2,947

TR250
1967–68 (US only)
As TR5 except:

ENGINE:

Compression ratio	8.5 to 1
Fuel system	Twin 1.75 Stromberg
Power	104bhp net at 4500rpm
Maximum torque	143lb ft at 3000rpm

WHEELS/TYRES:
185 x 15 radial-ply tyres

NUMBER BUILT:
8,484

TR6 PI
1968–75
As TR5 except:

ENGINE:
From January 1973 (CR series):

Power	125bhp (DIN) at 5500rpm
Maximum torque	143lb ft at 3500rpm

TRANSMISSION:
Overdrive standard fitment from 1973

SUSPENSION:
Front: Anti-roll bar standard

WHEELS/TYRES:
5.5in wheel rims still with 165 x 15 tyres

DIMENSIONS:

Length	13ft 3in
Width	4ft 10in

KERB WEIGHT:
22.1cwt

PERFORMANCE:
(Source: *Autocar*)

Max speed	119mph
0–60mph	8.2sec
30–50mph in top	7.0sec
50–70mph in top	7.7sec

PRICE INCLUDING TAX WHEN NEW:
£1,339 without overdrive (April 1969)

NUMBER BUILT:
91,850 (injected and carb)

TR6 Carburettor
1968–76 (US only)
As TR250 except:

ENGINE:

Compression ratio	7.75:1 (1972–73)
	7.5 to 1 (1974–76)
Power	106bhp at 4900rpm (1972–73)
	104bhp at 4900rpm (1974–76)
Maximum torque	133lb ft at 3000rpm (1972–73)
	131lb ft at 3000rpm (1974–76)
	All bhp figures net

SUSPENSION:
Front: Anti-roll bar standard

WHEELS/TYRES:
5.5in wheel rims replace 5in rims

DIMENSIONS:

Length	13ft 3in (1968–72)
	13ft 6in (1973–74)
	13ft 7½in (1974–76)

KERB WEIGHT:
21.1cwt

PERFORMANCE:
(Source: *Road & Track*)

Max speed	109mph
0–60mph	11.6sec
0–100mph in top	39.0sec

PRICE WITH TAX WHEN NEW:
$3,375 (February 1969)

---

car league. It was calculated that 150bhp would be needed, sufficient to give 0–60mph acceleration in under nine seconds instead of the 11.5 seconds of the TR4A.

The engine of the Triumph 2000 of 1963 provided the means, especially as the works rally 2000s had already proved capable of such outputs, albeit with the loss of civilised road

manners. Fortunately for Triumph, the mid-1960s saw the development by Lucas of a cost-effective mechanical fuel-injection system, the accurate fuel metering of which allowed the use of a hotter camshaft with racing-type overlap without any loss of tractability. Ancillary benefits were improved fuel consumption and a smooth power delivery above

2000rpm, albeit at the cost of a rather lumpy idling speed.

Along with the fuel injection the engineering team in Coventry stretched the 2000 engine to 2½ litres by lengthening the stroke: the 'six' was already at its maximum practical bore, so stroking it was the only inexpensive solution. This had the additional benefit of greatly increasing the

Below: The full convertible hood of the TR5 is being folded, a much easier operation than with some of the earlier TRs. Once down, it takes up quite a lot of the rear space.

torque, and although a long stroke militated against high revs, the 2.5 engine proved capable of a sustained and reliable 5500rpm. An improved and less restrictive design of cylinder head also assisted, and the new engine ended up giving almost 150bhp, with torque of 164lb ft at 3500rpm.

The 'six' was no heavier than the old four-cylinder engine but it was several inches longer. This did not cause too much difficulty: the radiator was redesigned and moved forward and with revised engine mounts and chassis cross-bracing the new engine mated easily with the existing TR gearbox. The bonnet power bulge was kept, even though the lack of carburettors meant that it served no purpose.

In other respects it was the formula as before. Some small cosmetic changes were incorporated, however, such as a new radiator grille, the addition of reversing and side-marker lights, and chromed strips below the doors. Inside were a new steering wheel, new seats, and a matt-finished wood dashboard with eyeball fresh-air vents and revised instruments and switchgear. Finally, there were fake-alloy Rostyle wheel discs – a real boy-racer fad of the time – on cars without wire wheels.

To cope with a power upgrade of nearly 50 per cent a brake servo became standard, the brakes were uprated, and the suspension and damper settings revised, while the differential received two additional mounting points. The transmission benefited from a raised axle ratio, which at 3.45 to 1 proved easy for the powerful engine to pull.

Introduced into the UK at a price of

£1,212 including Purchase Tax, the TR5 was terrific value. The TR2 had been the UK's cheapest 100mph car, and now the TR5 was the country's cheapest 120mph car as well as being the first mass-produced British vehicle with fuel injection, a fact which Triumph publicity made much of at the time. Sadly, as it turned out, the Lucas PI system was problematical and not fully understood even by Triumph's own dealer network; customers queued up for the TR5 unaware that they would be shortly doing the final development work on the PI engine. Limited supplies of the TR5 reached other markets at the same time, but the one place that ironically never saw the car was the TR's most important market, the United States.

In the late 1960s the first stirrings of US environmental restrictions on cars were causing consternation throughout the automotive world. It was initially thought that petrol injection, with its accurate control of fuel, would enable the TR5 to meet the new US requirements, but the primitive Lucas system proved incapable of this without additional expensive and relatively untried technology. This would put up both weight and cost, while it was by no means certain that the US market was ready for the complication of fuel injection on a modestly-priced sports car.

For such reasons the injected TR5 was never sold in the States and the seemingly retrograde step was taken of producing a carburettor-fed six-cylinder TR for North America, called the TR250. Triumph's engineers found that by using very accurately tuned tamperproof Stromberg carburettors the TR could meet the new emission standards and be sold for several hundred dollars less than an injected version. It did not seem to matter that the TR250's performance was only a little better than that of the TR4A, for with very restrictive speed limits in the US speed was not everything – and a

It's what's up front that keeps you out front.

good percentage of TRs were sold as second or 'shopping' cars anyway. It was in Europe that the real power boost was needed, and the TR5 amply provided that.

The TR250 sported a gaudy triple stripe across the bonnet and front wings, plus fatter 185-section tyres. In carburettor form the 2.5-litre 'six' produced exactly the same 104bhp as had its four-cylinder ancestor. However, an increase in torque to 143lb ft did provide a little more speed and acceleration. Times of around 10.5 seconds for 0–60mph were achieved and 110mph was attainable in overdrive. Despite its relative lack of urge, the TR250 sold quite well, 8,484 examples finding homes, all left-hand-drive and virtually all to North America. The TR250 and TR5 were only produced for 14 months, between July 1967 and September 1968, and so were true stopgap models. Just 2,947 of the injected TR5s were built, the majority in left-hand-drive form for continental

Europe. An unknown number of these was assembled from CKD kits at the British Leyland plant in Belgium. Of the 1,400 or so right-hand-drive cars made, something over 1,200 stayed in the UK, with Australia taking most of the remainder. Because it was both the fastest production TR – including the Federal TR8 – and also the rarest, the TR5 has become much prized in recent years and commands a premium over both the TR4/4A and the TR6.

Press reaction to the TR5 was enthusiastic: in *Autosport* John Bolster called it 'without doubt the best Triumph yet'. He managed 0–60mph in 8.8 seconds, 0–100mph in 28 seconds, and an exact 120mph flat-out, all on a fuel consumption approaching 25mpg. In another comment he referred to the TR5 as not merely up-to-date but leading the fashion for sophisticated sports cars, in that it was 'quieter and much more flexible than most saloons'. He criticised the amount of understeer but thought the rear suspension coped

Six-cylinder racers in the US

Ever since the mid-1950s RW 'Kas' Kastner had been making Triumphs of all sorts go indecently fast – faster indeed than the factory – and in 1963 he became competitions manager for Triumph in the US; in 1971 he left Leyland, but his newly-formed company Kastner-Brophy Racing was given a two-year contract to prepare Triumphs on behalf of BL in the States.

Although he and Triumph-supported privateer Bob Tullius of Group 44 had enjoyed much success in Sports Car Club of America racing with the TR4 and TR4A, the TR250 with its bigger engine caused problems, because its engine size moved it up a class in racing from the old four-cylinder. Additionally, SCCA rules did not allow fuel injection, as the US-market car did not feature it.

Fortunately, Kastner was able in 1969 to discover a way in which injection could be used on the TR6 and yet the car remain eligible for the very close and competitive SCCA racing. This was essential if the

Triumph were to have any chance against works Datsun 240Zs and other cars with much more power. By dint of his tuning expertise and sheer hard work, Kastner was eventually able to persuade the Triumph 'six' to produce in excess of 250bhp at 7500rpm – the sort of output undreamed of at Canley – yet still stay all of a piece. This was enough to make the TR6 fully competitive in its class, and eventually it won the Category C championship.

The successes on the track of Kastner-prepared cars and of those of Virginia-based Group 44 did much to aid Triumph sales in the US and give the importers a good return on the modest investment they made in supporting Kastner and Tullius, especially as Spitfires and GT6s were also campaigned, with excellent results.

It is arguable that the two have never fully received the recognition that they deserve for their part in the Triumph sports car story in the marque's principal market.

well with the power, despite a tendency to squat under hard acceleration. Comfort and controls were of a high order and Bolster thought the flexibility of the long-stroke engine 'quite fantastic'. Like many others, he found the idling too lumpy, with a tendency to stall, and felt that the hum of the high-pressure fuel pump was intrusive. 'Smooth' was the adjective that time and again was used to describe the engine, and the splendid exhaust note was remarked upon. Brakes were said to be powerful and well up to the performance, and the ride was deemed excellent; noise from the hood at speed, however, was criticised. The car was felt to be an excellent blend of performance, comfort and practicality, at a realistic price.

Not surprisingly, US press reaction to the TR250 was less than overwhelming. 'Something less than a Triumph' was the headline of Car and Driver in 1968. When the magazine put the TR250 through its paces, it found it slower than a TR4A, albeit smoother. 'To pay an extra $500 for a nearly identical but slower car doesn't make much sense,' it wrote – and who could really disagree?

Michelotti displayed this one-off TR5 at the 1968 Geneva show.

The TR5/250 had only ever been meant to hold the fort until a revised TR body style could be made available, but the problem that beset Triumph's management in 1967 was how to get a modernised TR body into production not only swiftly but at minimum cost – and, more to the point, whom to employ to do it. Giovanni Michelotti was the obvious choice, as he was still engaged on various projects for Triumph, but in the end he was not able to take on the work.

To save time and retooling costs, the new TR6 had to retain not only the TR4/5 inner bodyshell but also the entire centre section. Despite this, a wholly new and modern look was sought. Add to these parameters the compressed timescale, and one can see that the task of styling and tooling the TR6 was not going to be easy. The job went to German coachbuilder Karmann, more used to building convertible VW Beetles, who rapidly produced a new squared-off front and rear that blended with the old centre section so cleverly that one had to look very hard to recognise vestiges of the TR5 body. The design was both timeless and modern, and still looks good today.

With the style approved in September 1967, the first production cars were

being built exactly a year later, which was an amazingly short gestation period. Mechanically the early CP-series fuel-injected TR6s were all but identical to the TR5s, although wider 5½J wheel rims were employed and for the first time a front anti-roll bar was standard; the interior was also largely as that of the TR5, while early TR6s still sported their predecessor's rather tasteless fake-alloy Rostyle wheel trims.

Not surprisingly, the US market had to make do with a non-injected TR6 using the same twin-Stromberg set-up as the TR250. Increased weight and a proliferation of emission control equipment made the US version even slower than the TR250, sadly, despite power being up slightly to 106bhp. As with the TR250, the great majority of TR6s built – 77,938 in total – were to carburettor specification with left-hand drive. Production of the rest-of-the-world injection TR6 amounted to a further 13,912 cars, the majority of which were again left-hand-drive. For the first three years, 1969 to 1971, the injection TR6 was also assembled from CKD kits at the British Leyland plant at Malines, Belgium; after this was closed down in 1971, all cars were Coventry-assembled.

Apart from minor trim, paintwork and ornamentation revisions, the non-

US TR6 stayed the same in appearance for the six and a half years of its production. Mechanically there was one surreptitious and retrograde alteration, this occurring at the start of 1973 when the CR series of cars arrived. Regular complaints from customers and dealers concerning the difficulty of keeping the 150bhp engines in tune and in setting up the Lucas PI system led Triumph to de-tune the TR6 by quite a considerable extent, to 125bhp. This was largely achieved by substituting a milder camshaft, and did nothing for the TR6's performance although it certainly made for easier maintenance and servicing. Acceleration times for 0–60mph increased from 8.5 seconds to around 10 seconds, with a good 7–8mph being shaved from maximum speed. Triumph of course failed to mention this loss of nearly 25bhp in

This extraordinary device is the TR250K, created at the behest of 'Kas' Kastner, Standard-Triumph's US competitions manager. Intended as a publicity exercise, the TR250K was styled by Pete Brock, responsible for the lines of the Shelby Daytona Cobras. Completed in 1968, it was entered in that year's Sebring 12-hour race – retiring after a wheel failed. BL never capitalised on the car's publicity value, and it ended up in a museum.

Driving the injection TR6

'Smooth and potent' ran the headline of the original *Motor* road test of 1969, and I see no reason to disagree. The TR6 even today has the legs on many current models. I do not doubt the magazine's 0–60mph in 8.5 seconds claim, as the TR6 I have been sampling for this book feels quite rapid enough. It also feels surprisingly high-geared, the 3.45-to-1 rear axle, coupled with 185-section tyres, giving nearly 27mph per 1000rpm in overdrive top gear.

Relaxed 80mph cruising at under 3000rpm is good both for the eardrums in terms of relative silence, and for the wallet in terms of 27mpg overall, an excellent consumption from a heavy and fast 35-year-old car. Brakes are excellent – progressive, light yet powerful – and accompanied by a decent handbrake. Fierce acceleration can easily provoke the notorious tail-squat, the bonnet rising quite noticeably. Many cars these days have had this tamed by the fitting of stronger rear springs and dampers.

Steering is light at all but the lowest speeds although inevitably parking with fattish tyres requires some effort. The TR6 runs dead straight, with no tendency to wander, but fast cornering shows up the age of the chassis. The best approach is to keep the power on into the corner, thus keeping the tail down and maintaining negative camber on the rear wheels. Lifting off in a corner provokes some nervousness and a slight twitch. Inevitably, ultimate grip cannot equal that of a modern fwd saloon, but if one is positive the TR6 can still be hurried along very rapidly, the fierce acceleration making up on the straights what one loses in the corners. Surprisingly, the car feels somewhat softly sprung – at least to the writer, who has always preferred his TRs with a rigid rear axle and cart springs.

The 'A' type overdrive operates on second, third and top, and overdrive second is terrific fun, being a gear in which one can go from walking pace

to 70mph at 5500rpm in very few seconds, though for how long the driveshafts and the remainder of the transmission would stand up to this is a matter of conjecture. Gear selection is inevitably notchy, always a trait of the all-synchro Triumph gearbox, but the overdrive comes in and out instantaneously.

The engine, meanwhile, still exudes that smoothness that only a well tuned 'six' can offer – top-down one finds oneself blipping the throttle just to hear the sound. The legendary lumpy idling is of course there, though the car I tried showed no tendency to stall, nor to overheat for that matter.

The TR6 driving position is comfortable, and the instrumentation clear and concise, while luggage room is surprisingly good both in the boot and in the space behind the seats. The TR6 comes across as an impressive, fast and sporting car offering loads of fun – it really doesn't feel 35 years old.

their advertisements, and in 1973 there were many puzzled and disappointed TR6 purchasers in Europe and elsewhere. Today, with the benefit of 30 more years of development, it has proved possible to make the PI system run reliably with the 150bhp camshaft, and many of the later 125bhp TR6s have been uprated to the earlier specification.

These changes did not of course affect the US-market cars, which staggered on with 105bhp or so and an ever-increasing weight to pull. Further restrictions on exhaust emissions led

Opposite: A very early US-specification TR6 is seen here in a 1969 works publicity photograph. This car has the US-market high-backed seats. Note the Rostyle wheel covers found on the very earliest cars.

Above: Later TR6s sported this bib spoiler; wire wheels were always an option though octagonal 'safety' nuts were usually supplied.

Right: Hard acceleration demonstrates the TR6's notorious tail squat under power, the rear wheels adopting pronounced negative camber. This factory demonstrator is fitted with the new style of steel hard top introduced for the TR6: the centre no longer detaches, as on the old Surrey top.

to more than one lowering of compression ratio, this finishing for 1974–76 cars at a lowly 7.5 to 1. At this point, the cars were slower than ever, and almost certainly the slowest TRs ever made. Nor was it only in respect of power output that US legislation affected the TR, for front and rear bumpers had to be made progressively

more substantial to pass the notorious 5mph-impact test, a process which culminated in post 1974 US TR6s having a raised front bumper height and giant rubber overriders grafted on both front and rear. These nonsenses did nothing for the looks of the car, but they did at least enable the TR6 to be marketed in the US for a further two

Buying Hints

1. Comments made regarding the TR4 and TR4A apply equally to the body and chassis of the TR5 and TR6; brave restorers of badly corroded TR6s should note, though, that a brand-new body is available, made on original tooling by British Motor Heritage.

2. With regular oil changes, the six-cylinder engine is usually good for 100,000 miles, but the rocker gear is prone to oil starvation and wear. As ever, excessive crankshaft end-float caused by the break-up of the thrust washers can be a major problem. Oil pressure should be 70psi hot, and if it is much lower and down to around 10psi at a hot idle, there could well be crankshaft and bearing problems.

3. The Lucas fuel-injection system is not as unreliable as legend has it. Properly set up, it will work well for long periods. The boot-mounted fuel pump can overheat, but the cure is to substitute a Bosch pump; these usually prove totally reliable. Metering units can fail, but an exchange is surprisingly cheap, as are exchange injectors should these be required. One point to check is the condition of the short flexible fuel pipe on the nearside of the engine. If this leaks, high-pressure petrol will cover everything rapidly, creating a major fire hazard.

4. The central handbrake on these models is often weak, and the cables can seize.

A high standard of finish was achieved for the TR6 interior. The early cars did not have head restraints, and several designs of seat were used over the seven-year production period, plus at least four different steering wheels.

being available alongside. Clearly there was still a demand for a traditional open roadster even if by 1976 the TR6 was something of a dinosaur from a previous age. The US-market cars continued to be built until July 1976 and new examples were available from stock until well into 1977. Production of the injected car ceased 17 months earlier in February 1975, by which time demand in Europe had all but evaporated and the pioneering Lucas petrol injection system was in the process of being phased out in Triumph's big saloons. It was to be 1980 before another Triumph model, the US-market TR7, was to appear with fuel injection.

The TR6 was in production for considerably longer than any other TR model. It also outsold all of its ancestors, more than 90,000 TR6s finding buyers. The demise of the TR6 signalled the end of TRs with separate chassis frames, and thus of a long and distinguished line of sports cars stretching back 23 years and accounting for more than a quarter of a million units all told – an impressive total and a major export earner for Britain.

seasons at relatively minimal extra tooling cost. During this period a surprising number of this more than somewhat emasculated version were sold, this despite the all-new TR7

Above: Triumph's Lucas-injected 2½-litre 'six' looks good installed in an immaculate TR6. Below: A very late UK-market TR6 in Mimosa Yellow, carrying a 1974/75 registration. This would have been built with the 125bhp de-rated engine brought in surreptitiously in early 1973. From late 1969 onwards, TR6s came with this type of road wheel as standard.

The *Spitfire*

A very well preserved example of the original Mk1 Spitfire 4 – as it should correctly be called. This car is finished in Triumph's Conifer Green, a colour widely-used at that time.

Mention the word 'Triumph' to any sports car enthusiast and immediately they are likely to say 'TR', but in truth the name 'Spitfire' should be their first thought, for this model was more important to the company's coffers than all the traditional TRs put together, the Spitfire actually outselling the TR2–6 range by a factor of two to one. In its

18-year life and through five phases, the Spitfire sold in excess of 314,000 units, a tremendous number for what was a pure two-seater rather than a mass-market family car – only the MGB outsold it in those pre-MX5 days.

Back in the late 1950s when the Herald with its separate chassis was in development, it was realised that a small sports car using a version of the

Spitfire MkI
1962–65

ENGINE:
Four cylinders in line, cast-iron block and head

Capacity	1147cc
Bore x stroke	69.3mm x 76mm
Valve actuation	Pushrod
Compression ratio	9.0:1
Carburettors	Twin SU
Power	63bhp (net) at 5750rpm
Maximum torque	67lb ft at 3500rpm

TRANSMISSION:
Rear-wheel drive; four-speed, non-synchro first gear; optional overdrive from early 1963

SUSPENSION:
Front: Independent by coil and wishbone; anti-roll bar; telescopic dampers
Rear: Independent by transverse leaf spring and swing axles, location by radius arms; telescopic dampers

STEERING:
Rack-and-pinion

BRAKES:
Front: Disc
Rear: Drum

WHEELS/TYRES:
Steel disc or wire wheels on 3½in rims
Tyres 5.20 x 13in

BODYWORK:
Two-seater sports; separate chassis with steel panels

DIMENSIONS:

Wheelbase	6ft 11in
Track, front	4ft 1in
Track, rear	4ft 0in
Length	12ft 1in
Width	4ft 9in
Height	3ft 11½in

KERB WEIGHT:
14.25cwt

PERFORMANCE:
(Source: *The Motor*)

Max speed	91mph
0–60mph	15.4sec
30–50mph in top	11.5sec
50–70mph in top	14.0sec

PRICE INCLUDING TAX WHEN NEW:
£730 (November 1962)

NUMBER BUILT: 45,753

Spitfire MkII
1965–67

As MkI except:

ENGINE:

Power	67bhp (net) at 6000rpm
Maximum torque	67lb ft at 3750rpm

PERFORMANCE:
(Source: *Autocar*)

Max speed	92mph
0–60mph	15.5sec
30–50mph in top	12.5sec
50–70mph in top	14.6sec

PRICE INCLUDING TAX WHEN NEW:
£678 without overdrive (August 1966)

NUMBER BUILT: 37,409

Spitfire MkIII
1967–70

As Mk I except:

ENGINE:

Capacity	1296cc
Bore x stroke	73.7mm x 76mm
Power	75bhp (net) at 6000rpm
	68bhp at 5500rpm (US, 1969–70)
Maximum torque	75lb ft at 4000rpm
	73lb ft at 3000rpm (US, 1969–70)
Compression ratio	8.5:1 (US, 1969–70)

KERB WEIGHT:
15.5cwt

PERFORMANCE:
(Source: *Motor*)

Max speed	95mph
0–60mph	14.5sec
30–50mph in top	11.1sec
50–70mph in top	12.8sec

PRICE INCLUDING TAX WHEN NEW:
£717 (August 1967)

NUMBER BUILT: 65,320

Spitfire MkIV
1970–74

As MkI except:

ENGINE:

Capacity	1296cc
	1493cc (US, 1973–74)
Bore x stroke	73.7mm x 76mm
	73.7mm x 87.5mm (US, 1973–74)
Compression ratio	8.0:1 (US, 1972)
Carburettor	Single Stromberg (US, 1972)

Power	63bhp (DIN) at 6000rpm
	58bhp (DIN) (US, 1971)
	48bhp (DIN) (US, 1972)
	57bhp at 5000rpm (DIN) (US, 1973–74)
Maximum torque	69lb ft at 3000rpm
	74lb ft at 3000rpm (US, 1973–74)

WHEELS/TYRES:
145 x 13 on 4.5in rims
Tyres 5.20 x 13 (US, 1971–73)
155 x 13 (US 1974)

DIMENSIONS:

Track, rear	4ft 2in (1973 onwards)
Length	12ft 5in
Width	4ft 10½in

KERB WEIGHT:
15.2cwt

PERFORMANCE:
(Source: *Autocar*)

Max speed	90mph
0–60mph	16.2sec
30–50mph in top	11.7sec
50–70mph in top	16.3sec

PRICE INCLUDING TAX WHEN NEW:
£995 without overdrive (March 1971)

NUMBER BUILT: 70,021

Spitfire 1500
1975–80

As MkIV except:

ENGINE:

Capacity	1493cc
Bore x stroke	73.7mm x 87.5mm
Compression ratio	9.0:1 7.5:1 (US)
Carburettor	Single Stromberg (US)
Power	71bhp (DIN) at 5500rpm
	57bhp (DIN) at 5,000rpm (US)
Maximum torque	82lb ft at 3000rpm
	74lb ft at 3000rpm (US)

WHEELS/TYRES:
Tyres 155 x 13 on 4.5in rims

DIMENSIONS:

Length	13ft 1½in (last US cars)
Width	4ft 10½in

KERB WEIGHT:
15.9cwt

PERFORMANCE:
(Source: *Autocar*)

Max speed	100mph
0–60mph	13.2sec
30–50mph in top	10.0sec
50–70mph in top	12.1sec

PRICE INCLUDING TAX WHEN NEW:
£1,689 (May 1975)

NUMBER BUILT: 95,829

Above: The rear of the Spitfire is as pleasing as the front – Michelotti at his best. The central instrument panel was a great convenience in production.

Left: The same basic dash was carried through to the MkII, but with the surrounding metal being vinyl covered; for the MkIII the central instrument panel changed to a wooden item.

Opposite: The Spitfire's one-piece front gives excellent access to the mechanicals; the radiator is fitted with a remote header tank positioned above the inlet manifold.

same chassis and similar mechanicals would be comparatively simple to produce. Michelotti presented several proposals based on a shortened 83in-wheelbase Herald chassis, one particular design appealing instantly to Standard-Triumph's top brass, who resolved in April 1960 to go ahead. The Austin-Healey Sprite had already been available for two years and was doing well both in the showrooms and on the track, so clearly the market was there – and Triumph needed to be in on it. By the time construction of a prototype, codenamed Bomb, had been authorised in September, Michelotti in Turin was was already building up his proposal, and before the end of October a car very like the production Spitfire was sitting in the Canley works. It gathered dust during the early days of the Leyland takeover, but in July 1961 the project was given approval for production.

Having toyed with the idea of building the car in glassfibre, wiser counsels prevailed and a conventional pressed-steel body was decided upon, to be built by Triumph subsidiary Forward Radiator. The Herald-style one-piece front was retained, and winding glass windows were provided, a luxury unknown to BMC's offerings at the time. Clever design meant that a central instrument panel sufficed for both lhd and rhd models, and a cost saving was made by using the TR4 windscreen frame and glass. The car had an excellent hood which with the glass windows made it infinitely more weathertight than was the sports car norm in the early 1960s.

The outer longitudinal members of the Herald chassis were eliminated, body strength coming from the shell's exceptionally deep and stiff sills. A version of the Herald swing-axle independent rear suspension was of course employed, with the locating radius arms hung directly on the body rather than on the chassis crossmember as on the saloons. Front disc brakes were standard, as was an anti-roll bar and rack-and-pinion steering, the Spitfire – as it came to be known – thus benefiting from the same 25ft turning circle as the Herald.

The Le Mans Spitfires

Seeking to counter BMC's campaigning of special Sprites and MGBs, Harry Webster persuaded his fellow directors in late 1963 that a major attack on Le Mans should be mounted for June 1964, and that Spitfires were the cars to use as they had a good chance of doing well in their class.

Well before this time Michelotti had been encouraged to style a 'Spitfire GT' road car, a fastback coupé which eventually saw production with a six-cylinder engine as the GT6. It was immediately obvious that Spitfires with this aerodynamic shape would not only look good but prove swifter than open cars on the long Le Mans straights. Accordingly, a run of four racing Spitfires was laid down, eventually being registered as ADU 1B to ADU 4B. The cars were constructed not in the competition department but in the experimental department,

under the direction of John Lloyd – who was to be in charge of the new racing programme.

The decision was taken to run the cars as prototypes, which enabled them to deviate more drastically from production cars, which indeed they did. Aluminium bodyshells with faired-in headlamps and grafted-on glassfibre hard-tops were used, mounted on chassis that were both lightened and strengthened. TR4 gearboxes were mated to the 1147cc engines, which were extremely highly tuned, as over 100bhp was needed for any chance of a class win. Twin dual-choke Weber carburettors, a gas-flowed cast-iron eight-port head and a camshaft with really wild timing were used, this latter making the cars both difficult to start from cold and very intractable at anything under 3500rpm. However, these engines

really flew at the top of the rev range, the best of them producing around 102bhp at 7000rpm, or nearly 100bhp per litre from a pushrod engine originally designed for a small economy saloon. A great deal of development had to go into ensuring that the racing Spitfire engines not only stayed together at 7000rpm, but stayed together for 24 hours – a tall order, but one that was met.

On test these fierce little British Racing Green cars proved able to reach 134mph and to lap the eight-mile Le Mans circuit in under five minutes. The roadgoing Spitfire's handling deficiencies were dealt with by stiffening the suspension to such an extent that the cars barely rolled at all, although they could still lose adhesion suddenly at very high cornering speeds. All-up weight was around 14.5cwt, which was very similar to the

Engine and transmission were from the 1147cc Herald, but with twin SU carburettors plus a revised camshaft and manifolding boosting output to 63bhp net. In a lightweight car this gave 90mph and a 0–60mph time of around 15 seconds, figures that trounced the 948cc Sprites and Midgets handsomely.

When finally announced in October 1962, the Spitfire was a thoroughly

modern, well-engineered and desirable package using reliable components; small wonder that it sold well straightaway in all markets, despite costing around ten per cent more than BMC's more primitive offerings. It took the Sprite and Midget a further two years to gain winding windows, and they never did acquire independent rear suspension. However, the Spitfire nearly did not

happen at all, for at the eleventh hour Leyland considered shelving the whole Bomb project as part of the huge cost-cutting exercise when they took over the bankrupt Standard-Triumph concern at the start of 1961. How pleased they must ultimately have been that the bold decision to finance this car in the dark post-takeover days paid off so well.

The Spitfire was launched at a price of £730 including Purchase Tax and initially the only extra available was a heater. However, in January 1963 a particularly neat steel hard top arrived as did wire wheels and, surprisingly, an overdrive unit. Quite possibly the smallest engine that was ever coupled to an overdrive transmission, the Spitfire's 1147cc 'four' proved gamely able to pull the resulting high gearing of 19.1mph per 1000rpm without

The interior of a MkII Spitfire, photographed in 1965. The MkI's rubber floor mats have given way to a full set of carpets; the rather basic plastic steering wheel remains, however. The MkII looks externally like the MkI.

road-equipped production car.

The Le Mans cars were built to stay the course, and in the event itself ADU 2B managed to do just that, David Hobbs and Rob Slotemaker bringing the Triumph home in 21st place, third in its class, at an average speed of 94.7mph. The other two entries, ADU 1B and ADU 3B, both retired as a result of accidents rather than any mechanical deficiency, which was comforting for the development team. ADU 4B remained the spare car, and did not race.

As US sales were so important, all four Le Mans Spitfires were shipped to Florida for March 1965's Sebring 12-hour race, the team being run under the direction of 'Kas' Kastner. ADU 3B was spare car on this occasion, and in the race ADU 1B again suffered an accident, being comprehensively rolled by Peter Bolton. ADU 2B and ADU 4B

both finished strongly, at second and third in their class, a further demonstration of mechanical reliability despite the high state of engine tune.

Hopes were high in June 1965 for a good result at Le Mans, as the cars were around 110lbs lighter than in 1964: a thinner-gauge chassis frame, an aluminium cylinder head and a lighter Vitesse gearbox accounted for this. A little more power had been conjured from the highly-stressed engines – around 107bhp from the best of them, and enough to produce a truly impressive top speed of around 137mph. All four cars started the event and two completed it. ADU 2B retired with an oil-cooler problem, the only time that a mechanical problem caused one of the reliable little Spitfires to scratch. The unlucky ADU 1B had yet another accident, but ADU 3B and ADU 4B

both survived to finish 13th and 14th, and first and second in their class – an excellent achievement, the Spitfires beating main rivals the Alpine-Renaults and Austin-Healey Sprites; it was one of Triumph's best racing results ever.

That event was however the end of it, for these works Spitfires did not run again for the factory although they were lent to a private team to contest the Silverstone six-hour relay race later that year. The 1147cc engine was really at the limit of its development and due to be replaced by an enlarged version, and Triumph felt that the limited competition budget would be better spent on rallying rather than racing. In any event, the Le Mans Spitfires had achieved what they had set out to do, which was securing a class win at Le Mans.

protest, although acceleration in overdrive top was hardly much to write home about.

The motoring press was immediately enthusiastic about Triumph's new baby, *The Motor* calling it 'an outstanding new sports car'. The only major criticism surrounded the designed-down-to-a-price independent rear suspension. As with the saloons, hard cornering followed by lifting off the throttle could provoke a rapid spin as the inside rear wheel tucked under, leading to lack of ground contact. On balance, though, the general feeling was that the trait would not worry normal drivers and that a cheap form of independent rear suspension was better than no IRS at all. The Spitfire became particularly popular with enthusiastic female drivers – in some markets it was estimated that a majority of Spitfires had lady owners, doubtless impressed by the small Triumph's combination of chic looks, practicality, ease of driving and cheap 38mpg running costs.

Having found a winning formula, Triumph was content to leave the Spitfire almost unchanged for long periods. In early 1965 a slight power boost to 67bhp was accompanied by a new diaphragm clutch and an upgrade to the relatively spartan interior, which gained carpets and the vinyl trimming of previously-exposed metal. Having been launched as the 'Spitfire 4', the '4' – which had been regularly ignored

by everyone from the factory downwards – was finally dropped at this juncture, the car becoming simply the Spitfire MkII.

By 1967 the first safety and environmental restrictions were materialising in the US, one of the proposals being a uniform bumper-height for cars. As a result the MkIII Spitfire introduced in March 1967 had to suffer the raising of its front bumper

The Spitfire chassis laid bare. The bodyshell provides a considerable amount of stiffening: unlike the Herald, the Spitfire frame has no peripheral outriggers.

The Macau Spitfire

This enigmatic vehicle was probably the nearest thing Triumph ever made to an out-and-out racing car. In 1965 Standard-Triumph's Hong Kong dealer, Walter Sulke, commissioned the works to build him a one-off Spitfire racer based on the Le Mans coupés, to be entered at his expense in events in south-east Asia. Unlike the Le Mans cars, the Macau car was an open roadster, well streamlined and with a faired-in driver's headrest after the fashion of the D-type Jaguar. Wide alloy wheels were fitted, plus headlamp covers, and there was a rigid tonneau over the passenger seat and a wraparound half-height windscreen. The finished car looked very racy, particularly as it sported a broad centre stripe. Mechanically it was as the 1965 Le Mans cars, and with the full-house 109bhp engine proved capable of exceeding 130mph. A long-distance 22.5-gallon fuel tank was provided, as were racing-type quick-lift jacking points.

This unique Spitfire enjoyed some success locally, but it was not long before it had found its way to 'Kas' Kastner's California workshop where a full-race 220bhp GT6 engine and TR6 gearbox were installed, making it very rapid indeed although handling was considered marginal. The car enjoyed a fair bit of success in SCCA racing in the modified class, but the difficult handling prevented it from being an outright winner.

The unique 130mph 'Macau' Spitfire racing car. It was said to be 410lbs lighter than the production car and had nearly 110bhp at its disposal.

to above the indicators and sidelights and to a point where it ran right across the front of the old radiator grille. This arguably did nothing for Michelotti's stylish original design, but the US market was important, so a 'bone-in-teeth' bumper it had to be. In compensation the engine increased in capacity to 1296cc, and with a new eight-port head a very adequate 75bhp resulted. The little Spitfire was rapidly catching up on its TR brothers, for the MkIII could approach 100mph and had a 0–60mph acceleration time of around 13 seconds. A full convertible hood also arrived with this new model.

Triumph's junior sports car sold better than ever in MkIII form, and by late 1967 the 100,000th Spitfire had been built – this in just five years. The UK tax-paid price had risen to £717 as compared with £684 for the MG Midget. That the Spitfire was always a little dearer than its rival did not seem to matter: it was more spacious, a little faster, and perceived as more modern. Further minor improvements took place in August 1969 when a matt-black windscreen surround was introduced along with better seats, a padded steering wheel and a zip-out window for the hood as on the TR6. Wheel width increased to 4½in, with radial tyres finally becoming a standard fitment.

With demand still good, the opportunity to restyle the body was taken for the 1971 model year, Michelotti devising a new look for the Spitfire based on his design for the Stag. As with the TR5-to-TR6 transformation, the inner body structure, doors and centre section of the old car had to be re-used in the MkIV, but the front and rear ends Michelotti was allowed to update. The new Spitfire was 4in longer and was a much more major revision than might at first have been thought. It had all new panelwork for the wings, bonnet, boot and valances, together with a redesigned hard top which incorporated opening rear quarter windows. The previously visible bonnet rib-joints disappeared while the flatter top to the boot allowed a touch more luggage space and more modern and larger light clusters that aided safety. At last, too, a full-width rear bumper appeared.

Inside, the much-criticised suits-all-countries central instrument panel disappeared, and the instruments were placed directly in front of the driver in a revised dashboard with the latest 'safety' rocker switches; this type of dash had been introduced for

Above: Wire wheels were rarely specified on new Spitfires but have been retro-fitted on many examples.

Right: The raised bumper of the MkIII Spitfire is very obvious.

US-market MkIIIs during 1969, incidentally. A steering lock arrived, as did much better seats and a higher standard of trim and soundproofing. Mechanical upgrades included an all-synchro gearbox, a higher 3.89-to-1 rear axle ratio, and – above all – significant improvements to the somewhat doubtful swing-axle rear suspension. The key change was to allow the transverse spring to pivot about its centre mounting. This 'swing-spring' arrangement eradicated much of the previous dramatic wheel camber changes and consequent dicey handling.

The works rally Spitfires

Harry Webster gained authority to build not only the Le Mans racers, but also a team of four rally Spitfires, these to be built up in the competition department as opposed to the experimental shop. The original plot was to use the basic steel inner body structure for strength, but with aluminium exterior panels and the normal production hardtop. It was resolved to push the rally regulations to the absolute limit to gain competitiveness, the same ultra-hot 1147cc Le Mans engines being employed, albeit with aluminium cylinder heads. Vitesse overdrive gearboxes were installed and the axle ratio was lowered compared to the Le Mans cars. Wide steel wheels were fitted, and conventional rather than faired-in headlamps ensured that the four cars looked not too different from production Spitfires. They were finished in powder blue, registered consecutively as ADU 5B to ADU 8B, and were ready in time for the June 1964 Alpine Rally.

To be strictly accurate, there was a fifth car, ADU 467B, built by the works to a similar specification but at British Petroleum's expense, for Stirling Moss's 'SMART' rally team. This pea-green car was to be driven by the relatively inexperienced Valerie Pirie on the same rallies as the works cars and to be maintained by the competition department alongside them. Sadly, of the five major events entered, this car only finished one, coming home in a lowly position in the 1965 Tulip.

As to the works cars in the 1964 Alpine, only Terry Hunter in ADU 7B finished, coming third in class. Two others retired after accidents, and the third car broke a connecting rod, one of the few mechanical failures on this engine and a failure which led to production Spitfire engines being beefed up.

Later that year the same ADU 7B (running with a Le Mans bonnet) did exceptionally well in the gruelling Tour de France, a combination of a major rally with a number of races. The car, crewed by Rob Slotemaker and Terry Hunter, won its class, beating all the French opposition and finishing tenth overall. The other two entries did not finish, both of them suffering from engine maladies. All three of these cars were given fastback hardtops for this event, although the tops were not quite the same as those of the Le Mans racers.

In October 1964 ADU 5B, despite being to rally specification, won its class in the Paris 1000km race, and then ADU 7B and ADU 6B managed first and second in class (and second and fifth overall) in the Geneva Rally, one of the team's best results. The team prize was also secured, with the help of a privately-owned Spitfire: it must not be overlooked that amateur drivers were also doing well the world over in Triumph's small roadster.

For 1965 Simo Lampinen was persuaded to join the team and a new left-hand-drive rally Spitfire was built for him, registered AVC 654B. Three works cars contested the Monte Carlo Rally, two finishing at 14th and 24th places overall, and second and third in class. In May's Tulip Rally the sole works entry of Lampinen's car suffered clutch problems although Val Pirie in the 'SMART' car did finally manage to finish an event. June's Geneva Rally saw the blue Spitfires finishing first and second in class and then the final event in which the works cars competed as a team took place in July, this being the always-difficult Alpine Rally.

This was arguably the team's finest performance, for the rules allowed prototype cars to run sporting almost any modifications. Taking advantage of this, Triumph constructed a 1296cc version of the 1147cc engine which produced 117bhp at 7000rpm, increasing the torque proportionately to 97lb ft at 5500rpm. Tractability was thus much improved, a great benefit for what was basically a roadgoing vehicle. Brakes were uprated to cope with the extra speed and the cars were in with a real chance of high placings. ADU 5B, ADU 6B and ADU 7B were all entered, as was Lampinen's lhd car.

Although the Fidler/Robson car crashed as a result of broken wheel studs and Slotemaker's car had an engine blow-up, the other two cars succeeded handsomely, Lampinen winning the prototype class outright in AVC 654B, with Thuner and Gretener finishing second in class driving ADU 6B. Sadly, this was to prove the works Spitfire's swansong, and the only factory use of the 117bhp engines, for thereafter it was decided to concentrate on rallying the Triumph 2000 saloons.

Fortunately for today's enthusiasts, several of the works race and rally Spitfires have survived, so that the scream of that highly-tuned little engine can still on occasions be heard.

Simo Lampinen presses on in his left-hand-drive works rally Spitfire 'AVC 654B' during the 1965 Alpine Rally.

Above: The factory hardtop merges well with the Spitfire's lines – this is a MkIII.

Below: Oops! A MkIII Spitfire demonstrates the limitations of the Herald-type swing-axle rear suspension when one lifts off mid-corner. The nearside rear wheel has lost contact with the ground altogether.

The Triumph Fury

A Spitfire on steroids is how one might describe the unique Michelotti Triumph Fury prototype of 1965. In side view it really did resemble an overgrown Spitfire, but from the front it was unmistakable in that it had pop-up headlamps, an idea originally considered for the Spitfire itself. The rear had echoes of the yet-to-come MkIV Spitfire and Stag and along the body sides was a prominent crease line. The TR4/Spitfire windscreen was incorporated, as were wrap-around bumpers at both ends, but the revolutionary thing about the car was that it had a monocoque body, and was thus the first Triumph sports car with no separate chassis frame. This followed MG's lead with the MGB, a car at whose market the Fury was clearly aimed.

Mechanically the Fury borrowed heavily from the Triumph 2000 saloon, whose engine, transmission and suspension (including the independent rear) it utilised. An interior that was luxurious for the time incorporated winding windows with front quarterlights, and a decently weatherproof hood: the whole package was meant to be upmarket and to upstage the MGB. Performance was also apparently up to TR levels, as monocoque construction had saved much weight.

The unique pale blue prototype was registered and extensively tested in 1966, but with the successful Spitfire and TR ranges in full production, it was filling a market gap that was simply too slender, being too near the TR in terms of size, performance and likely selling cost. Despite the fact that those who drove it reportedly liked it, the project was soon shelved. As often happened with Triumph prototypes, it fortunately escaped destruction and still survives as a fascinating footnote in Triumph's history.

The Fury anticipated Michelotti's restyle of the Spitfire/GT6 for 1971; eventually it became clear that there was no sense in such an intermediate model.
(Ken Chisholm)

The MkIV Spitfire of 1970 had its swing-axle suspension modified to the swing-spring system shown here; it is a big improvement on the original set-up.

Right: The 1970 MkIV Spitfire has a modified rear with distinct echoes of its larger brother, the Stag. Heavier than the MkIII and with slightly less power, it is noticeably slower but in compensation is better equipped and handles more safely.

Right centre: The well-trimmed cockpit of a later MkIV. The car has come a long way from the somewhat basic layout of the 1962 version.

Right bottom: The early MkIVs — and the very last MkIIIs — have this style of black-finished dashboard.

One retrograde step was that power on non-US cars dropped to 63bhp (DIN) from the previous 75bhp (net). This was allowed to happen despite the addition of nearly 100lbs in weight. Even taking into account the differences in power calibration, this made for a slower car. Whereas a good MkIII Spitfire could approach 100mph, the best that the British magazines could persuade from the MkIV was around 91mph. Almost all the acceleration times were inferior too.

A slight downgrade in power might not have been too noticeable in Europe, but this was as nought compared to the situation in the US, where each successive season saw the 1296cc engine further emasculated by ever-tightening emission controls. For 1971 the US version was down to 58bhp with use of only a single Stromberg carburettor, but for 1972 power drooped to a dire 48bhp, and this in a so-called 'sports' car. Clearly the situation in the car's biggest market was a nonsense and something had to be done rapidly. Even changing the rear axle ratio back to the original 4.11-to-1 couldn't save the 1972 US Spitfire's embarrassingly slow performance.

Fortunately since the introduction of the Triumph 1500 saloon in 1970 there had existed a further stretched version of the engine, and this 1493cc unit was adopted for the North American market for the 1973 and 1974 seasons, and helped to restore some measure of liveliness, although this was inevitably at a cost of extra fuel consumption. At least the ever-stricter emission standards could be met and sales to the US could continue; without these, the Spitfire was hardly a viable proposition. The 1500 engine remained exclusive to the US until the 'MkV' cars brought it to other markets in December 1974.

Despite all this, the greatly improved rear suspension drew such praise that this masked criticisms of poorer performance. Bill Boddy from *Motor Sport* weighed into the perennial Spitfire-versus-Spridget debate by stating after testing a MkIV that he found the Triumph more of a motor car for road use than the Spridget: it was simply bigger all round, yet cost no more to run.

To keep the Spitfire ahead in the small sports car stakes, further revisions arrived in 1973. In February came restyled instruments in a new wooden dashboard, along with fully-reclining seats and optional head restraints. The rear suspension was further revised, to provide a 2in increase in track and reduce wheel

camber angles. Later in the year wire wheels ceased to be an option, having dramatically declined in popularity, and the optional overdrive was now a stronger unit, while in December a matt-black front spoiler was added. Despite these regular upgrades, sales were declining, particularly in the home market. What had once been a cheap, cheerful and swift little roadster had put on weight and cost. The 1973 Spitfires, although more practical and comfortable than those of ten years earlier were no faster, and performance ultimately is what sports cars are about. It was the TR2 to TR4A story all over again.

Happily there was a reasonably effective remedy, one that had already been used in the US. Thus it was that for the 1975 model year the MkIV disappeared and the Spitfire 1500 replaced it. To the great dismay of MG supporters, this same 1500 engine surfaced at the same time in the MG Midget, which not only had to suffer a Triumph engine but also giant black bumpers and a raised ride height that destroyed its handling. It was as if

British Leyland's product planners and engineers were resolved to make the Spitfire's great rival a laughing stock. Luckily the non-US Spitfire did not need to resort to horrid afterthought bumpers, retaining its good looks to the end – although some of the mid-to-late-1970s paint colours were particularly vile ...

In US form the 1500 engine had to be equipped with only a single Stromberg carburettor, but other markets were able to have a twin-SU tune which was good for 71bhp (DIN) and a reasonable 82lb ft of torque at 3000rpm. This was finally enough grunt to put the 1975 Spitfire back where the 1967 MkIII had been: it could just top 100mph, albeit at the cost of a ten per cent increase in fuel consumption, which was now 32mpg overall. The 0–60mph time achieved in the 1975 *Autocar* road test was a very respectable 13.2 seconds, not much slower than the US-specification TR6. All magazines which tested the 1500 were full of praise for the improved handling, for the 1970 and 1973 rear suspension revisions taken together

Driving the Spitfire

Whichever Spitfire you choose, there are some 'givens' with Triumph's baby sportster. In essence they come down to this: a Spitfire will always be a more civilised car than its deadly rivals the Sprite-Midget duo. Even a MkI is more spacious and more comfortable than a comparable Spridget – and of course gains by having wind-up windows – and a 1500 with overdrive is almost in a different class, with its relaxed performance and pleasant interior.

The MkI is no ball of fire, but is reasonably sprightly up to 60mph, with the high third gear a good ratio for twisting country lanes; it will settle happily at 70mph, but wringing a final 10mph out of the mildly-tuned 1147cc 'four' is something of a struggle.

Brakes are firm and the gearchange

is light and loose, with a slightly odd diagonal movement from third to fourth. The steering is nicely fluid but lacks a little in feel. On poor surfaces the MkI rides firmly but not uncomfortably, and the overall feel is of a car lacking the edge of the more instantly responsive Spridget.

What about the famed swing-axle handling? Set the MkI up for a bend, power through without lifting the throttle – and don't indulge in any rapid direction changes before the suspension has found its feet again – and you'll not have any problems. Drive with less prudence, and there's no margin of forgiveness.

Move up to a MkIII and there's a more plush cockpit and a beefier, freer-revving engine – it really is a nice unit – but otherwise the recipe

remains the same. But with the extra performance you do need to be more aware of the rear suspension's failings. Go in to a bend too fast, change your mind and decelerate, and you could be in for an interesting time as one of the swing-axles starts to tuck under and the car flicks into oversteer.

These vices were eliminated on the MkIV; add a 1500 engine and the last Spitfire is a manifestly superior car to a late Midget, with secure handling, an acceptable ride, decent levels of refinement, and a spacious cockpit with comfortable seats, all this matched to a good-sized boot and an easy-to-use hood. In the late 1970s it still felt surprisingly modern, and in today's conditions it still stacks up as a pleasing and practical roadster with more than acceptable pep.

Above: The hardtop on the MkIV and 1500 is more angular – but still attractive. (Jon Pressnell collection) Below: Late US-market Spitfire 1500.

Buying Hints – Spitfire and GT6

1. As these cars are derived from the Herald, many of the points relevant to these cars are applicable, particularly as regards the mechanicals.

2. The structure relies on short chassis outriggers to support the body rather than a perimeter box frame as part of the chassis. The three-part sills are thus far more structural than those of the Herald, and considerable attention must be paid to their integrity. The chassis has a good reputation and is rarely badly corroded. In fact, acknowledged experts suggest the car is best scrapped if the frame is terminally rotted.

3. All body support points should be thoroughly inspected for deterioration; in particular the front outriggers rust, but these can be repaired without removing the body.

4. The door gaps give a good clue as to the body's integrity. They should be even all round; if not, suspect a bodged repair.

5. Rear wheelarches rot, and if this is the case it is usually better to replace the whole wing. Inner wheelarches and wings rust, as does the floorpan – including the boot floor. The bases of the A-posts, the floorpan-to-sill joints and the trailing edge of the Spitfire boot lid are other favourite rot-spots.

6. The one-piece front itself is usually pretty sound; but beware misalignment, which will always look wrong.

7. Virtually all body panels are still available new and at reasonable cost, as is most of the brightwork.

8. The driver's seat tends to collapse with long usage, but again nearly all interior trim is available, as is weather equipment. Window and wiper mechanisms sometimes give trouble.

9. Mechanically, it is the suspension, particularly at the front, that will cause most grief. A well-worn system can disintegrate and collapse, with dire results. The brass trunnions that form the bottom pivot of the system

should be lubricated with EP90 oil every 3,000 miles. This is frequently neglected, leading to partial seizure and eventual breakage of the vertical link. All front suspension joints should be checked, although fortunately a home rebuild of the system is straightforward and relatively inexpensive.

10. The rear suspension also causes problems, again having trunnions each side that can wear. Rear hub bearings need regular greasing and omitting this can cause the driveshafts to eat into the bearing cages, necessitating an expensive specialist repair. On the later GT6s the Rotoflex couplings should be carefully looked at: they are prone to cracking and only last 25,000 miles at the best.

11. Brakes are straightforward and cheap to overhaul, the exception being the dual-circuit master cylinder of late cars, which can be expensive.

12. Engines and transmissions are dealt with elsewhere and are tough and long-lasting.

really worked, albeit at the cost of a harder ride. The rear axle ratio, 3.89-to-1 in US 1500s, was raised to 3.63-to-1 for rest-of-the-world Spitfires, and with the optional overdrive engaged this produced the very high gearing of 22.6mph per 1000rpm, making for relaxed motorway cruising.

Externally the non-US 1500 remained largely unchanged although rather tacky matt-black 'Spitfire 1500' transfers were added, in the fashion of the time. For US cars the impact-absorbing black overriders grew in size again, adding several unwanted inches to the car's length and yet more weight: by the time production finished the Federal Spitfire weighed 16.7cwt, over 20 per cent more than the original 1962 car.

March 1977 saw a further clutch of revisions, with new nylon-upholstered seats, TR7-type column switches, a smaller steering wheel, a cigar lighter and an extra courtesy light. Apart from an increase in wheel rim width to 5in in 1978, for the non-US cars that was it. The model was allowed to continue for a further three years almost unchanged, picking up what sales it could without British Leyland having to expend cash on tooling or development. However, yet more stringent US legislation meant a drop in compression ratio back to 7.5-to-1 in 1977, while regulation changes forced a move to bulky impact-absorbing bumpers during 1979. A catalytic converter had also been found necessary although the date of

its introduction varied according to each individual state's emission standards. In fact California's standards were so stringent that the final 1980 model-year Spitfires could not be sold there at all as they were simply unable to comply.

The Spitfire 1500 soldiered on until the late summer of 1980, the final car (to UK specification) driving off the production line amid some ceremony in August that year. The car remained available from stock both in Europe and the US well into 1981, but once these were sold the small Triumph sports car was no more, after 314,342 examples had been built, of which 77 per cent (242,918) were exported. It was a low-key end to a great little car.

Above: The interior of a late 1500 displays the patterned fabric seat centres introduced in 1977. The Spitfire cockpit was always more spacious and better appointed than that of the rival Spridget. Below: From 1979 the US-market Spitfire (power unquoted!) was obliged to carry these clumsy moulded bumpers – a sad desecration of the car's elegant lines. (Graham Robson collection)

The GT6

A *factory publicity shot of the original GT6 in left-hand-drive form. The bonnet bulge necessary to clear the lengthy engine adds to the car's mini E-type looks. The production body changed hardly at all from Michelotti's 1963 GT design, although it was found necessary to add bonnet louvres to extract engine heat.*

The 'poor man's E-type' or the 'mini E-type' were two of the epithets given to Triumph's GT6 in its day. A great deal more than a Spitfire with a roof, the GT6 is arguably the most underrated of all the company's post-war products. The GT6 was sired by a prototype Spitfire being sent to Italy for Michelotti to work his magic on. When it returned it looked almost exactly as the

production GT6 – another example of Michelotti getting the styling right first time. Originally the idea had been to sell this GT version of the Spitfire in the same 1147cc form as the roadster, but the extra weight of the top and the superior trim meant that it was significantly slower than the open car and yet would be more expensive. That the Spitfire GT had a marginally higher top speed on account of its better aerodynamics was not enough to square the equation. Accordingly, the proposed release date was put back whilst some re-engineering took place.

Within a few months a 1600cc Vitesse unit had been installed, but with the Vitesse being uprated to 2-litres, what could be more natural then than installing the same power unit in the Spitfire GT and creating something really rapid? An obvious difficulty was the sheer length of the engine, but the 'six' was just wangled in by moving the radiator right to the front of the car and adding a not-unpleasing power bulge to the bonnet. Originally blooded in the rally Spitfires (even though not yet homologated), a new all-synchromesh gearbox with optional overdrive was coupled to the engine, which produced 95bhp on a 9.5-to-1 compression ratio with twin Stromberg carburettors.

Compared to the Spitfire, the GT6 – as it came to be called – had its mechanicals strengthened in almost all areas to deal with the greatly increased torque. The differential although superficially similar was beefed up and an especially high 3.27-to-1 ratio was used for non-overdrive cars. Those sold new with overdrive normally had a 3.89-to-1 ratio, but some cars were sold with overdrive and a 3.27 axle, leading to extremely high-geared and relaxed cruising in overdrive at a slight cost in acceleration. Being relatively light and yet torquey, the GT6 was particularly economical, better than 30mpg frequently being obtained. In fact driven gently it could produce fuel consumption figures as good as those of its smaller stablemate.

Suspension was basically as for the Spitfire, but spring rates and damper settings were uprated and a thicker anti-roll bar used. The swing-axle rear suspension, criticised from the start in the Spitfire, was amazingly left virtually unmodified, something that Triumph would have cause to regret. Wider 4½in steel wheels with 155x13 radial ply tyres were the usual fitment, but wire wheels were optional. Larger-diameter front discs with bigger

GT6 MkI

1966–68

ENGINE:
Six cylinders in line, cast-iron block and head
Capacity   1998cc
Bore x stroke   74.7mm x 76mm
Valve actuation   Pushrod
Compression ratio   9.5:1
Carburettors   Twin Stromberg
Power   95bhp at 5000rpm
Maximum torque   117lb ft at 3000rpm

TRANSMISSION:
Rear-wheel drive; four-speed all-synchromesh gearbox; optional overdrive

SUSPENSION:
Front: independent by coil and wishbone; anti-roll bar; telescopic dampers
Rear: independent by transverse leaf spring and swing-axles, location by radius arms; telescopic dampers

STEERING:
Rack-and-pinion

BRAKES:
Front: Disc
Rear: Drums

WHEELS/TYRES:
155 x 13 tyres on 4.5in rims

DIMENSIONS:
Length   12ft 1in
Wheelbase   6ft 11in
Track, front   4ft 1in
Track, rear   4ft 0in
Width   4ft 9in
Height   3ft 11in

KERB WEIGHT:
17.5cwt

PERFORMANCE:
(Source: *Autocar*)
Max speed   106mph
0–60mph   12.0sec
30–50mph in top   6.9sec
50–70mph in top   8.5sec

PRICE INCLUDING TAX WHEN NEW:
£1,007 without overdrive (September 1967)

NUMBER BUILT:
15,818

GT6 MkII

1968–70

As GT6 MkI except:
ENGINE:
Compression ratio   9.25:1
Power   104bhp at 5300rpm

TRANSMISSION:
Optional overdrive now also available with 3.27 to 1 rear axle

SUSPENSION:
Rear: Independent by transverse leaf spring, lower wishbones, radius arms; telescopic dampers

DIMENSIONS:
Track, rear   4ft 1in

KERB WEIGHT:
17.8cwt

PERFORMANCE:
(Source: *Autocar*)
Max speed   107mph
0–60mph   10.0sec
30–50mph in top   6.7sec
50–70mph in top   7.9sec

PRICE INCLUDING TAX WHEN NEW:
£1,158 without overdrive (April 1969)

NUMBER BUILT:
12,066 (incl GT6 Plus)

GT6 MkIII

1970–1973

As GT6 MkII except:
ENGINE:
Compression ratio   8.0:1 (US, 1972–73 models)
Power   90bhp (US, 1971 model)
                     79bhp (US, 1972–73 models)
Maximum torque   116lb ft at 3400rpm (US, 1971 model)
                     97lb ft at 2900rpm (US, 1972–73 models)

SUSPENSION:
Rear: As GT6 MkII until February 1973, when rear suspension becomes as Spitfire MkIV, with pivoting transverse spring

DIMENSIONS:
Track, rear   4ft 2in from February 1973
Length   12ft 5in

PERFORMANCE:
(Source: *Autocar*)
Max speed   107mph
0–60mph   10.0sec
30–50mph in top   6.7sec
50–70mph in top   7.9sec

PRICE INCLUDING TAX WHEN NEW:
£1,373 (August 1972)

NUMBER BUILT:
13,042

All three models of GT6 on show, the MkI nearest the camera; unusually this car is fitted with the optional wire wheels. In the background can be seen a racing GT6.

callipers looked after front braking, while at the rear the drums were increased in diameter, but the braking system remained unservoed. Rack-and-pinion steering was of course used, the ratio being slightly lower than that of the Spitfire to counter the increased weight of the engine.

The front grille was a single-piece unit, and front quarterlights complemented the opening rear quarter windows. The interior was clearly meant to be a cut above that of the usual sports car, with a polished wooden dash carrying a full set of instruments in front of the driver – rather than in the centre, Spitfire-style. A leather 15in steering wheel was a nice touch, as was thick pile

carpet throughout, including in the load space. Sensibly no attempt was made to provide any rear seating, as the car was physically very small inside, being nowhere near as large as its MG rival. The GT6 was definitely not a car for big people, as the tight rally-style seats made clear. Still, luggage accommodation was adequate for two, and very convenient to reach through the tailgate. The whole car was very neat, compact and racy-looking.

After the usual delays, the GT6 was finally launched at the London Motor Show in October 1966, to instant acclaim. The price was £985 including Purchase Tax, exactly the same as that of the TR4A, which was a car with similar performance but a different way of achieving it. The old and trusted formula of putting a relatively large and torquey engine into a small car had worked again; if only the rear

suspension and handling had been up to the power.

Once the motoring press came to drive the car, criticism of the shortcomings of the rear suspension became overt and rather negated all the car's good points. The engine was smooth, powerful and provided both relaxed cruising and strong acceleration, the interior was well-appointed and practical, the all-synchro gearbox a delight with its close ratios and high gearing, and with good luggage accommodation for two the GT6 well deserved its Grand Touring appellation. But countering all these positives was the simple fact that Spitfire swing-axle rear suspension was not up to coping with the additional power of a 2-litre 'six'. Lifting off in mid-corner caused the inevitable rear-wheel tuck-under and resultant loss of adhesion. While many average drivers would never reach this

Above: In profile the MkI GT6 is lithe and elegant; a shame, then, that its roadholding was so open to criticism.

Right: A step up from the Spitfire, the MkI interior has a full-width wood dashboard and rally-style seats. The grab handle doubtless came in useful on high-speed corners.

point, nevertheless the problem was sufficiently serious for more than one magazine to imply that the GT6 was potentially dangerous, and urgently needed revision. This apart, performance was good and indeed better than that of the more expensive MGB GT which had already been on sale for a year: 60mph came up in 10.5 seconds and top speed was105–107mph.

Despite the criticisms, the GT6 sold strongly from the start, and by early 1967 around 150 cars a week were finding homes, a rate that remained

The GT6 in competition

As far as the UK goes, the GT6 really has no competition record. Although it could have been made into a reasonably competitive racing car it had the misfortune to appear just at the time when the company under Donald Stokes was turning away from motor sport and running down the competition programme. There was however one abortive attempt to build a racing GT6, the Le Mans GT6 R project.

The plan was to build what was in effect a Le Mans Spitfire fitted with a race-tuned six-cylinder engine, this to run at June 1966's Le Mans as publicity a few months before the GT6's October launch. Harry Webster commissioned Ray Henderson to build the car and as something near to 200bhp could have been expected on triple Webers, the GT6 R would have been a fearsome machine. With almost double the power of the Spitfires, it might have been good for 150mph on the Mulsanne straight, but it would have had to have competed in the prototype category, against Porsches and the like, and reliability might have been a problem. For whatever reason, the running chassis was never properly bodied and early in 1966 the project was sadly abandoned. Rear suspension was unique for a Triumph in employing a MacPherson strut arrangement in the manner of the Lotus Elan, while a TR transmission and final drive were used for strength. The body was intended to be similar to that of the 1965 Le Mans Spitfires, which as we have seen were very GT6-like in outline. Had the highly-tuned 2-litre engine held together for 24 hours, which was doubtful, it could have done very well. But as it was, the GT6 R was just another Triumph might-have-been.

In the US Kastner and Tullius transformed the GT6 into a very successful SCCA racer. In the 1967/68 period the GT6 racers did moderately well, but in 1969 and 1970, with the latest rear suspension and further development, they won the SCCA Class E Championship outright – resulting inevitably in the car being put into the next class up for 1971, where it was less competitive. Nevertheless the racing MkIII GT6 still managed to win two Class D races in 1972 against fierce opposition. All this showed that the GT6 could have been made into a formidable racing car by the Coventry factory had the cash and the desire been there – it is a pity that they were not.

But darling, does it handle? Late 1968 saw the introduction of the MkII GT6 compete with extra louvres and a raised front bumper – and a comprehensively re-jigged rear suspension.

Above: A MkII GT6 of the road-test fleet is seen here showing off its Jasmine Yellow paint finish.

Right: The MkII GT6 has sophisticated lower-wishbone independent rear suspension with Rotoflex rubber couplings. This tames the wayward behaviour for which the MkI car quickly became notorious. This system is also found on MkIIIs made before early 1973.

consistent throughout the car's seven-year life. What has come to be known retrospectively as the MkI GT6 was on sale for two years, from October 1966 to October 1968, and in that time 15,818 cars were built, more than 80 per cent of which were exported – most, as usual with sports Triumphs, to North America.

Triumph engineers were well aware of the limitations of the swing-axle GT6. The same problem also afflicted the 2-litre Vitesse and clearly required urgent attention. As ever, cost was the major factor and a way had to be found to tame the independent rear and limit camber changes without major chassis or body alterations. This was achieved most ingeniously: the transverse spring was retained but lower wishbones were added to each side, pivoting on the chassis rails and located by adjustable radius arms. The presence of lower wishbones kept the rear wheels more parallel to each other and reduced the camber change that occurred between full bump and full rebound from 21 degrees to 7 degrees. The height of the rear roll centre was also drastically lowered and the transverse spring stiffened up,

Driving the GT6

With that lovely turbine-smooth straight-six and compact Spitfire-derived body – beautifully equipped, too – the GT6 seems to have everything a lover of sports GTs might desire. On the road this seems true enough – provided you are not too big to fit in the cosy cockpit. The straight-six gives torquey relaxed performance and confident overtaking, and overdrive knocks back the revs to aid refinement. The steering is slightly slow-witted rather than razor sharp, the gearchange notchy but cooperative enough, and the brakes short-travel and firm.

So much is true of all GT6s, the only difference to this blend of characteristics being the more haphazard but less bland interior of the MkI. Where the cars differ, though, is in their cornering comportment.

The MkI genuinely is a handful if not treated with the utmost caution: slow in and faster out – with gentle progression – is the only way to tackle corners. Any hesitation, lifting off or sudden change of inputs will unsettle the rear and make the car hard to catch. Adding to this lack of control is a looseness to the rear on bumpy roads which makes it difficult to hold a steady line.

The good news is that the MkII is a car transformed, with safe handling and all the predictability the MkI lacks. The car still squats under acceleration and dives on deceleration, and it is still the strong understeerer you'd expect – no Spitfire agility here – but you won't get the hairs standing up on your neck if you miscalculate your approach to a corner. Interestingly, late MkIIIs with the simpler swing-spring rear are little different from the more elegant Rotoflex-rear MkIIs and early MkIIIs.

With the suspension so effectively tamed, the GT6 is a seductive pocket-sized GT, marred only by intrusive wind noise. One can't help feeling it's an under-rated motor car.

leading to much more stable rear-end handling. What made all this possible at realistic cost was the use, for the outer universal joint, of a rubber 'doughnut' Rotoflex coupling, as originally developed for the front driveshafts of the Triumph 1300 saloon. These couplings not only accommodated plunge and angle changes but also, being rubber, absorbed shocks and transmission wind-up. The result was a car whose handling was totally transformed – at an additional cost per car of only around £25. At a stroke the Achilles Heel of the GT6 had been dealt with, and all the other features of the little coupé could shine through.

The MkII GT6 may have risen in price by £101 but a number of other improvements helped justify this increase. In particular, a further 9bhp was released from the straight-six by using a TR5 cylinder head. Known as the 'full-width' head, this had TR250-type manifolds and was matched to a redesigned camshaft. For the UK market the high 3.27 axle ratio was standardised, with or without overdrive, although the 3.89 axle, as fitted to all US cars, was an option.

Cosmetic touches for the MkII included fake-alloy Rostyle wheel covers when wire wheels were not ordered, extra louvres on the bonnet sides, and ventilation louvres behind the rear quarter-windows. In common with the MkIII Spitfire the front bumper was raised, while inside there was a revised matt-finish wooden dashboard in the TR5 style, complete with rocker switches, clearer instruments and eyeball vents, plus a new padded TR5-type steering wheel. The whole package added up to a greatly improved car, a fact not lost on the road-test fraternity, who could now find little to criticise – at a price of £1,125, the GT6 was still tremendous value. For reasons not clear, the new GT6 was badged for the US market as the GT6 Plus, and emission regulations

Hard cornering in a MkII GT6 does not produce the alarming wheel lift-off that can be experienced in the MkI. This is a road-test photograph taken in 1968.

Bob Tullius, the US racing driver who had major success in various models of Triumph, is seen alongside his Group 44 GT6 Plus. This is the US name for the Mk II GT6: the 'Plus' badge can just be seen on the bonnet. In the States the MkIII was called just that, somewhat illogically.

meant that it remained with the old 95bhp engine.

The MkII had a two-year life, but despite being a much better car it did not sell as well as the MkI. The only notable changes in specification were that in October 1969 fully-reclining seats and more padding and sound insulation were introduced, along with a matt-black windscreen surround. A year later the MkIII version arrived, after 12,066 MkII and GT6 Plus cars had been built – as ever the great majority (over 80 per cent) being exported.

The MkIII GT6 arrived at the same

time as the MkIV Spitfire and shared its square-tail styling. Along with the new front grille and slimmer bumpers, the GT6 also received slightly flared wheelarches, the bonnet louvres disappeared, and the bonnet itself was slightly re-profiled. The tacky fake-Rostyle wheel covers thankfully disappeared and in common with the Spitfire a deeper windscreen was

incorporated, while the fuel filler moved from the tail to the nearside wing. For the US, power dropped again, to 90bhp, but rest-of-the-world cars continued with the 104bhp engine and in other mechanical respects the MkIII was as the MkII. Interior revisions were few: the overdrive switch was now in the gearlever, new heater controls arrived,

Buying Hints

1. Structural points are all as the Spitfire, with the addition that the tailgate can rust as a result of defective seals causing water ingress, and that the seam along the top of the windscreen can also cause trouble.

2. Mechanically, the running gear is as the Spitfire, but for the engine and gearbox, where the remarks on the 2000/2.5 and TR5/TR6 largely apply. As always with the six-cylinder unit, beware of the dreaded crankshaft end float.

Above: This late 1973 car is one of the last of the breed and has the later swing-spring type of independent rear suspension as fitted to 1973 cars. To counter this retrograde step these 'phase two' MkIIIs incorporated a brake servo, tinted glass, a smaller steering wheel, restyled instruments and improved, fire-resistant trim.

Left: A red GT6 and the open road – what more could one want? Except perhaps a sun roof?

and there was yet another new steering wheel. A new range of bright and supposedly fashionable colours was offered, some best forgotten today – lurid purple Magenta anyone? The wire wheel option was still available, but was rarely seen.

The MkIII was a clever and inexpensive updating of the earlier car, and succeeded in making the GT6 look more modern, even if some of the old 'mini E-type' look had been lost. Sales were much as the earlier cars and ran at around 500 a month – it appears that there was a finite market for a small sports coupé that no amount of improvements to the product could increase. The GT6 continued almost unchanged for the 1971 and 1972 seasons although US cars for 1972 sadly had to make do with a further drastic power reduction to a pathetic 79bhp to keep abreast of legislation. Even for other markets quoted power

Right: The dashboard of the MkII and the MkIII are very similar, and feature a matt finish; this is a MkIII.

Below: Restored to perfection: the engine bay of a MkIII GT6.

dropped to 98bhp, and then to 95bhp by 1973, although whether this was a true drop or merely as a result of recalibration is not entirely clear.

There remained one final batch of revisions, revealed in February 1973. The principal change can hardly be regarded as beneficial, at least in cold technical terms: the Rotoflex rear suspension was deleted, presumably on cost grounds. The Vitesse models sharing it had by then disappeared, and the Spitfire had never used this excellent system, so the GT6 was out on its own. In its place, the Spitfire swing-spring rear was used, with a wider track. While this was certainly better than the original swing-axle suspension, it could never be ultimately as good as the Rotoflex/wishbone type. A victory for the cost accountants!

The GT6 carried on for a further nine months until lack of sales and the difficulties of complying with US legislation meant that there was no point in continuing. The final few cars were built in November 1973 and that was that; there was never any GT6 replacement, for the MGB GT was also in the British Leyland corporate fold and fulfilled much the same function, albeit with less speed and slightly more expense.

In its three years of production 13,042 of the MkIII GT6 were made, of which just 4,218 had the February 1973 revisions. In fact the build rate of the MkIII was lower than that of the two previous models despite all its improvements, which leads one to suspect that the GT6 was appealing to a falling market faced with the inexorable rise of the sports saloon. In total 40,926 GT6s were made, and as a car that is perhaps more appreciated today than it was in its time, a goodly number survive and are cherished. There is nothing else quite like the 'poor man's E-Type'...

The *Triumph Stag*

This lovely Stag sits on the correct optional alloys and wears the second style of grille; all the trim add-ons – sill finishers and coachlines – have, however, been removed.

The distinctive and upmarket Stag was a delightful concept: a car that was ideal for the man with a growing family who had been obliged to forsake his TR on space grounds. Alas, it was an ambitious project marred by a lack of development, indifferent build quality and poor reliability – not for nothing was it

known colloquially as the 'Triumph Snag'. Happily, with 30-plus years of further experience the Stag's problems are behind it and today can be seen the excellent vehicle that was always hiding in the fog of British Leyland politics, cash crises and labour problems, for it was the Stag's misfortune to have been produced

A brace of early Stags, in both open and hardtop form. Note how the soft top is fully hidden by the tonneau panel.

during the turbulent years of the British Leyland conglomerate.

The Stag's origins date back to a 1964 Michelotti design exercise for a drophead Triumph 2000. This was a project that the Italian devised on his own account and not as a result of a Triumph commission, although the company was happy to make a prototype 2000 saloon available. What he produced looked remarkably like the production Stag of six years later: it had headlamps concealed under sliding covers that proved impractical, and the T-bar had yet to be added, but in all major aspects – as was his fashion – Michelotti had got it right first time.

Certainly Triumph's head of engineering, Harry Webster, thought so when he saw the finished vehicle in Italy in 1966. Rather than allow Michelotti to exhibit the car publicly Webster swiftly arranged for Triumph to acquire the concept, and this unique prototype was ferried back to Coventry.

Had sufficient resources been available, the car could have been on sale as early as 1968, albeit with the 2½-litre TR5 engine: market research had indicated that there was a large demand worldwide for an upmarket four-seater convertible that could be sold at a realistic price – around half the cost of the Mercedes SL being

Triumph's aim. It was a market with very few players and those that there were all tended to be exclusive and inevitably pricey. If Triumph really could produce Michelotti's lovely convertible at half the cost of the German or Italian equivalent, a queue would form, as indeed it did in 1970 when the Stag finally appeared.

The 1966-67 period was the time when Leyland and Rover were merging, ahead of the 1968 takeover of BMC and the creation of British Leyland. In its dowry Rover brought with it the ex-Buick 3½-litre V8 that it was then productionising for use in the P5B saloon and later the P6. Triumph was at the same time developing the V8 spin-off from the Dolomite 'slant-four', initially in 2½-litre fuel-injected form, the idea being that this would go into the big saloons and also possibly the Stag. Although a running Triumph V8 existed by 1966, the Rover unit was far further down the road than Triumph's embryonic engine, and had rational thinking prevailed after the merger the Triumph unit would have been sidelined in favour of the Rover V8.

But rational thinking was in short supply at British Leyland. Motor-industry politics played a greater role, and Triumph was allowed to continue with its own V8 in parallel with the Rover engine. The Triumph V8 was formed in effect by two of the new 'slant-four' engines (see Chapter 6) initially designed for Saab, the two cylinder blocks on a common

Triumph Stag
1970–77

ENGINE:
90-degree V8, cast-iron block and alloy heads

Capacity	2997cc
Bore x stroke	86mm x 64.5mm
Valve actuation	chain-driven single ohc per bank
Compression ratio	8.8:1 (later 9.25:1) 8.0:1 (US)
Carburettors	Twin Stromberg
Power	145bhp (DIN) at 5500rpm 127bhp (DIN) at 6000rpm (US)
Maximum torque	170lb ft at 3500rpm 148lb ft at 3200rpm (US)

TRANSMISSION:
Rear-wheel drive; all-synchromesh four-speed with optional overdrive (overdrive standard from October 1972), or automatic

SUSPENSION:
Front: Independent by MacPherson struts; anti-roll bar
Rear: Independent by coil springs and semi-trailing arms; telescopic dampers

STEERING:
Rack-and-pinion, power-assisted

BRAKES:
Front: Disc
Rear: Drum
Servo assistance

WHEELS/TYRES:
Tyres 185 x 14in on 5½in rims

DIMENSIONS:

Length	14ft 6in
Wheelbase	8ft 4in
Track, front	4ft 4½in
Track, rear	4ft 5in
Width	5ft 3½in
Height	4ft 1½in

KERB WEIGHT:
25.1cwt

PERFORMANCE:
(Source: *Motor*)

Max speed	117mph
0–60mph	9.7sec
30–50mph in top	7.6sec
50–70mph in top	7.7sec

PRICE INCLUDING TAX WHEN NEW:
£2,108 without overdrive (hardtop version, July 1970)

NUMBER BUILT:
25,877

The fastback Stag

With Michelotti's help Triumph had successfully converted the Stag's junior sibling the Spitfire into the attractive GT6, so why not do the same to the Stag? This plot was hatched in late 1968 and was the brainchild of Spen King, Harry Webster's replacement as Triumph's chief engineer. The original prototype Stag that Michelotti had built from a 2000 saloon in 1964 went back to Turin and Michelotti turned it into a fastback coupé. Unusually, though, his styling was not well received back in Coventry, and King commissioned an alternative design to be submitted back to Michelotti.

Eventually, after much to-ing and fro-ing, a compromise style was reached in March 1969 and Michelotti was given the task of building a bodyshell to the agreed design. This reached Coventry for approval in mid-1969 and a running prototype was built, with a six-cylinder injected 2½-litre engine. This car was in use for evaluation by management early in 1970, but was rapidly sidelined so that all energies could be concentrated on getting the open Stag into production. The effort was not wasted, however, as King revived the idea at the end of 1970

and had a third fastback Stag built by his engineering department, this time a V8 carrying prototype number X815.

The tail styling was slightly modified to echo the new GT6 MkIII design and the result was an elegant and practical car, with a large tailgate opening to reveal a spacious luggage area which became positively huge with the rear seats folded down. Headroom for adult rear passengers was adequate, although there was no more rear legroom than on the normal Stag, as the car was still built on the same wheelbase. The fastback would no doubt have sold well enough, had cash been available to productionise it, and had the factory not been too busy coping with the flood of Stag warranty claims. Fortunately, this third car survives, and appears on occasion at Triumph shows, so enthusiasts can still judge in the metal yet another excellent Triumph idea that failed to materialise.

The fastback Stag was not unlike an overgrown GT6 MkIII. This is the sole survivor of the three prototypes and represents the finalised design. Sadly this rapid and useful coupé never reached production.

crankcase being at 90 degrees to each other. Aluminium cylinder heads were topped with a single overhead camshaft on each side, these being chain-driven. The camshafts operated the valves via bucket-type tappets, the valves being inclined in their heads so that as installed they were nearly vertical.

The proposed 2½-litre V8 was sidelined in the late 1960s by the then technical director, Spen King, when it became obvious that its torque would be inadequate to provide the required performance in the heavy Stag, and the engine emerged as a 2997cc unit with the very over-square dimensions of a 86mm bore with a 64.5mm stroke. This allowed high revolutions, the production unit being safe to 6500rpm, a high speed for a 3-litre engine in the 1960s. On an 8.8-to-1 compression ratio and with twin 1¾in Stromberg carburettors, the power output was 145bhp at 5500rpm with a maximum torque of 170lb ft at 3500rpm, not dissimilar figures to those of the TR5 PI.

Although in the 1966–1969 period there were several occasions when the Stag project was nearly cancelled, it did thankfully survive and was very much seen as a prestige product by Triumph's management. One of the reasons for its survival may be that the Stag did not clash with any other existing or projected British Leyland vehicle – even Jaguar did not make a four-seater convertible.

Although Michelotti's original design was closely based on the 2000 saloon, in the production Stag not a single body panel was shared with the big saloons despite the fact that there were a number of obvious similarities. One of the reasons was that at 8ft 4in the Stag's wheelbase was 6in shorter than that of the Triumph 2000. This lack of commonality caused further delay, as the body had to be tooled from scratch. Most body panels were pressed at Triumph's old Number 1 factory in Speke, Liverpool, but they were actually assembled at the new Number 2 factory there, a place not noted for good quality control or labour relations. The finished bodies

The Federal Stag

The US version of the Stag was not a sales success, principally because of the car's mechanical difficulties. Also, unlike Europe, the States had a good number of reliable home-grown four-seater convertibles available for less than the Stag, so it was not such a unique proposition. Nor was the Stag a sports car, something which many Americans expected of any car with the Triumph badge. Finally, the engine had to be detuned to comply with emissions legislation, thereby losing nearly 20bhp. One can see that there was a lot militating against the Stag in North America.

The model was available in the US from September 1971. As the known problems occurred swiftly once the car was in service, one can only marvel at Triumph's rashness in marketing the Stag at that time at all, for Americans are not noted for tolerating mechanical unreliability in a new car. In the 1972 model year fewer than a thousand examples were sold, and about 75 per cent of these suffered mechanical difficulties. For 1973 a federalised MkII was marketed and sales improved somewhat, but continuing warranty claims finally led to Triumph throwing in the towel in late 1973 and withdrawing the car altogether, after 2,871 examples in total had been imported. It took a further two years to dispose of stocks.

Federal Stags always had lower-compression engines with additional emission control devices which further sapped power.

Horsepower was additionally reduced by the fitment in most cases of air conditioning. High-backed seats which differed from the rest-of-the-world cars were used and there were also minor differences in dashboard layout and switchgear. The 1972 model-year cars had wire wheels as standard, with octagonal knock-on caps, whereas alloy wheels were the norm on MkII Federal models. There were many other minor differences, and one is left wondering why British Leyland ever bothered. Had it known how few examples would be sold no doubt it would have avoided the US altogether – but then without the possibility of sales in the US, the Stag probably would never have been produced at all.

were then transported to Canley for the cars to be fully built up, something of a logistical nightmare. Another cause of delay was that by 1967–68 it was obvious that the big saloons would need an urgent revamp and as they greatly outsold any potential four-seater convertible, this was given priority. The late-stage decision towards the end of 1968 by the new head of engineering, Spen King, that the engine must be enlarged to three litres also contributed to delay, as most of the Stag's mechanical parts consequently needed strengthening. A stronger gearbox and differential were required, as were bigger brakes which then necessitated 14in rather than 13in wheels. In fact, much re-engineering was needed in a hurry if even the postponed release date of mid-1970 was to be achieved. The T-bar roll-over protection was a further late arrival when it became obvious that there would be severe body shake without it; there was also the feeling that proposed US legislation might make the T-bar a legal requirement in the States.

Ever since the Stag concept had been considered it was always envisaged that it would be a well-equipped car, with the best specification that Triumph could offer. Items that are commonplace today but rare in 1970 were featured, such as power steering, reclining seats and

There is a surprising amount of room in the Stag's rear seats – two average-sized adults can travel quite comfortably, although legroom can be a little short at times.

electric windows. The whole interior was beautifully trimmed,soundproofed and padded, as befitted a £2,300 car – even the T-bar was fully padded. Full instrumentation was set into Triumph's characteristic matt-wood dashboard and on MkI models opening the glovebox activated a maplight – a nice touch. Good-quality carpet was used and although the seats were upholstered in PVC, at least it was in an attractive basket-weave finish.

The hood dropped down into a well behind the rear-seat backrest, and once stowed a neat lift-up cover hid it from view and gave the car a well-finished appearance. A very substantial optional hardtop was supplied with most cars although this was an extra-cost option, as was the hood itself on hardtop cars. The hardtop sported a heated rear window, and could be fitted with the hood remaining on the car. Other optional equipment included overdrive, which became standard from late 1972, and automatic transmission; in fact most Stags were sold as automatics, despite the extra cost. Tyres were wide for the time, being of 185-section on 5½in rims; MkI cars had 14in steel wheels with dummy Rostyle covers but knock-off

wire wheels were available as a (rarely specified) option. US cars strangely had wire wheels as standard until early 1973 and thereafter received five-spoke alloy wheels – as did all Stags from 1975.

Suspension on the Stag followed that of the parent saloons, with struts at the front and an independent coil-sprung semi-trailing rear, but with the addition of a front anti-roll bar. Large 10.6in front disc brakes arrested the Stag's considerable weight, aided by 9in rear drums and a vacuum servo.

Production began in March 1970 for a June launch. On paper the Stag's specification looked superb and at a UK tax-paid price of around £2,250, depending on extras, it did indeed handsomely undercut any continental competition. Even before any test results were published, a waiting list built up, despite the surprising fact that the vast majority of the first year's production was for the UK market.

Before long several of the authoritative magazines had received Stags for test and all applauded Triumph for trying to provide something really different. But was it a sports car, a grand tourer, a boulevard cruiser? Nobody seemed able to decide, and those who saw the Stag as

a sports car and treated it as such were destined to be disappointed. Surely they missed the point? Those who viewed it as a relaxed long-distance cruiser, with a surprising turn of speed if pressed, got it right, for that is what the Stag really was – and is – all about. Much criticism was directed at what was seen as over-light and vague power steering and too-soft rear suspension, but everyone loved the engine's splendid V8 burble and the way that it would rev right round the clock. Wind noise was criticised, whether with the hardtop or the hood in place, while rear-seat accommodation was felt too restricted; in fairness it is definitely possible for two normal-sized adults to occupy the rear.

As to performance, again reading the reports one senses a slight tinge of disappointment which is hardly fair. A 0–60mph time of ten seconds, with 100mph coming up in half a minute, is hardly slow even today, and fully wound-up a Stag with overdrive could just touch 120mph. Because of the high 6500rpm rev limit, speeds in the gears were unusually high, too. It was generally agreed that the fuel consumption of around 23–25mpg was very reasonable given the car's

Driving the Stag

The character of the Stag is dominated by that splendid V8, and one finds oneself revving the engine needlessly just to hear it. As well as sounding good, the engine produces plenty of power. Acceleration is not startling but certainly rapid enough, and does not disgrace this heavy 30-year-old car in the modern-traffic grand prix. The pull in top gear is especially impressive and even after slipping into overdrive there is still some muscle left for acceleration.

The expected notchy gearchange is present and the clutch is heavier than one is used to on modern cars. On the move the car rides very

comfortably and feels quite softly sprung. The power steering is disconcertingly light and until you have the gauge of it you are unsure exactly what the front wheels are doing. Once you have its measure it is surprising how fast you can hack the car along on give-and-take roads, but this is not really what the Stag is about: it is more long-legged grand tourer than nervous sports car.

On a motorway the Stag is more in its element, and cruises beautifully at 80mph in a most relaxing fashion and both the car and driver can keep this up all day despite the inevitable wind noise and back-draught. Brakes are reassuringly powerful and quite as

good as most modern cars.

The basketweave plastic seats are comfortable enough, but the material inevitably feels outdated and sticky – no surprise that some owners give their car a full retrim in leather. As for the rear seats, someone of average height would be able to occupy the seats without discomfort for at least a couple of hours, if not for all day.

The whole car strikes one as more modern both in looks and in feel than its years. My brief drive simply made me want a Stag again and wonder why I have been without one for so long – clearly it is a car still capable of everyday year-round use.

weight and speed, and the whole package was felt to be good value for money.

As the writer can personally testify, the Stag is a car of which one grows fonder the more it is driven, so a quick road test will never initially impress. An alternative longer-term view was given in *Autocar* by its publishing director, who after a year's ownership and 13,000 miles emphatically confirmed that with hindsight he would still have bought a Stag – a car he found relaxed and relaxing to live with but which could be readily wound up to give a lively burst of acceleration.

Unfortunately the production Stags had not been on the roads long before problems occurred. The author well recalls in the early 1970s seeing cars stranded on verges enveloped in steam and being eyed disconsolately

by their owners, made all too well aware that overheating was the Stag's Achilles Heel.

The radiator's capacity to cool the V8 was marginal at best. Unless a very close eye were kept on the temperature, any loss of coolant – or use of the wrong type – caused a rapidly escalating cooling problem that could easily culminate in warped aluminium cylinder heads and a very expensive repair, either for Triumph or the owner, depending on whether the warranty had expired. In export markets with hot climates the problem was of course worse.

Stretching timing chains was another ill – these needed to be replaced at 25,000 miles, but some were failing even before that mileage. If the chains were not changed the cam timing could jump, with catastrophic results. It is said that

A Stag in its final 1976–77 form, with alloy five-spoke wheels and polished sill-finishing panels. In its seven-year life the Stag changed remarkably little – but went through 35 different paint colours, some being very rare indeed.

three-quarters of all Stags sold in the US suffered from valvegear maladies, and if this is only half true it must have cost the company a fortune in warranty claims work to say nothing of the poor reputation engendered.

These two failings gave the Stag such a poor reputation that within two years of its launch owners were already fitting alternative engines in a desperate attempt to make the car what it should have been. Piston and bearing problems also occurred, and advertisements for Stags for sale with blown-up engines became commonplace. It was a public-

Re-engined Stags

The Stag's engine maladies meant that within a few years of its launch desperate owners were looking for alternative power units that could be made to fit, and quite a cottage industry of Stag conversion firms developed. One engine that would of course fit easily was Triumph's own 2½-litre straight-six as used in the big saloons and the TR6 – not surprisingly as the car was initially designed around this engine. The 'six' mated easily to the Stag's TR6-derived transmission, but even in its most highly tuned TR5 form, the six-cylinder engine could not equal the creamy torque-rich power delivery of the Stag's V8. Provided, however, that ultimate performance wasn't sought, the 'six' was a good conversion, with the added bonus of retaining the car's integrity as a Triumph.

One engine that produced roughly the same amount of torque as the V8 was Ford's cast-iron 3-litre V6 as used in the Granada and Capri. It was also compact, and so fitted the available space easily, and had the advantages of cheap spares, easy servicing and proven reliability. A special bellhousing was made to mate it to the Stag gearbox although some Ford V6s were installed complete with their own automatic transmission. It was however a heavy engine, and upset the Stag's handling by promoting understeer.

By far the most widely used engine was the all-aluminium 3½-litre Rover V8. This produced the car that many felt the Stag should have been all along – indeed there is a strong argument that had the Stag been given the Rover unit from the start it would not have had its reputation destroyed by engine woes, and would have sold much better and maybe even remained in production for many years longer.

There were problems, though: the Rover V8 was bigger than the Stag

unit and in common with some other conversions required both a bonnet bulge (a sure sign of a converted Stag) and the radiator being repositioned. It was also much lighter, and this caused handling difficulties, provoking front-end lift at speed and a degree of wander unless modifications were made to the suspension. Many owners fitted the Rover engine complete with its automatic transmission, but it could also be mated to the Stag manual gearbox – although this could only just handle the Rover V8's greatly increased torque. Alternatively the manual 'box of the 3500S could be fitted, or the the later SD1 engine and its related five-speed gearbox.

A further snag that afflicted all conversions was caused by the Stag V8's high 6500rpm rev limit. With its 3.7-to-1 rear axle ratio, the Stag had been geared to take account of this level of revolutions, but the engines used for conversion all revved lower, the Rover for instance having a 5200rpm limit. As a result, to achieve a truly successful conversion the Stag's axle ratio needed raising to the 3.45-to-1 used in the TR6 which inevitably increased the cost and complication of the job.

In the US a good many cars received American small-block V8s

and a number of other engines were tried in Stags over the years, even a diesel or two. However, the whole episode now tends to be history, for in modern times the trend has been for Stags to be re-converted to their correct engines in the name of originality.

Now that Triumph's V8 can be made fully reliable and the cars are for the most part in the hands of enthusiasts, this is obviously a sensible route to take – even if there are not enough genuine Stag V8s to go around, as so many were scrapped years ago when they expired. This led to scruffy Stags being raided simply for their power units, with the rest of the car being scrapped as not worth the cost of restoring. Proving the new-found reliability of the Triumph engine, one specialist, Hart Racing Services, produced a full-house racing Stag with a highly-tuned 220bhp power unit.

In conclusion, one is left wondering at just how good a 'factory' Stag with a Rover SD1 engine and a five-speed gearbox would have been, had BL knuckled under and developed such a car. Pretty good, the author can't help thinking…

The unique V8 engine (never used in any other model) is crowned by twin Stromberg carburettors.

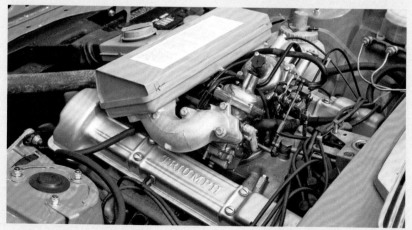

Right: The Stag's luxurious interior was never bettered on a Triumph; the instruments – always a Triumph strong point – are a model of clarity.

Below: The hardtop is a very substantial affair and is definitely not a one-man job to lift. A heated rear window is included.

Buying Hints

1. The inner body usually survives well, and rot in the main rails under the body is rare, but the outriggers and the crossmember under the radiator both rust, as does the cradle for the differential. Look too at the top of the rear damper mountings. The bottoms of the A-posts and front floors are also susceptible, as are the structural sills – so beware of polished sill covers hiding rust.

2. The outer wings, front and rear valances and the headlamp panel are rot-spots; check the wheelarches carefully, too, as filler is common here. Doors rot at their bases, both the skins and the frames, and the windscreen frame should also be checked. A place often missed is the floor of the hood well, which can rust through as a result of the hood being folded away damp. The rear edge of the boot lid rusts, as does the boot floor.

3. The hardtop is steel, and can also rust: examine the bottom edges for corrosion. Another perhaps unexpected point to check is the petrol tank, which can rust, and is hard to replace.

4. Virtually all body panels are available, making replacement possible if not cheap. Post-1973 Stags are significantly more rustprone than earlier examples.

5. All the engine shortcomings can be overcome. The V8 will still need more than average attention though,

and must always be run with a correct corrosion-inhibiting anti-freeze coolant. Not to do so will soon lead to corroded and warped cylinder heads, and this is twice as expensive as normal as there are two heads on a V8 engine. Silted-up radiators and leaking water pumps also cause overheating. Uprated pumps and radiators will assist, but a normal system in top condition should work properly.

6. Oily water in the expansion bottle and gurgling sounds when running are sure signs of impending trouble.

7. The engine should run quietly with no tapping or clicking sounds. If you remove the oil filler cap it should slow down or stall – if not, the carburettor breather pipes are leaking.

8. Timing chains have a life of only 20,000-30,000 miles: rattling at hot idle is a sure sign of wear. Not to renew them is to invite slipped timing and a big bang…

9. The original ignition system is difficult to keep in tune and most cars now have a much superior electronic system.

10. Rumbling from a hot engine when blipping the throttle to 3500rpm is a sure sign of main-bearing wear, bearings being a further weakness of the Stag engine. That said, a well-built engine should cover 100,000 miles with no trouble

– although if the crankshaft hasn't been properly hardened 1,000 miles will be nearer the mark.

11. Gearboxes are pretty bulletproof, the auto being particularly strong and reliable. Overdrive problems are usually just down to faulty electric controls.

12. A whining differential indicates wear, but in general the final drive is strong and durable. Driveshafts are long-lasting if to the manufacturer's specification, but beware of cheaper imitations.

13. Suspension rubbers need regular renewal and can produce mysterious knockings if worn. Polyurethane replacements are available. Poor handling could be nothing more than worn trailing-arm bushes.

14. The power steering is light, but if it is over-light the spool valve in the rack will have failed. Don't forget that to change a Stag's battery partial dismantling of the power steering system is necessary – yes, really – so a strong battery is a plus point.

15. Seats can sag badly and this is not easy to cure. The interior is expensive to restore: some trim materials cannot be sourced and a number of rebuilt cars have thus been re-trimmed in leather. Beware also misaligned hoods and bent hood frames.

relations and an engineering disaster that should never have been allowed to occur, but which was alas to become symptomatic of British Leyland. The engine was simply not ready to be sold to the public and sadly it was the buyers who had to complete the

development process. When owned by a careful enthusiast the Stag could prove perfectly reliable, but it was simply not ready for everyday service with the average owner.

Nor was this all, for perennial quality-control problems at the

Liverpool plant caused other irritations. Badly-fitting and leaking hoods, drooping doors, non-functioning electric windows and various electrical gremlins were common, especially on the earliest cars. It got so bad that production was halted altogether in late 1970, for two months, whilst procedures were improved. To be fair, later Stags were significantly better in virtually all respects, but the damage to the car's reputation had been done, the model never fully recovering. Things got so bad in the States that by 1973 the car was unsaleable, and was withdrawn from the US market at the end of that year.

Despite all its difficulties, the Stag gained a loyal following in the UK. There was indeed nothing else quite like it, especially at the price, and a coterie of owners persevered with their Stags, some purchasing two or even three cars during the model's seven-year currency. Subsequent developments have countered the engine and cooling problems, and today a well-maintained Stag, suitably endowed with a larger-capacity radiator and a more efficient water pump, is a delightful classic – although it will not tolerate abuse.

The Triumph Stag stayed in production virtually unchanged until July 1977, there unsurprisingly being no replacement. During those seven years it was given only cosmetic improvements, firstly when the MkII version arrived in February 1973. This featured an increase in compression ratio to 9.25-to-1, and together with modified cylinder heads and pistons gave a modest power increase; additionally a more modern J-type overdrive replaced the old A-type. Externally there was a new range of colours, a double coachline, matt-black sills with a beaded edge, a matt-black tail panel, slightly different wheel trims and badges, and stronger bumper mountings. The instruments were restyled, a smaller steering wheel arrived, and there was an intermittent wiper setting, a driver's footrest, and provision for headrests, while a courtesy light was fitted into the underside of the T-bar. Options included alloy wheels, Sundym glass, a laminated windscreen and headrests.

The only other slight revamp occurred in October 1975, for the 1976 model year: polished extruded-aluminium sill finishers were fitted and five-spoke alloy wheels, Sundym glass and a laminated screen now became standard. A grand total of 25,877 cars are believed to have been built, of which 8,120 – just under a third – were exported, with 17,757 remaining as home-market sales, a reversal of the usual position with Triumph products.

Given the Stag's traumas, Triumph's unique V8 never had the wider use for which it was intended, it being originally conceived for use in the large saloons as well. Several prototype V8 'Innsbruck' saloons were built, and there was also at least one 2500 estate car fitted with the Stag V8: by all accounts this was a superb vehicle, much in demand by Triumph management who valued its Q-car performance. What a shame they did not see fit to release a production version to the public once the engine was sorted.

This late car with hardtop carries the optional alloy wheels so often found on surviving cars.

The TR7 and TR8

One of the early design sketches for the TR7 produced at Longbridge by Harris Mann. The car as finally produced bears a striking resemblance to this sketch.

What can one call the always controversial TR7 but an enigma? Was it a proper TR or – as some suggested – a Dolomite coupé? The TR7 had nothing in common with its predecessors except the TR name, and even 30 years later it is not accepted by many in the TR or Triumph fraternities. The jury is still out on the question of its styling: you either love it or hate it, although many initial detractors were mollified when the convertible version came along five years later. Whatever one's feelings about the car, the fact is that more were made than any previous model of TR, by many thousands, and today it has a loyal following, particularly in V8 form.

As with the Stag, the TR7 had the misfortune to be developed and produced during the dark days of the British Leyland empire and as a result many aspects of its history owe more to internal factory politics than to engineering. It was not a bad car, but it was often badly put together. It was also strikingly different, and perhaps too different for many customers. How did it all happen?

In the late 1960s work began on a new generation of Triumph sports cars, a two-seater with lift-out roof panels, codenamed Bullet, and a fastback two-plus-two coupé coded Lynx. The initial idea was that Lynx should go on sale in 1972, about a year before Bullet. However, after prototypes had been made, for the time being the promising Lynx was sidelined, leaving Bullet to carry on as Triumph's sole future sports car. It was to be as simple a car as possible, in reaction to previous Triumph sophistications such as independent rear suspension and fuel injection, and would have a rigid Toledo-type rear axle, carburettors, and a plain four-speed transmission. The 'slant-four' Saab/Dolomite overhead-cam engine was to be the power unit, but enlarged to a full 2-litre capacity.

By early 1971 the mechanical details were settled and the car could possibly have been on sale by 1973. But there were still uncertainties over the styling, which was felt too bland. At this point Harry Webster happened to mention to Harris Mann, in charge of styling at Austin-Morris, that the design of the proposed new Triumph was still not finalised. Mann duly submitted his own thoughts in the form of sketches of a wedged-shaped fixed-head coupé with concealed headlamps. It was more than modern – it was verging on the futuristic. The top brass at British Leyland liked this revolutionary design so much that Triumph's own proposal, honed by Michelotti, was passed over, as was an alternative by freelance William Towns.

By this time it was quite obvious that British Leyland was making too many sports models, and that rationalisation was essential. Work on

a putative new mid-engined MG having been abandoned, it was suggested that Bullet should also appear as an MG – with revised styling – to replace the MGB. This never happened, of course.

It still seemed very likely that US legislation would outlaw open cars altogether, hence British Leyland

resolved to make only a fixed-head version of Bullet, to be manufactured in unprecedentedly large numbers in the modern Speke plant; a long-wheelbase 2+2 Lynx was expected to follow. Launch of the US version of the TR7 – as it was to be called – was given priority and set for January 1975, the rest of the world having to wait more

TR7
1974–81

ENGINE:
Four cylinders in line, cast-iron block and alloy head

Capacity	1998cc
Bore x stroke	90.3mm x 78mm
Valve actuation	Single overhead cam
Compression ratio	9.25:1
	8.0:1 (US)
Fuel system	Twin SU carbs
	Twin Stromberg carbs (US)
	Fuel injection (late US cars)
Power	105bhp (DIN) at 5500rpm
	92bhp (DIN) at 5000rpm (US)
Maximum torque	119lb ft at 3500rpm
	115lb ft at 3500rpm (US)

TRANSMISSION:
Rear-wheel drive; four-speed, all-synchromesh gearbox. Optional five-speed gearbox (later standard) or automatic transmission

SUSPENSION:
Front: Independent by MacPherson strut and anti-roll bar
Rear: Live rear axle with coil springs, radius arms; anti-roll bar; telescopic dampers

STEERING:
Rack-and-pinion

BRAKES:
Front: Disc
Rear: Drum
Servo assistance

WHEELS/TYRES:
Steel disc or alloy wheels
Tyres 175 x 13in or 185/70 x 13in

DIMENSIONS:
Length	13ft 4in
	13ft 8.5in (US)
Wheelbase	7 ft 1in
Track, front	4ft 7.5in
Track, rear	4ft 7.3in
Width	5ft 6in
Height	4ft 2in

KERB WEIGHT:
19.7cwt (coupé)
21.1cwt (convertible)

PERFORMANCE (convertible):
(Source: *Autocar*)
Max speed	114mph
0–60mph	10.7sec
30–50mph in top	11.3sec
50–70mph in top	12.4sec

PRICE INCLUDING TAX WHEN NEW:
£3,000 (coupé, May 1976)
£5,959 (convertible, March 1980)

NUMBER BUILT:
112,368*

TR8
1979–81

As for TR7 five-speed except:

ENGINE:
V8, aluminium cylinder block and aluminium cylinder heads
Capacity	3528cc
Bore x stroke	88.9mm x 71.1mm
Valve actuation	Single central camshaft
Compression ratio	8.1:1
Fuel system	Twin Stromberg carbs
	Fuel injection (Californian and 1981 cars)
Power	133bhp (DIN) at 5000rpm
	137bhp (DIN) at 5000rpm (Californian cars)
Maximum torque	174lb ft at 3000rpm (carbs)
	168lb ft at 3250rpm (injection)

WHEELS/TYRES:
Alloy 13in wheels
Tyres 185/70 x 13in

STEERING:
Rack-and-pinion, power-assisted

PERFORMANCE:
(Source: *Road & Track*)
Max speed	120mph
0–60mph	8.4sec

NUMBER BUILT:
2,722*

*see page 173

Special TR7s and 'might have beens'

Left: The surviving late 1970s Lynx prototype is seen resplendent in Java Green; a V8 Rover SD1 engine is installed. The huge black rear bumpers do nothing for the car's looks.

Centre: Two versions of the aborted Broadside concept – on the left is the fastback coupé, and on the right the 2+2 open car. Both are based on the TR8 and both survive in the BMIHT collection at Gaydon.

Bottom: The unique Crayford-converted 'estate' TR7 caught at a car show in later years. (TR Register Archive)

The idea of a fastback 2+2 coupé, codenamed Lynx, goes back to the original Triumph styling exercises of 1969–71 and was revived as part of the Harris Mann family of designs. Eventually it was decided that a TR7-based Lynx would enter production in 1978, powered by the Rover V8; built on a wheelbase extended by 11in, it featured a lift-up tailgate and split fold-down rear seats, and did away with the TR7's controversial side swage in favour of horizontal scalloping. Rear accommodation was good for a coupé and at least on a par with that of the Stag, for which the Lynx was alleged to be a potential replacement.

A number of prototypes were built, one of which survives. But like so much at that time, the project ran aground as BL fought for its survival. Lynx would have been built at Speke, and the closure of the troublesome and unviable Liverpool plant saw the project cancelled; in any case, there were doubts about the model's likely appeal in the key US market.

This was not quite the end for the concept though, as in 1979–80 a 2+2 coupé was looked at in the context of a project called Broadside, which envisaged a restyled TR7/TR8 on a 4in longer wheelbase, using the Lynx doors. If anything this effort looked even more bland than the Lynx, and was certainly no replacement for the elegant Stag.

One private attempt at providing a TR7 with a load-carrying rear was built by Crayford to the order of Page Motors Ltd. A TR7 was converted to have an estate-car back with a full lift-up tailgate and folding adult-sized rear seating, rather on the lines of Reliant's Scimitar GTE or the Lynx Eventer based on the Jaguar XJ-S. Sadly though, the conversion was not as attractive visually as either of these. As a result the planned production run never materialised and only the one car, known as a TR7 Tracer, was built. As always with such conversions, cost was a factor – this spiritual successor to the GTR4 Dové would simply have been too expensive.

One TR7/TR8 conversion that did see a good number built over a lengthy period was that by Grinnall. These conversions were even officially recognised by British Leyland and were sometimes performed on brand-new cars. Major bodywork alterations included 11 modified panels, a restyled front and rear, widened wings with flared arches, sill extensions, and the removal usually of the unloved swage line from the bodywork. A deep front spoiler and wide alloy wheels complemented these beefed-up looks. Although some Grinnalls remained as TR7s, the majority were given a full TR8 mechanical conversion as well, often with uprated V8s producing well in excess of 200bhp. In such cases rear axle location was improved by adding a Watts linkage and/or torque tube. A luxurious interior retrim in leather with an optional polished walnut dashboard was complemented by a top-quality mohair hood. There were numerous individual options and accessories an owner could commission for a Grinnall conversion, with the result that no two cars were the same. The company succeeded in giving the TR7/TR8 convertible a much more modern and attractive look and had TR production continued British Leyland could have done well by adopting many of the Grinnall's features. Cars with the full Grinnall conversion, especially V8s, are highly sought-after today – but because of the car's highly individual nature and the fact that second-hand cars were often converted, it is not possible to be sure exactly how many were built.

than a year until May 1976. This meant that in the UK, where the TR6 was withdrawn in spring 1975, a whole year passed with no TR being available.

The transformation of Mann's avant-garde concept into production reality was less than happy, not helped by huge black plastic-covered impact bumpers – those on US cars in addition having moulded-in over-riders at the rear. Nor did the plain steel wheels with their matt-black hubcaps do much to lift the body's controversial styling with its pronounced swage along the flanks and ribbed-plastic rear-pillar

Above: US-spec cars have side marker lights and over-riders on the rear bumper.

Below: A rare car now is the original four-speed coupé as introduced on the home market in spring 1976. To the writer's eye the car is too wide in relation to its length.

trim. At least the high-tailed lines allowed a capacious boot – which was just as well in view of the lack of interior space.

The TR7 used a 1998cc version of the eight-valve Dolomite engine, mated to the Dolomite/Marina four-

speed all-synchro gearbox; there was no overdrive option, but an automatic was offered although few were sold. The rear axle – with a ratio of 3.63-to-1 which made the car hopelessly undergeared and fussy – was suspended on coil springs and located by radius arms and an anti-roll bar. At the front, the suspension, which was meant to have been shared with the stillborn SD2, was by struts controlled by an anti-roll bar, while the steering was unassisted rack-and-pinion. Brakes, servo-assisted, were 9.7in discs at the front with 8in rear drums.

As installed in non-US cars the engine used twin SU carburettors and produced 105bhp on a 9.25-to-1 compression ratio, with 119lb ft of torque at 3500rpm. The Federal version with all the emission-control equipment, Stromberg carburettors, and an 8.0-to-1 compression ratio, turned out a puny 92bhp, further eroded by the air conditioning fitted to many cars. As the Federal TR6 before it, the US-market TR7 was not fast, strangled as it was by anti-

pollution legislation. Performance of the rest-of-world TR7, however, was about on a par with the detuned 125bhp TR6, and brisk enough to be fun but a long way behind the TR5 of nearly ten years previously. A conscious attempt was made to provide an up-to-the-minute and comfortable interior, although unlike all previous TRs there was no possibility of squeezing children, small adults, or luggage into the rear: it was strictly a two-seater, and there was very little space behind the TR7's brushed-nylon seats.

British Leyland corporate switchgear and controls were used, there was a full set of clearly legible instruments, and an excellent heating and ventilation system was installed – fortunately, as the compact interior could get somewhat claustrophobic unless specified with the optional fabric sunroof. Federal models were burdened with a steering wheel with a grotesque central crash pad whereas other TR7s had a distinctly tacky-looking wheel with moulded plastic spokes – the 1970s were not

renowned as an era of good taste...

With hindsight, the TR7 coupé was a brave but misguided attempt at providing something sporting yet totally new and different from its predecessors. Had the car been built as a drophead right from the start things might have turned out differently. Looking at contemporary road test reports it is obvious that there was general disappointment at the lack of an open version, but that was not BL's fault given the legislative climate of the times. Rereading those first tests it is clear there was dismay at what was seen as technical regression, in abandoning independent rear suspension and fuel injection; there were also criticisms of the loss of space behind the seats, and a general feeling that the car was undergeared and could do with either overdrive or a five-speed transmission. It was also regretted that the car was too quiet, and sounded more like a saloon than a sports car.

On the positive side the TR7 was felt to be the most comfortable and convenient TR yet, with the driving

The TR7 Sprint

This more rapid TR7 would have been a sort of halfway-house to the TR8. It is a car that has always caused controversy, in particular concerning how many were made and why it never became a production model. Given that the TR7 was already using the bottom end of the 1998cc Dolomite Sprint engine, it seemed natural that the next step would be to offer the full 127bhp Sprint engine in the TR7. This is indeed what was always planned. Several promising prototypes were made and in early 1977 authority was given for a pre-production batch of cars to be constructed. It is thought that around 60 TR7 Sprints were made, in three separate batches. There was even a proper driver's handbook produced – the author having one of these in his collection – and the car was

scheduled to enter production in mid-1977.

All cars were of course fixed-head coupés and all had the five-speed gearbox and stronger rear axle from the Rover SD1. A number were in left-hand-drive form, though none actually reached the USA. Larger brakes of the kind being developed for the TR8 were used and there were minor modifications to the suspension settings. By all accounts it was an excellent car, capable of 120mph and 0–60 mph in 8.5 seconds, but it unfortunately collided with the labour troubles at Speke and was shelved before any true production examples had been built.

At first the delay was said to be temporary, but when TR7 production restarted at Canley nearly

a year later, there was no sign of the TR7 Sprint: effort instead was concentrated on productionising the convertible and the TR8. None of the 60 or so Sprints were sold as new cars through official channels, but many of them did reach customers after having been used first as management, demonstration or development vehicles. British Leyland officially denied that the cars even existed but fortunately for owners they were an amalgam of existing Triumph parts, so service presented few difficulties.

A number of Sprints have survived but potential buyers should always be cautious as a fair few eight-valve TR7s have had the 16-valve engine inserted over the years. A genuine TR7 Sprint should have a chassis number with the prefix ACH.

Right: The cockpit of the home market coupé TR7 as introduced in May 1976. Brushed nylon seats are in evidence along with a particularly nasty design of steering wheel.

Below: The production TR7 convertible as built at Canley in early 1980. The hood tucks away very neatly, and alloy wheels are standard.

position, controls, instruments, and the standard of the interior fitments generally being liked. There was good if not tremendous performance, particularly if the potentially excellent fuel economy was taken into account, and the roadholding and general handling were much admired – proving that a well-located rigid rear axle could be at least as good as many of the independent rear suspensions available, while avoiding extra cost and complication. It was felt that the chassis could definitely handle more power but in the meantime the TR7 as a package was judged good value.

The major criticism made was dealt with at least partially in later 1976 when a five-speed option was introduced. This used the gearbox newly developed for the Rover SD1 saloon, the only problem being that the company could not make enough of them. This shortage led to the five-speed option being withdrawn from non-US markets in December 1976 just a few months after it had arrived, but it soon became standard in the US – and

eventually reappeared as an option for other markets in October 1977. This was more theoretical than real, however, because very few cars were then being made, as the Liverpool plant had been on strike for months...

It was only when, after the most appalling labour problems in Liverpool, the whole TR7 production

Special-edition TR7s

The late 1970s were the pioneer days of limited-edition models, a car-selling ruse that became more popular in the '80s and '90s. Triumph was in early with six different special TR7s, four for the US and two for the home market. First off, in July 1976, was the Southern Skies model. This was only offered in the southern states of the US and featured factory-fitted air conditioning and a bronze-tinted glass sliding sunroof. Twin side-stripes were added, plus special 'Southern Skies' decals. An unknown number were made. The TR7 Victory edition followed closely and was sold throughout the US. Equipment included a set of white-painted six-

In their desperate efforts to shift TR7s, British Leyland in the US confected several limited editions, among them this Victory Edition, which sported a spray-on vinyl roof, so-called racing stripes, and 'competition-type spoked wheels'. (Jon Pressnell collection)

spoke steel wheels which proved prone to cracking, necessitating their early replacement, and a spray-on vinyl roof, along with bold black triple striping running along the rear wings, across the tops of the doors and finally across the bonnet in front of the windscreen. It is thought that as many as 3,500 of these Victory models were made – hardly a limited edition!

The TR7 Premium was again only on the fixed-head coupé and emanated from Canley in the winter of 1979–80. Four hundred were built for the UK market, all in black with either silver or gold side-striping. Alloy wheels, halogen headlights, twin driving lamps, twin rear fog lamps, a front spoiler (not yet a standard fitting on ordinary TR7s) and a folding fabric sunroof marked the car out externally, while plaid cloth seats in navy or tan, a radio/cassette unit, and a Moto-Lita steering wheel upgraded the interior.

Before this model an unknown but small number of Jubilee TR7s had been made in 1977 to celebrate Queen Elizabeth's silver jubilee. Alterations were very modest, running only to jazzy striped seats and double striping along the car's flanks.

The first limited-edition convertible TR7 was the Thirtieth Anniversary model built at Canley in 1979 for the US. Supposedly celebrating 30 years of Triumph roadsters, starting with the never-produced TRX of 1950, this essentially phoney exercise gave the buyer $900-worth of

extras all for the same price as the standard car. These included side pinstriping, polished aluminium trim rings on hubcap-less wheels, a stereo radio/cassette, front fog lamps, a chromed boot rack, a padded black leather-covered steering wheel, coconut matting for the floors, and a Union Flag dash plaque. Again it is not known how many such cars were built.

The final TR7 limited edition was the Spider, 1,200 of these dolled-up convertibles being built at Canley in 1980. The great majority were sold in the US, but a few reached other export markets. The Spider had black paintwork with a red laurel front decal, red side-striping, and the word 'Spider' in red ahead of the rear wheels. Alloy wheels, a radio/cassette and air conditioning were provided, as was a leather-covered steering wheel. Pewter grey seats with darker striping distinguished the interior as did a black-moulded dashboard.

Inevitably, with all these special editions the fancy bits were mainly cosmetic and frequently failed to survive resprays, accidents and general wear and tear. Thus original examples are rare now and command something of a premium over a normal TR7.

Perhaps the most special of all TR7s were the three especially narrow convertibles built for the restricted-width roads of the isle of Bermuda. These cars had 6in cut out lengthwise from their centre, something that must have been a major and expensive job. Other TR7 oddities included cars built in special finishes as advertising tools or competition prizes for major companies. Levi Strauss and Coca Cola both commissioned these, while the unique Sheaffer TRZ was a fixed-head TR7 given the full Wood and Pickett luxury treatment for use as a competition prize.

WE BEAT THE STRIPES OFF OUR COMPETITION.

THE TRIUMPH TR7
VICTORY EDITION
FREE Spoiler Wheels
FREE Vinyl Roof
FREE Racing Stripes

AT CHARLOTTE, LIME ROCK, BRIDGEHAMPTON, POCONO, NELSON LEDGES AND PUEBLO, TR7 IS THE SHAPE THAT WON.

TRIUMPH
TR7

THE SHAPE OF THINGS THAT WIN

Right: A late convertible shows the greatly improved trim of the later cars

Bottom: This is a genuine pre-production rhd TR8 convertible – complete with power steering as standard.

line was transferred to Coventry in October 1978 that the five-speed gearbox properly reappeared, this time as a standard fitment. Five-speed TR7s also received the stronger SD1 rear axle, which had a 3.9-to-1 ratio, along with low-profile tyres and larger rear brakes – all of which improved the car no end. In March 1977, meanwhile, the car was given lowered suspension, revised wheel trims and some supposedly fashionable tartan interior trim.

This was possibly British Leyland's most turbulent period. The Liverpool-built TR7 gained a terrible reputation for poor quality and continual strikes ultimately led to the entire plant being shut down in May 1978. The TR7 was lucky to survive at all, but when production restarted at Canley in October 1978 quality thereafter improved greatly. Canley-built cars were recognisable by a laurel-wreath nose transfer and revised badging.

It was at this period that frantic work was going on behind the scenes at Canley to develop the TR7 convertible now that the threatened US legislation had not materialised. To convert the monocoque shell entailed major re-engineering to avoid scuttle

shake and preserve rigidity: even the bumper mounts on the convertible were structurally different from those of the coupé. All this took time and it was only in summer 1979 that the convertible was launched in the US, with other markets having to wait until February 1980.

At last the TR7 had become the car it should always have been. Above all, the convertible TR7 looked infinitely better than the fixed-head version and this soon showed in the sales figures, those for the closed car tailing off to almost zero by the end of production. The convertible's hood proved weathertight and not too noisy at speed, the relaxed cruising now available in fifth gear aiding comfort, as did upgraded seats and trim materials. In an attempt to

promote the closed car, in March 1980 it was given a sunroof, alloy wheels, halogen headlamps, and a radio/cassette unit as standard; sales, however, still dwindled.

The wait for the V8-powered TR8 was even more exasperating – and when it finally arrived it proved to be for North America only, although a few development and publicity cars did escape to the home market.

The TR8 had a chequered history, first appearing in Speke-made 'pilot-build' form as early as the first half of 1977 – as a fixed-head, the convertible then being two years in the future. What happened was that in the wake of the Speke closure a batch of trial-production TR8s was sent over to the US for evaluation and demonstration.

The works rally TR7s and TR7 V8s

British Leyland had always envisaged that the new TR could be a rally winner and to this end the TR7 was homologated as early as October 1975 – before the car was even on sale in Europe. Not only that, but some judicious rule bending saw it homologated with the Dolomite Sprint's 16-valve head and its overdrive gearbox, plus a heavy-duty Salisbury rear axle that never appeared in a production TR7.

The cars were prepared at the corporate competition department at Abingdon. Tony Pond was newly engaged to drive one TR7, with old BL hand Brian Culcheth having the other, the cars first appearing on May 1976's Welsh Rally amid much over-blown publicity.

Running on twin Weber carburettors, the 16-valve engines produced a reliable 180bhp or so in Group One form and the cars were fast in a straight line. But much work needed to be done on handling, suspension, transmission and brakes; in truth the TRs were not yet ready to rally, but pressure from British Leyland's management and from an over-zealous publicity machine prevailed. In the Welsh Rally both cars rapidly blew up their engines and exactly the same thing happened on the Scottish Rally the next month – a most inauspicious start.

Fortunately the Manx Rally in September was an all-tarmac event and – as was soon obvious – the TR7 was much more competitive on hard surfaces than on the loose stuff in forests. Both cars finished at third and fifth overall and when combined with the sole Dolomite Sprint entry this enabled Triumph to win the team prize. Development of the cars continued and reliability improved, but the power was not there for victory in a major event. In November 1976's RAC Rally, Culcheth finally managed to finish ninth after his car had consumed three gearboxes, but

A works TR7 driven by Tony Pond, here on its way to a second place overall in 1977's Scottish Rally. These cars were generally at their best on tarmac events.

Pond had to retire with rear suspension maladies.

For 1977 John Davenport became British Leyland's director of motorsport and great things were expected. A full programme of 12 events was planned and rear disc brakes were finally ready. In addition work had commenced on making the V8 engine rally-worthy. Highlights of the year included Pond finishing first overall on the Belgian Boucles de Spa event, third in the Mintex Rally, third in the Tour of Elba, second on the Scottish Rally and eighth on the RAC event. Brian Culcheth's best result was second overall on the Manx Rally.

By this stage the 16-valve TR7s had done pretty well, but not outstandingly so, as there were still too many mechanical failures, with neither the engine nor gearbox proving totally reliable. When the cars held together, and particularly on road events, they were in contention, but two full seasons of development had yet to make them the potential world champions the pre-launch publicity had promised. The

Abingdon team was much derided in the motoring press and even patriotic enthusiasts were sceptical that the TRs would ever fully come good.

Finally, in April 1978, the TR7 V8 was homologated (prematurely as it turned out) and the much-needed power boost was at last available. The V8 engine ran on twin Weber carburettors on an American Offenhauser manifold, giving a reliable 270bhp–280bhp, with bags of torque. A close-ratio gearbox and the new SD1 axle were fitted, and not surprisingly the V8 was considerably quicker than the TR7 Sprint.

Tony Pond was the only contracted driver for 1978, other big names being hired as required and as available. The V8 TR started well, with Pond winning its first event outright, the Scottish Granite City Rally. In June 1978 came one of the best of all TR7/TR8 results when Pond won the Belgian Ypres Rally – a tarmac event ideally suited to the TR. Likewise the Manx Rally, which Pond also won outright although the second Abingdon car suffered an engine problem.

The main weakness in the cars by late 1978 was the gearbox, but when both entries retired from the Tour de Corse just after the start, each car having lost its gearbox drain-plug and oil, sabotage was the prime suspect – though this was never proven. Great things were expected of the TR in Britain's main event, the RAC Rally, in November. Three TR7 V8s were entered, for Pond, John Haughland and Simo Lampinen. The latter sadly retired with clutch failure but Pond managed to finish fourth behind the works Escorts, despite losing time when the handbrake linkage came adrift and locked a rear wheel. This was the TR's best-ever result in its home rally, bolstered by John Haughland bringing his car home twelfth.

Tony Pond left the team for Chrysler at the end of 1978, all the same, disillusioned after three seasons of trying to make the TR a world-beater. The team struggled on, and top Scandinavian drivers Eklund and Lampinen did much of the 1979 driving. The engines received Pierburg fuel injection, which gave them about 300bhp, but lack of suspension movement was still causing poor handling on rough non-tarmac events.

That year the best result was a second overall for Per Eklund on the Mintex Rally. On the Scottish he finished third, a position also achieved on the Manx event by team-driver Graham Elsmore. On the RAC Rally three out of the four V8s finished in the top 20, but the highest placing was Eklund at thirteenth. There were no first places at all in what was a relatively disappointing season with a great many engine failures and not a few accidents. The 300bhp TR7 V8 was not at all easy to handle on loose surfaces, and it showed.

What turned out to be Triumph's last year in motorsport was 1980 and for this season Davenport had not only signed up Roger Clark but Tony Pond also returned to the team. The cars were running on a four-Weber set-up rather than the injection of 1979 and although they still produced the same 300bhp the engine's torque was greatly improved.

Unfortunately the V8 continued to have problems with its lubrication system and not one TR finished in the first six events entered, most retiring with engine maladies. Finally, in June 1980, Pond managed to finish fourth overall in the Scottish Rally, with Roger Clark ninth.

Fortunes changed for the Ypres Rally where Tony Pond again won outright, with Eklund managing a third in the difficult Thousand Lakes Rally. Pond and his co-driver Fred Gallagher chalked up a further outright victory on the Manx Rally but other than these shining exceptions the dismal string of mechanical failures continued.

In the team's very last event, November 1980's RAC Rally, only one of the four TRs finished, Pond managing to come in seventh. Two retired from engine failure and one with a broken axle. The writer well recalls watching all the late 1970s RAC rallies in the Welsh forests and how eagerly enthusiasts awaited the TR7s, only to have hopes continually dashed by yet more mechanical failures.

Immediately after the RAC, the plug was pulled on MG's Abingdon factory and the competition department lost its home. Simultaneously, continued production of the TR7 and TR8 began to look doubtful and a top-level decision was taken to concentrate thereafter on the Rover 3500 for racing and the forthcoming Metro 6R4 for rallies. That, for Triumph, was that.

When they were going, the V8s were fast, noisy and spectacular – but they usually only went for limited periods. It was all a great shame, for with wholehearted management support such as Ford enjoyed, and with similar finance, the TR7 V8 could have been a top-class rally machine and the car to beat. On its day it could and did win but far more often than not it retired. It was not so much a 'might-have-been' as a 'nearly-was'.

One of the British Leyland works TR7s competing in the RAC Rally in 1978. By this time they were fitted with 280/300 bhp V8 engines.

The Group 44 racing TR7s and TR8s

Ever faithful to Triumph, the Group 44 team started the process of making the TR7 a competitive US racer as soon as cars were available, and for 1976 Sports Car Club of America racing the TR7 of Bob Tullius was tuned to give 170bhp. Uprated and much stiffer suspension, Koni dampers and competition brakes were added, and the car was lightened by removing all but essential equipment. Even in this state and with a top driver, the racing TR7 was not competitive enough for outright wins, but it proved very capable in SCCA Class D, winning an impressive ten races out of 12 starts in that class in 1976. A similar car was developed by the Huffaker organisation and this too proved competitive, taking on the TR7 racing mantle when Bob Tullius moved to an XJ-S in 1977. The Huffaker car eventually won the SCCA Class D Championship, proving that within the limits of its capacity the TR7 could indeed be made into a racing car.

When the TR8 became available for US racing, Bob Tullius and Group 44 took up the challenge and the car was modified to the limit of the regulations. The engine was taken to a full 4-litre capacity and given fuel injection based on that of the UK's TR7 V8 rally cars. In this form it produced 330bhp reliably, with even more available in a Sprint version. A special four-speed version of the usual gearbox was fitted, though with the fifth ratio removed, as it was not strong enough, while wheels,

suspension and brakes were of course modified to cope with the substantial power, tamed by a limited-slip differential. The TR8 racer proved a winner in the Trans Am racing series, but this led to the SCCA penalising the car to such an extent that Bob Tullius turned to the IMSA series – where again the TR8 proved sufficiently competitive to win.

Although rallying was primarily a European sport, the SCCA did run a rally series in the US in which John Buffum was a prime contender. His

Bob Tullius in his Group 44 TR7 at its racing debut in Charlotte, North Carolina.

private TR7 won the Pro-Rally series in 1977, following which he was offered a Triumph-US works drive for 1978 in the course of which he won no fewer than eight events. He continued the run of success in a 280bhp Huffaker-prepared TR8 in 1979 and 1980 and was also on occasion to be seen in European events at the wheel of one of the Abingdon-prepared works TR7 V8s.

Their construction may also have had something to do with homologation of the V8 engine for use in the Abingdon competition department's rally TR7s, for these were fast becoming prominent at the same time. These early TR8s had chassis numbers in the ACN series and something over 100 were made, the exact number being uncertain.

In spring 1979 Canley built a further series of fixed-head V8s, these having

TCN chassis number prefixes. Records indicate that 141 of these reached the US, with a further 63 in theory released to the home market, although this figure is doubtful and probably includes development and competition cars.

The convertible TR7 was released to the US market in the summer of 1979 but it was not until 1980 that any convertible TR8s reached the market. That year 2,088 examples were

delivered in the US and Canada, the only places where they were officially sold, and a further 405 TR8 convertibles were built for the 1981 model year, exclusively for the US. As for the UK, between 18 and 25 right-hand-drive TR8 convertibles are thought to have been built, most eventually being sold off. There are no records of any coupé TR8s being built by Solihull.

The TR8 was not just a TR7 with a

The V8 engine is a neat fit in the TR7's engine bay – not surprising really, as the car was designed with this engine as a possible future fitment.

large engine slotted in, a considerable amount of re-engineering being required. The principal differences include a 3.08-to-1 rear axle ratio, the addition of power steering, a redesigned front subframe to accommodate the larger engine, uprated suspension bushes and spring and damper rates, thicker front brake discs with larger pads and callipers, a different exhaust system, the standard fitment of alloy wheels, greatly

increased radiator and cooling system capacity, and modified instrumentation. The SD1 gearbox and axle were of course already fitted to the TR7 by 1978. Some TR8s had automatic gearboxes; almost all also had air conditioning, and 1980 cars for California and all 1981 cars had Bosch fuel injection built under licence by Lucas. Externally the TR8 was distinguishable by its twin exhaust system and extra bonnet bulge,

although many later TR7s also had this. The factory TR8 was a rapid car despite the anti-pollution equipment restricting power to 134bhp, with 0–60mph taking around 8.5 seconds, and an easy 120mph being obtainable. Home-market cars with 155bhp were never magazine-tested, but would have been significantly quicker.

Owing to the TR8's rarity and desirability, a TR7-to-TR8 conversion industry arose in the early 1980s, and cars are still being converted today. Strictly speaking these are all TR7 V8s, but most – perhaps unsurprisingly – sport TR8 badges. Buyers should be aware that there are good conversions, bad conversions and many in between. In addition a number of TR7 conversions have been passed off by the unscrupulous as genuine TR8s, a factory TR8 being worth considerably more than a home-built V8-powered TR7. A good conversion will have all or virtually all of Triumph's own modifications, and it will certainly have uprated brakes, as even the correct TR8 brakes are barely adequate. The rear axle ratio needs to be raised, too, as otherwise the car will be undergeared, while all the cooling system mods need to be in place, as the 3½-litre V8 produces a good deal more heat than the four-cylinder engine. Again because it is so much faster, any V8-powered car should have uprated suspension. Reputable conversion specialists will have undertaken all these tasks, or furnished kits with all the necessary parts, but a number of private conversions consist of little more than dropping an old Rover V8 into the TR7's engine bay and these cars are positively unsafe.

There was one final chapter to come in the manufacture of the TR7: as a result of the decision in 1980 to shut the Canley plant, TR7 and TR8 production was transferred to the Rover plant at Solihull. The final Coventry-built TR came off the line in

Driving a five-speed TR7 convertible

Borrowing a late-model Solihull-built TR7 convertible for a brief drive on a sunny day has made me conclude that this is indeed a pleasant way to travel. The top stows rapidly and without fuss, the driving position and seats are comfortable, and the controls are conveniently laid out if with that overwhelming 1970s sense of being somewhat fragile. On the road the car feels slightly faster than expected although it is necessary to wind the engine up well for real progress – a certain lack of torque is apparent. The engine and exhaust notes are distressingly bland and I think I'd go for the V8 version if only to hear the sound.

The gearbox has the usual slightly obstructive synchromesh and notchy feel but improves as it warms up, while the clutch is surprisingly heavy. At speed, five-speed gearbox notwithstanding, the car feels undergeared and fussy – again the V8 with the 3.08 axle would cure all that – and I dread to think what an original four-speed TR7 would be like. The '7' pulls well and runs straight and true but suffers a certain measure of scuttle shake plus a rattle from the windows, but then we're talking of a car that is 25 years old. Windows-up and hood-down, cruising at 65–70mph is all very pleasant if undramatic.

Hood-up, the wind noise is obvious, but no worse than with many other soft-tops.

Brakes feel a little less than positive – they stop the car well enough, but do not inspire confidence. Handling and cornering are excellent: on a TR7 there is all the adhesion you'd expect, plus a comfortable ride thanks to the long-travel suspension.

One could perfectly happily use a TR7 as an everyday go-to-work car, but for a little extra capital outlay and slightly increased running costs I would really want the V8 version – in properly sorted form, that would be quite a car.

The ultimate TR7/8? This is the Le Mans racing turbocharged TR8 built by ADA Engineering for the 1980 race. Sadly it did not prove to be reliable.

August 1980, with some US cars being built in Solihull during the April–August transfer period before full production for the 1981 model year began at Solihull in September 1980.

Quality continued to improve at Solihull and minor trim and badge revisions moved the TR7 further upmarket. Additionally plans were in hand to fit the Austin-Morris

Buying Hints

1. Working from the car's front, check for rust where the seams of the front panel join the wings. The alloy headlamp pods don't rust, but can react with the surrounding steel and cause bubbling. Bonnets of early cars are usually reasonable, but the later bonnets with the extra bulge can rust badly, particularly in the front corners. Under the bonnet inspect the tops of the suspension turrets, a vital MoT point. The coverplate at the base of the windscreen rusts through, as does the scuttle panel, this ensuring that rain enters the car, filling the footwells and helping the floors to rust.

2. Doors rust, both skins and frames, as does the spare-wheel well and the boot sides – this as a result of faulty boot seals.

3. The front subframe can rust around its mountings, an MoT failure point, and corrosion can also appear in the front chassis legs and floorpan. Mounting points for the trailing arms are safety-critical and have often deteriorated, and the sills themselves are vital to the car's integrity, particularly on the convertible.

4. Windscreen frames on both coupés and convertibles can rot, leading to further water-ingress problems.

5. The engine and its faults are described in the Dolomite section. It suffers in the same way, so beware of warped alloy heads and overheating. Oil leaks are common and difficult to cure. Water pumps can fail regularly and to fit them demands removal of the inlet manifold.

6. Any car with a V8 conversion should be thoroughly checked. Has it been done properly, and have all necessary changes been made? The V8 engine itself is inherently reliable but requires frequent oil changes if sludge problems are not to affect the rocker gear, a common failing.

7. The early four-speed gearbox is weak, but virtually all cars still running will have the much stronger five-speed unit, along with the Rover rear axle. These are simple and robust and should not give problems.

8. Electrics can be doubtful, particularly the operation of the pop-up headlamps. Each lamp has a motor and as these gather muck at the front of the car, their life tends to be short. Try them several times to ensure correct operation. Other electrical difficulties are often down to bad earthing, though the 1970s switchgear is not of the highest quality.

9. New convertible hoods are readily available and inexpensive. The interior lasts quite well, but the entire cockpit can be re-trimmed at modest cost, so condition is not critical. You may well want to replace that awful 1970s tartan anyway…

10. Values of the TR7s have been low now for years. Convertibles are worth at least twice what fixed heads are in the same condition, with well-executed V8 conversions up to double again. Genuine factory TR8s fetch a high premium, but are very rare in the UK. It is not cost-effective to attempt to restore a poor or rusty car, which means that doggy TR7s are still being scrapped or cannibalised for spares. Good condition original cars are getting rarer and prices will in future only go up. Buy now whilst they're still good value.

O-series engine in place of the Triumph 'slant-four'. Prototypes were already running, but the fact was that by mid-1981 every TR7 or TR8 built was losing British Leyland more money than ever. The ratio of the pound against the dollar had risen greatly, making the TR much more expensive in the US, its principal market. Faced with mounting losses from all directions in the crumbling British Leyland empire, boss Sir Michael Edwardes saw no alternative but to stop making the TR altogether – just when the factory had finally got the product right. The plug was pulled on 5 October 1981, and the author well recalls being interviewed that day on BBC news about the history and demise of the TR.

As to numbers of TR7s and TR8s built, this has proved to be both a controversial and complex subject, incapable of a precise answer. Around 115,000 examples of all types were built, this including roughly 2,850 factory-built TR8s. Of this grand total, around 15,600 were convertibles, approximately 2,450 of these being TR8s. Thus it can be seen that the vast majority of TR7s were coupés, the great bulk of these being built at Speke in the early years of production. As always with the TR series, a large majority of cars were exported, principally to the US.

Writing in 2006, many years down the road from British Leyland's troubles of the late 1970s, one can see that the TR7 did its best in a difficult market at a difficult time. Today the many surviving examples are finally being restored and cherished, and are regarded as being as much a part of Britain's sports car heritage as their ancestors. Fortunately for the impecunious, the TR7, especially in fixed-head form, remains inexpensive and forms a useful entry-level classic vehicle for the younger enthusiast.

The demise of *Triumph*

Triumph as a maker of cars died on several occasions. You could argue that it first died in 1939 when bankruptcy forced the cessation of production just as war arrived. You could say that it almost died in early 1961 when Leyland stepped in to rescue the ailing Standard-Triumph company from imminent collapse. Or possibly in 1968 when Triumph as part of Leyland Motors was absorbed into the ill-fated maw of British Leyland. Or what about November 1980 when the last Triumph cars left a genuine Triumph factory in Coventry? Or perhaps it finally died on 5 October 1981 when the last British-designed cars left the production lines – albeit at Solihull and not at Canley? The TR7 had a genuine Triumph engine design that dated back to the mid-1960s and for all its Morris Marina door handles and Rover rear axle it was still very much a Triumph, even if not quite as most enthusiasts knew it.

What cannot be allowed, however, is any half-baked argument that Triumph only died as a car maker in 1984 when the final Triumph-badged Acclaim saloons were made. These were not Triumphs: they were licence-built Hondas. They may well have been worthy little cars but to a true enthusiast it sticks in the throat that they carried the Triumph name.

In truth, though, the Triumph marque did not really die so much as slowly fade away. The process can be seen as beginning in the mid-1970s, when no direct successors were planned for the 2000/2500, Dolomite, Stag or Spitfire ranges. Even those

projects that BL did come up with were almost all shelved, whatever their merits. The cash evaporated and the personnel and ideas simply drained away. It was a sad but seemingly inevitable story and one that did not need compounding by the ultimate hijacking of the name for totally cynical commercial reasons.

A revival of the Triumph name has been the subject of rumour on several occasions over the past few years. But whatever it resurfaces on, if it ever does resurface, will not be a Triumph, so let us remember the Triumph company from its heyday. As to when that was, again one could argue the toss, but my suggestion would be 1967, a moment or two

before British Leyland engulfed it. A splendid product line-up was in production or just about to be – the TR5, the 2.5PI saloon and its 2000 brother, the two-litre Vitesse, the MkIII Spitfire, the GT6, and the members of the Herald family. All were proper Triumphs, and were respected, durable cars of quality, most of them with sporting overtones and competition ancestry. They were what Triumph was all about…

The sales catalogue for the Acclaim made much of the car's supposed Triumph-ness, but the last car to bear the famous name was nothing more than a re-badged Honda. (Jon Pressnell collection)

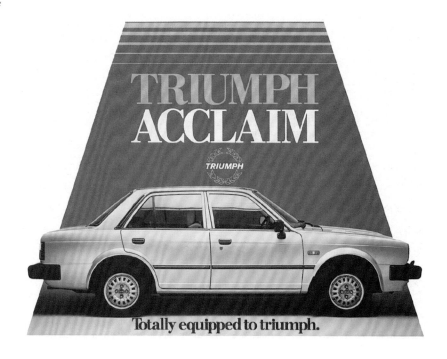

Index

Acknowledgements

I must thank all those members of the various Triumph clubs who have assisted me in the preparation of this book, in particular my friends and colleagues in the TR Register and those members of other Triumph clubs who have kindly provided both information and cars for photography and driving impressions.

In any book of this nature one draws on many secondary sources, and in this connection I am happy to acknowledge my debt to noted Triumph author Graham Robson, whose pioneering research on the marque, across many books, has been an invaluable aid.

Thanks are also due to the staff at Haynes Publishing, in particular Mark Hughes, Flora Myer and James Robertson. Jon Pressnell has done an excellent job in both editing and improving my text, as well as in sorting out a vast quantity of Triumph photographs and illustrations.

Finally, I must thank Rosy Pugh for deciphering my poor handwriting and typing up the manuscript.

Bill Piggott, Rutland, 2006

ILLUSTRATIONS

Unless otherwise indicated, illustrations are from the LAT Photographic archive, and are mainly being drawn from the files of *Motor*, *Autocar* and *Classic & Sports Car* magazines. For details of the archive's services, write to LAT Photographic, Teddington Studios, Broom Road, Teddington, Middlesex TW11 9BE, visit website www.latphoto.co.uk, or phone 0208 251 3000.